A Conceptual Introduction
to Modeling:
Qualitative and Quantitative
Perspectives

A Conceptual Introduction to Modeling:
Qualitative and Quantitative Perspectives

David W. Britt
Wayne State University

LEA LAWRENCE ERLBAUM ASSOCIATES, PUBLISHERS
1997   Mahwah, New Jersey

Lawrence Erlbaum Associates
10 Industrial Avenue
Mahwah, New Jersey 07430-2262

Cover design by Kathryn Houghtaling

Library of Congress Cataloging-in-Publication Data

Britt, David W.
    A conceptual introduction to modeling : qualita-
tive and quantitative perspectives / David W.
Britt.
        p. cm.
    Includes bibliographical references and index.
    ISBN 0-8058-1937-1 (c : alk. paper). — ISBN
0-8058-1938-X (p : alk. paper)
        1. Mathematical models. I. Title.
    TA342.B75 1997
    300'.1'1—dc20   96-25124
                                              CIP

Books published by Lawrence Erlbaum Associates
are printed on acid-free paper, and their bindings are
chosen for strength and durability.

Printed in the United States of America
10   9   8   7   6   5   4   3   2   1

Contents

Preface

May you live in interesting times. (Old Chinese curse)

There is always that battle between preconceived notions of what the image looks like with respect to the found object and the discovery of form through the process of combining multiple nondescript shapes. (Guagliumi, 1994, p. 47)

This book is about modeling as an ongoing process. Models facilitate continuing dialogue about which concepts are important and unimportant, what their nature is and is not, and how they may and may not be related to one another. These dialogues lead to four forms of understanding: descriptive, interpretive, explanatory, and predictive.

Engaging in this multidimensional specification process is akin to Guagliumi's (1994) description of constructing a collage. There is a lot of tension and rediscovery from the variety of found objects whose relationships to one another give meaning to the overall construction.

After an overview of the critical realist framework within which mixed-method modeling is possible, the early chapters in this book discuss the disciplines involved in specifying and respecifying concepts and relationships. The next three chapters discuss ways of elaborating models to capture more of the complexity that characterizes situations that we are interested in understanding. The critical importance of feedback loops and context for describing, interpreting, explaining, and making predictions with respect to social life are emphasized in two of these chapters. The next two chapters focus on the tensions involved in evaluating and simplifying models, and a final chapter recapitulates the major themes.

These are interesting, even exciting times for social and behavioral scientists. On the one hand, the organization of our descriptive, interpretive, explanatory, and predictive understanding of situations remains a fundamental problem. On the other hand, all of our disciplines are confronting cleavages along at least two dimensions: quantitative versus qualitative, and basic versus applied.

As we experience these cleavages, the seemingly cursed aspects of living in interesting times challenge our search for professional identities and sane work environments. Minimally defined, *sane work environments* might be those in which quantitative and qualitative researchers can agree to disagree and struggle to find some common ground, and in which there can be appreciation of both applied and basic research. This book grew out of my own searches. It was stimulated most immediately by a desire to keep the worlds of graduate students from becoming too parochial by allowing them to fixate on only one style of research.

My commitment to working with graduate students grew out of a more collective commitment on the part of my Wayne State University colleagues to forge a civil and tolerant working environment for basic and applied, quantitative and qualitative sociologists. It also had deeper roots in my own past as a quantitatively trained sociologist who discovered, in working with organizations of various kinds, that there were never enough resources to do a definitive study. I learned that the world was a much more complex place than what could be captured with elegant designs and tools.

ACKNOWLEDGMENTS

Putting this book together has given me the opportunity to examine the work of researchers in a variety of disciplines and substantive areas. This by itself has been exciting, challenging, and stimulating of further thought and reflection. There are a number of people, however, who have directly or indirectly provided support and constructive feedback at different points in the process. David Jacobs, Larry Isaac, and David Maines read early versions of papers that eventually became chapters in much-revised form. I have benefited from discussions with LaRue Allen, Larry Aber, several other colleagues, and a host of students. Editorial feedback from anonymous external reviewers, and detailed editorial comments from Ebonya Washington and Susan Milmoe were very helpful in providing continuity. Finally, special thanks should go to institutional support from Wayne State University in the form of a sabbatical and the Greenwich Village Summer Camp for Textbook Writers for a place to work.

—*David W. Britt*

For LaRue

1

First Steps, Basic Dilemmas, Gulfs and Bridge Building

Every cobbler thinks leather is the only thing. (Trow, 1957)

. . . a slice of bread without caviar on top is still a slice of bread. (Lieberson, 1992)

Remember what it was like when we played with something like a logo set when we were children? Such sets have lots of names now, but they all came with simple blocks and sticks that could be put together to simulate buildings, cars, bridges, gargoyles and other imagined structures. We decided which blocks to use, either by ourselves or with the other kids with whom we were playing, and what they represented. When we decided which blocks should be attached, we connected them with sticks or piled them up in different combinations. When we decided which blocks should not be connected, we left the space between them empty or left the ones we did not want to use in the box . . . or scattered on the floor. There was constant reality testing, initially among ourselves and occasionally with others. If what we were building fell over, looked ugly, met with guffaws and chuckles from passers-by, or somehow did not match the scenario of our play activities, we changed blocks, sticks, spaces, and even where we played with the set.

Building models is a lot like playing with a logo set. There is a lot of simplification as we construct models to represent images of various realities. Instead of blocks, we have concepts, but the struggle to tentatively decide which blocks to use and what they mean is parallel. Instead of sticks, we have arrows. The struggle to tentatively decide how things relate to one another is similarly parallel. We decide what the nature of the variables is according to what we or the others with whom we are working think. We decide which variables should be related to each other and which ones should not, again in consultation. We wrestle with questions of context—and we do a lot of reality testing. You may think this is a lot of tentative decisions—you are right; the reason for this is that in the social sciences, there is no last word.

1

Causal models are collections of variables and assumptions about what the variables are and how they relate to one another. They simplify realities and focus our attention on certain aspects of situations as these situations change through time and place. Models may help us describe how aspects of situations are related to one another. In other cases, models may help us predict how events will unfold. If they capture the essence of the causal dynamics of situations, models may help us gain insight into how people and other social entities live through sequences of events. In still other cases, models may help us understand why things happen the way they do by providing a vehicle for pitting alternative explanations against one another. This book is an introduction to the process of modeling, with an emphasis on how to think about models, what to do with them, and what makes them credible. A continuing theme is the investigation of how the modeling process might be altered to create a bridge for the organization of knowledge from quantitative and qualitative sources. Creating such a bridge should facilitate a dialogue between assumptions and data from all sources or, to follow up on one of the quotes at the beginning, creating such a bridge will help us make shoes out of things other than leather.

There are a few biases that I should lay out before moving further. I see models primarily as *organizing devices for a continuing, explicit dialogue between multiple sources* of data and assumptions. In this light, models summarize what we believe we have learned about the dynamics of phenomena in patterns woven from different contexts, in different historical periods and with different individuals and social groups.

I believe we need to establish the legitimacy of modeling underlying realities that are approximately defined by the conjunction of context, history, and social entities (individuals and social groups). This objective of modeling is in opposition to simply modeling available data points to provide the best fit. By itself, this would be a leap of some magnitude beyond standard practice. In the context of considering models as organizing devices for both quantitative and qualitative data, moving toward underlying realities instead of only fitting models to quantitatively derived data points is a shorter leap, but a necessary one if we are to allow models to be more flexible and useful for researchers with different styles. Such an approach requires relentless rethinking of the meaning of context, and action no matter what the scale of the analysis or the sources of the data. For example, Isaac and Griffin (1989) reframed the nature of historical periods from arbitrary containers of numerical information to substantively meaningful and potentially different contexts. Only by doing so is it possible to appreciate how the relationship between union strength and U.S. labor militancy changes from one historical period to another.

On a smaller scale, the same issues apply. Modeling the effectiveness of different teaching strategies would, at a minimum, require detailed and rich knowledge of not only strategies and student behavior and attitudes but also an understanding of the school and community in which the classroom is located, as well as the interpenetrating histories of all of these factors and how they mutually define one another. This may all sound very abstract, but imagine how naive it would be to assume that schools do not set limits and create conditions that can either facilitate or retard what is happening in classrooms. Similarly, is it not much more reasonable to assume that the same strategies might work for some students in some communities, but be useless in other contexts? To simplify a bit, establishing the legitimacy of modeling underlying realities means starting with the assumption that social life is lumpy and that combinations of context, history and social entities must be examined.

A final bias concerns the process of making models credible and trustworthy. Standard practice in quantitative research judges the credibility of models by the confidence we may have in the estimates of coefficients. I believe that the credibility or trustworthiness of models and their relationships must rest on more than the preciseness of coefficients estimated from the statistical manipulation of large data sets. Coefficients have no inherent meaning. At the very least, they require an additional causal mechanism "that puts the substantive process in context and 'makes sense' out of it (Isaac, Carlson, & Mathis, 1994)." Isaac et al's (1994) plea is for greater richness and interpretive understanding about how social entities are dealing with the dynamics in which they find themselves, and for which they may have been in part responsible.

Much of this book is about credibly making sense of what is going on in situations of interest. After laying out a basic dilemma faced by researchers and developing a framework for doing mixed-method modeling, the next two chapters discuss the building blocks of concepts and relationships while keeping in focus the importance of spaces—the things we do not believe belong in concepts or things that are unrelated to one another. The three chapters that follow discuss various forms of elaboration, strategies for adding concepts and relationships to models in ways that embrace the complexities of what we are trying to understand. Chapters 7 and 8 discuss criteria for evaluating models and moving from elaborated to working models. A final chapter briefly reviews important lessons and discusses the limits of modeling.

EXAMINING ALTERNATIVE DEFINITIONS

Having stated these biases up front, consider some examples of how models have been defined over the last 25 years so as to put my approach in perspective. Richardson and Pugh (1981) gave a standard definition of modeling from a system dynamics perspective:

> The term 'model' stands for a representation . . . of some slice of reality . . .
> The purpose is to gain understanding . . . [by] exposing the model's
> assumptions about a problem to criticism, experimentation and reformu-
> lation. (pp. 2–3)

There are three key points contained in this definition: simplification,
explicitness, and reformulation. Models are collections of explicit, specified assumptions—not vague understandings regarding how the world
works. They simplify reality to bring the critical dynamics that shape
that reality into better focus. The Richardson and Pugh definition makes
clear that assumptions in models are always open to criticism and being
reformulated. This is the dialogue.

The nature of the assumptions that are being made explicit in models
does not stand out particularly well in the Richardson and Pugh (1981)
definition. Consider the following definition by Uslaner (1976), drawn
from the introduction to a popular statistically based book on modeling
by Asher (1976):

> Causal modeling is a technique for selecting those variables that are the
> potential [cause] of the effects—and . . . [isolating] the separate contribu-
> tions to the effects made by each [cause]. (p. 5)

Carving the world up into sets of variables is a key simplifying
assumption that cannot be taken lightly (Abbott, 1988). Modeling may
attempt to come to grips with causal dynamics, represented in this
definition as distinguishing between causes and effects and assessing
the relative importance of causes in generating effects. Such an approach hinges on the plausibility of assuming that these variables are
free to assume values independent of one another rather than occurring
in clusters. Modeling may also be used in situations where such an
assumption is not seen as being plausible. It might be more realistic, for
example, to think in terms of combinations of conditions that come
together in particular configurations to produce certain outcomes
(Ragin, 1987). Models may help graphically capture the explicit assumptions about configurations of conditions in ways that supplement either
the equations or the prose common in comparative analysis.

A more general definition that brings home another typical characteristic of models is the following by Land (1969):

> . . . the term path model is used to refer to the set of structural equations
> . . . representing the postulated causal and noncausal [i.e., merely asso-
> ciational] relationships among the variables under consideration. (p. 7)

As this definition makes clear—and the other definitions of modeling
suggest—models have almost invariably been tied to sets of equations
applied to quantitative data. The need to estimate coefficients with
certain statistical properties appears to have played a critical role in the

way in which the process of modeling is understood by most social scientists. Limiting modeling to those situations in which precise estimates of coefficients may be developed is, in the extreme handicapping. It diverts attention from the real business at hand. Tukey (1963) in an oft-quoted maxim, phrased the issue in normative terms:

> The most important maxim for data analysts to heed, and one which many statisticians has shunned, is this: 'Far better an approximate answer to the right question, which is often vague, than an exact answer to the wrong question, which can always be made precise.' (p. 13)

The real business of modeling is not estimating coefficients. The real business of modeling should be helping to ask the right questions and to organize answers. In fact, because the language of modeling—in the social sciences of the last 25 years—started with sets of equations, there are not many examples of qualitative studies in which the language of causal modeling is used (but see Miles & Huberman, 1994). Yet, if you talk with qualitatively trained, applied, or preventive-intervention-oriented social scientists, there is general agreement on the role that modeling plays in their approach to social phenomena. They are likely to say something to the effect of, "First, you model the dynamics of the phenomenon in which you are interested—because you cannot design an intervention until you know what you are doing—and then you develop an intervention on the basis of the knowledge summarized in the model."[1] I believe that by considering models as organizing devices that facilitate a continuing, explicit dialogue between multiple sources of data and assumptions, we can ask better questions and develop more valid answers in spite of having widely divergent methodological approaches.

A BASIC DILEMMA

The causal modeling process requires simplifying assumptions about the nature of the social world. Comparisons need to be made across cases, time, or different aspects of a phenomenon. Making simplifying assumptions immediately places researchers in a dilemma, however. If the assumptions we make do not reduce complexity and ambiguity to manageable bounds or make comparison possible across cases, times, or aspects of a phenomenon, causal analysis is not possible. On the other hand, if the assumptions we make are too unrealistically simple, if they presume to generalize all times and contexts or hinder our ability to get close to the phenomena of interest, the relationship of models to the complex realities being modeled becomes tenuous.

---

[1]From a conversation Dr. Andrea Sankar, an applied anthropologist.

How this basic dilemma is resolved has implications for the kinds of analyses that are possible, for the range of phenomena that are analyzable, and for the meaning of the results from either a practical or theoretical standpoint. Freedman's work (1985, 1987, 1991), for example, reminded us of the fragility of the assumptions necessary in using multiple regression analysis, still the industry workhorse for quantitative work with large samples. We must make constraining assumptions about the direction of causation, measurement error in our variables, the linearity of the variables in the analysis, and the impact of variables left out of the analysis. Because these assumptions are often violated, the credibility of the analyses is often suspect.[2] Part of the overall problem is an attempt to emulate the precision of the natural sciences, with results that occasionally expose the differences between the two. In discussing the appropriateness of using regression analysis for certain tasks, Freedman (1985) drew the following inference:

> ... insofar as the problem of planetary motion now looks clean and simple, that is the result of centuries of hard work ... The social sciences may be at the pre-Keplerian stage of investigation—the equivalent of figuring out which are the planets and which are the fixed stars. If so, using sophisticated analytical techniques like regression is bound to add to the confusion. The problem is to define the basic variables, to figure out ways of measuring them, to perceive the main empirical regularities. Estimating coefficients by least squares before the basic variables have been understood is like using a scalpel to clear a path through the jungle. (p. 352)

Precision may be a false goal for social science modeling. To justify the use of a scalpel, we have begun to consider only those larger-scale quantitative studies that have a chance of satisfying the assumptions of multiple regression analysis as credible. We have become enamored of large-sample studies that can compensate for the violation of statistical assumptions by having many cases. Yet some of those who are writing most thoughtfully about such large-sample studies argue that precision of estimation and functional form can be easily overdone. Achen (1991), for example, in a short monograph on interpreting and using regression, argued:

> *Functionally correct causal specification in social science is neither possible nor desirable.* Social scientists neither have nor want correct, stable functional forms for their explanations. Good social theory avoids such things. (p. 16)

---

[2]In a quote that brings home the truth of the old saw, "Don't fetch water in a bucket with holes in it," Freedman (1985) said this about the stochastic assumptions which regression analysis must make: "Regression analysis too [like models in the natural sciences] make quite strict assumptions, explicitly or implicitly, about the stochastic nature of the world. In most social-science applications, these assumptions do not hold water. Neither do the resulting models" (p. 345).

Many interesting phenomena cannot—or perhaps, should not—be studied with large samples. Some phenomena may be so context-dependent that to try to aggregate across contexts makes no sense. Further, there are only so many revolutions, so many shifts from centralized to market economies, or so many classrooms operating in contexts with particular configurations of school size and resources.[3] The important point here has less to do with sample size than with what the real business of modeling is about. Freedman's critiques are chastening. Achen's work sensitizes us to the resiliency of some quantitative tools under certain circumstances. Considering at least these parts of these scholars' larger work brings us almost to the same place as does a conversation with an applied qualitative scholar: Precision is not what modeling is about; modeling is about getting to the essence of the causal dynamics of a situation configured in time and space.

Claiming that we can get to the real business of modeling by starting from either the quantitative comparison of large data sets or the qualitative analysis of a few cases belies the difficulty of the journey. We must dig a bit deeper to appreciate the gulf that is created between research styles. These styles have tried to resolve the basic dilemma by trading off certain ways of disciplining investigations to maximize available leverage in others. A shorthand listing of the elements of these alternate styles, drawn from Isaac et al. (1994), is presented in Fig. 1.1.

One essential choice is between cases and variables or concepts. Cases are things like people, situations, groups, census tracts, economic time periods, and so on. They are the social, political, or economic entities whose actions and characteristics one is interested in understanding. Variables and concepts are characteristics of cases that are constructed from information available. Individual-level variables are things like income, dogmatism, and conservatism. Group-level variables are things like cohesion and morale. Census tracts permit construction of variables like percent of households below the poverty line.

• Quantity	• Quality
• Generality	• Particularity
• Variables	• Cases
• Outcomes	• Process
• Structure	• Agency
• External, Formal Relations	• Internal, Substantial Relations

FIG. 1.1. Creating the gulf.
Reprinted with permission from Isaac, Carlson, & Mathis (1994, p. 111).

---

[3]Skocpol (1979) framed the choice in a similar vein for macro-historical phenomena: "Comparative historical analysis is, in fact, the mode of multivariate analysis to which one resorts when there are too many variables and not enough cases" (. 36). An excellent introduction to the comparative method and the differences between it an more variable-based methods is Ragin (1987).

Figure 1.2 shows the relationship of cases (represented by the circles) to variables and concepts (represented by the capitalized letters within each circle). Case-based analysis focuses on the case as a whole: all of the individual, all of the group, all of the political entity (Ragin, 1987). Variable-based analysis focuses on a sampling of information available so as to make it easier to compare. Even with many variables constructed, however, variables always represent a simplification of the richness of cases in two senses. There is always more richness of detail than can be captured as variables. This is represented in Fig. 1.2 by the blank spaces not associated with variables. And the construction of variables implies that the meaning of the variable or concept may be appreciated independent of the context.

It would be massively expensive to gather huge amounts of data on many cases, so we are usually faced with having to do one or the other. Ragin (1987) phrased this as a choice between gathering a lot of information on a small number of cases as opposed to gathering a more limited amount of information on a lot of cases. Fundamentally, it is a choice about which kind of leverage one wants to develop. Choosing to study a large number of cases and focusing on variables and concepts gives leverage in comparing across cases on a limited range of the phenomena of interest. Choosing a small number of cases and focusing on the cases as wholes gives leverage in comparing across many aspects of the phenomena of interest.

A second consequence of the decisions represented in Fig. 1.1 focuses on how we talk about what we are observing. Focusing on several cases and studying how things vary increases the chances that we will examine outcomes and talk about the formal, structural relations among variables. If we focus on a smaller number of cases and learn as much as possible about them, we are more likely to focus on process rather than outcomes, the importance of agency (the intentional activities and decisions of social entities) as opposed to structure, and more internal, substantial relations.

FIG. 1.2. The relationship of cases to concepts and variables. Circles represent cases. Upper-case letters represent concepts and variables drawn from information on cases. Empty space within circles represents other information about cases.

The elements in the two columns of Fig. 1.1 have been given various names. For example, in trying to develop a case for the case study, Sjoberg, Williams, Vaughn, and Sjoberg (1991) called a set of preferences similar to the left-hand column the *natural sciences model*. In trying to meld realistic and theoretically useful assumptions about historical contingency (that relationships among variables differ depending on the time period and context) into quantitative historical analyses, Isaac et al. (1994) called this set of preferences the *extensive/variable-oriented mode*. In trying to move beyond traditional comparative and quantitative strategies, Ragin (1987, 1989) compared *variable-oriented* and *case-oriented* approaches, with the variable-oriented strategy containing a set of practices that overlap considerably with the list in the left column of Fig. 1.1. Guba and Lincoln (1989) would attach a *positivist* label to the activities in the left column, and perhaps an *interpretivist* label to the activities in the right-hand column. These only begin to describe the alternative ways of thinking about this widely and hotly debated gulf, as evidenced by the recent collections by Brannen (1992) and Reichardt and Rallis (1994).

The tradeoffs between these general research styles and the mutual reinforcement of the elements within styles have led some to believe that the gulf between these two styles cannot or should not be bridged (Guba & Lincoln, 1989). How can one embrace both subjectivity and objectivity at the same time? How can one believe that the concepts we use are both fixed and emergent at the same time? How can one simultaneously believe that facts have an independent existence—and that they do not? How can one simultaneously believe in the utility of researcher-oriented and participant-oriented perspectives? How can one hold sacred both explanation and understanding at the same time? And how can one believe that there are both single and multiple realities at the same time? Phrased this way, as House (1994) reminded us, there is less room for compatibility.

The apparent bias of the social science article review process along lines of this cleavage is one of many reflections of the fact that dogmas regarding this gulf die hard (Howe, 1985, 1988). There is inertia built into the training of students, an inertia based on the belief that each of these styles is so complex that specialized training and practice are necessary for gaining skill in either mode. Constructed around these elements are style-serving rationalizations for why one style is better than the other. The denigration of the alternative style may increase the commitment of recruits to one's own style. Given the often vitriolic exchanges between members of these two camps, cannibalism may not be much of a stretch. Converts to one's style are highly prized as if each proselyte added additional validation to one's perspective. Light and Pillemer (1982) summarized the hardening institutional boundaries of this debate as follows:

For many years researchers in education could be divided fairly clearly into two broad camps: those who preferred qualitative case reports, and others who favored quantitative, statistically based studies. Of course there has been some overlap, but even a cursory look at any major university's course listings on research methodology turns up courses that clearly emphasize one approach or the other. These different emphases in training are then reflected into how researchers organize and communicate their work. Major social science journals are categorized as "quantitative" or "qualitative," with a crossing of boundaries all too rare. (p. 2)

BUILDING BRIDGES
FROM SHARED ASSUMPTIONS

Ironically, the very problems that make this gulf so difficult to bridge also make it useful to try to do so. The more divergent the styles of research, the greater the chances of each style's being able to compensate for the biases of the other (Brewer & Hunter, 1989):

The multimethod approach is largely built upon this insight. Its fundamental strategy is to *attack a research problem with an arsenal of methods that have nonoverlapping weaknesses in addition to their complementary strengths.* (p. 7)

There has been a renewed debate during the last few years over the combining of qualitative and quantitative approaches. A long-standing commitment to multiple indicators is traceable to Campbell and Fiske's influential work on multitrait, multimethod matrices in the late 1950s (Campbell & Fiske, 1959). Although this commitment was relatively weak in the 1960s, it animated several provocative and insightful pieces in the 1970s, notably Sieber's (1973) discussion of qualitative and survey methods, Campbell's (1974) Kurt Lewin Award address at the American Psychological Association Meetings, and the seminal collection of articles in Cook and Reichardt (1979). The 1980s saw these discussions broaden to include a significant collection of papers on multisite field studies (Smith & Louis, 1982), the publication of the first edition of Miles and Huberman's (1984, 1994) *Qualitative Data Analysis: A Sourcebook of New Methods*, Rossman and Wilson's (1985) and Mark and Shotland's (1987) analyses of multiple methods, heated discussions in the educational journals (e.g., *Educational Researcher*) and Ragin's (1987) landmark work on *The Comparative Method*. The 1990s have been marked by Brannen's (1992) collection of essays from British researchers, Reichardt and Rallis' (1994) special issue of *New Directions for Program Evaluation*, and a number of conferences that have been devoted to the joint use of qualitative and quantitative data in the service of specific research questions.

A recent special issue of *New Directions in Program Evaluation* is especially encouraging for those seeking to develop a framework of assumptions conducive to the development and assessment of mixed-method models (Reichardt & Rallis, 1994a). Summarizing their own views and those of others, Reichardt and Rallis (1994b) laid out areas of agreement between quantitative and qualitative researchers that have been ignored or treated as background assumptions in the past.

Program evaluators (and applied or action researchers more generally) have a "commitment to understanding and improving the human condition" whether they come from a qualitative or quantitative tradition (Reichardt & Rallis, 1994b, p. 89). Further, both qualitative and quantitative researchers agree that rigor, conscientiousness, and openness to critique are essential for the creation of knowledge. Common commitments to quality and useful knowledge—perhaps fostered by the presence of qualitative and quantitative researchers on joint research teams (Delaney & Ames, 1993; Gilbert 1993; Singer 1993)—make it easier for us to respect one another's positions, exchange ideas, and constructively critique one another although some epistemological elements may separate us (Reichardt & Rallis, 1994b).

Reichardt and Rallis (1994b) built on earlier work by Phillips (1990) and others to document more specific points of convergence between qualitative and quantitative approaches that are especially relevant to the development and use of models. Central to their argument is the movement away from the logical positivism that characterized much early quantitative work in a postpositivist position. These more specific positions are concerned with how theory-laden facts are, how value-laden the whole research process is, how fallible we assume knowledge and the knowledge-building process to be, and what we imagine the nature of reality to be. Logical positivism believed that facts were untainted by theoretical concerns, that the scientific research process was immune to the intrusion of personal and cultural values (and therefore value-free), that knowledge is a simple matter to establish, that once established is unassailable, and that there is a single reality that is directly observable. Current positions are much more complex and flexible and it is important to understand the nature of these changes. The credibility of Reichardt and Rallis' claim that there has been movement to a postpositivist position is augmented with their documentation that Cook and Campbell (1979)—a quantitative bible if there ever was one—reverently embraced postpositivism. Borrowing some credibility from Cook and Campbell is good start, but let us explore these four areas of growth in more depth. They establish the framework for the development of the rest of the book.

Theory-Ladenness of Facts

The theory-ladenness of facts derives from the impossibility of divorcing the research process from the theoretical perspectives within which it occurs. If theoretical positions dull our sensitivities to what situations and people are trying to tell us, we may become deaf to the essential dialogue that must take place. That facts are theory-laden is a strong tenet of most qualitative researchers and procedures have evolved to minimize the intrusion of theoretical perspectives as much as possible. Strauss and Corbin (1990), for example, emphasize three strategies: being as sensitive as possible to one's theoretical biases before going into the field, consciously minimizing their impact, and constantly re-exposing one's conclusions and assumptions to new data. Altheide and Johnson (1994) suggested "developing accounts of the interactions among context, researcher, methods, setting and actors" (p. 489). Miles and Huberman (1994) suggested other compatible strategies such as checking for researcher effects, examining outliers, following up on surprises, looking for negative effects, presenting one's findings in public, and checking out rival explanations.

Quantitative researchers draw on a number of strategies to keep theoretical perspectives from driving their efforts to develop credible descriptions as well. For example, they incorporate multiple theoretical perspectives into their designs (Jenkins & Kposowa, 1990), allowing them to compete with one another or to synthesize them into specific models. They incorporate many versions of questions in their scale-development studies so as to minimize the intrusion of theoretical bias. They draw from qualitative research techniques to formulate survey questions in protocols that are more reflective of the lived experience of people, rather than theoretical perspectives (Sieber, 1973). And they make explicit reference to the risk of assuming that facts have some sort of independent existence (Cook & Campbell, 1979).

For both qualitative and quantitative researchers, then, the potential for theoretical bias is appreciated. Facts cannot be assumed to have an independent existence, and it is incumbent on the researcher to try to reduce the bias as much as possible. This may not be possible or even desirable in all cases. Different perspectives may generate irreconcilable facts. Put another way, the preconceived structures that our theoretical perspectives impose on what we observe may be incompatible. The discrepancies themselves may provide interesting grist for dialogue, but different researchers may be so wedded to their theoretical perspectives that they believe that alternative approaches just do not get it, so they spend their time talking past one another (House, 1994) rather than appreciating the potential for either integration or complementary viewpoints (Brannen, 1992a).

Patterns in data, characterized by things repeatedly occurring together in time and space, are a type of fact. Hence, they are inherently theory-laden as well. Implicit or explicit theoretical perspectives are inescapably involved in the naming of the phenomena that are associated with one another. For example, to notice that an adolescent who is nervous around other people is more likely to subsequently smoke marijuana than an adolescent who does not feel such nervousness is to impose a low-level pattern. But even at this low level of abstraction, such an observation is not stripped of theoretical inferences (Van Maanen, 1988). Framing is immediately involved in the definition of nervousness, for example. How do we know when someone is nervous? Our cultural values and social scientific theories organize the basic data for us to a certain extent, but there is still a lot that is vague. Do nervous people talk too much, too quickly, grind their teeth, stutter, sweat, fidget, or exhibit some combination of these? Collecting additional observations about similar patterns and concluding that adolescents who exhibit psychological symptoms (nervousness, trouble sleeping, mood swings, etc.) are more likely to subsequently experiment with drugs requires even more implicit or explicit theorizing. Miles and Huberman (1994) reflected this theory-ladenness in calling systematic representations of variables and their relationships "conceptual frameworks" (p. 38).

Defining models as summarizing devices acknowledges the inherent theory-ladenness of facts. By so doing, it keeps us from prematurely deciding which variables are important and unimportant, what the evolving nature of the variables we are considering may be, and how the meaning of variables and patterns may change depending on our theoretical perspective. Being sensitive to the theory-ladenness of facts, then, keeps us open to and dependent on a continuing dialogue between data and assumptions, an important component of the approach to models taken in this book.

Value-Ladenness of the Research Process

Another component of an emerging framework for model construction is recognizing the extent to which values shape the entire research process. The positivist tradition assumed that the values of the researcher made no difference in what was studied, how it was studied, what was analyzed, what theories were chosen as competing explanations, and how it was reported: Science was scientific by definition. To believe such a naïve position is to become blind to the multiple ways in which our values have an influence on the research process.

Qualitative researchers have been sensitive to the potentially pervasive impact of researchers on the research process because the researcher *is* the primary research instrument. Quantitative researchers may have studied smaller parts of the overall process—by asking how interviewer characteristics bias the interview process, for example—but they are increasingly aware of the implications of values in the research process (Campbell, 1979, for example).

The implications of value-ladenness and theory-ladenness for the research process are, then, strong and shared. Facts have no independent existence; they are shaped by the theories we explicitly or implicitly hold dear and by the values that we espouse. Their joint influence goes far beyond facts, however. They shape how we choose and frame a problem to examine, how we construct a design for attack, how we analyze the problem, and what we end up reporting. The entire research process is fragile and porous as far as values and perspectives are concerned. Saying a bucket does not have any holes in it does not make it so.

Models should force us to be more explicit and open about what we are assuming, how we frame problems, what we are attending to and ignoring, and how we think things are related to one another. It is undeniably true that where you sit determines what you see, but by increasing the openness and explicitness of the dialogue about the essential elements of a situation, models may increase the richness and rigor of that dialogue.

Fallibility of Knowledge

A third component of a framework of assumptions conducive to the development and evaluation of mixed-method models is an assertion of the fallibility of knowledge. If knowledge were infallible, we would not need to bother engaging in dialogue. We would already know everything that we needed to know. Such a position would be both naive and dangerous.

There appear to be two important subcomponents of fallibility: the assumption that all knowledge is tentative, and the assumption that many iterations are involved in reaching and verifying conclusions. However, not only qualitative researchers believe that knowledge is "subject to continuous refinement, revision, and, when necessary, replacement" (Guba & Lincoln, 1989, p. 104). Many researchers from both camps have argued that conclusions can never be proven (and, therefore, taken as absolutes), but must always be taken as tentative and subject to disconfirmation (Berry, 1993; Blalock, 1969; Cook & Campbell, 1979; Lofland, 1995). Consider, for example, how Cook and Campbell (1979), drawing heavily from work by Popper (1959), talk in their text on quasi-experimentation about the general question of validity:

> . . . we should always use the term 'approximately' when referring to validity, since one can never know what is true. At best, one can know what has not yet been ruled out as false. (p. 37)

Tentativeness has another aspect. For any given set of facts or patterns of relationships, there are a limitless number of theories that can plausibly explain them. Although it is true that many qualitative researchers share this assumption (Miles & Huberman, 1994; Strauss,

1987; Yin, 1994), contrary to the claim made by Guba and Lincoln (1989), it crosses the quantitative/qualitative divide (cf. Phillips, 1990). Reichardt and Rallis (1994) cited explicit support for this assumption in Campbell and Stanley (1963) and Cook and Campbell (1979), thus demonstrating continuity of support among more experimentally oriented quantitative researchers. Support for this assumption goes far beyond those quantitative researchers concerned with quasi-experimental designs, however. It is also a fundamental tenet among those concerned with nonexperimental quantitative research (Berry, 1993; Blalock, 1969). Eliminating rival hypotheses increases the tenability of our claims for particular ways of explaining facts and patterns, but we never get to the point of being able to categorically say that that we have proven a particular theory.

Iteration has several connotations and denotations depending on the particular elements being related and the scale of the discussion. As usually presented in quantitative and qualitative methods texts (Babbie, 1992; Pelto & Pelto, 1978), iteration refers to a cycle of deduction and induction, with the cycle focusing on the dialogue taking place between theories and data. Marshall and Rossman (1989) expanded this conception by explicitly bringing description, explanation, and prediction into a cycle that features a dialogue between theory and data to inform policy and practice.

Miles and Huberman (1994) described multiple dialogues among different phases of the research process as an interaction between data displays and analytic text (1994, p. 101), as an inherent characteristic of the qualitative data analysis process (1994, p. 308), as variations in sense making taking place between different components of an analysis sequence (1994, p. 85), and as a series of informational feedback loops between different components of the data analysis process (1994, p. 12). In their (1994) treatments, the multiplicity of the dialogues trying to make sense out of what is being observed and analyzed is especially prominent. Explanation is an important part of the overall dialogue, but so too is understanding the process in the same way that participants make sense out of it. Being able to engage in a dialogue of the prediction of events in different times and places is a facet of the overall dialogue traceable to earlier work by Huberman and Crandall (1982).

In sum, building knowledge is an uncertain task. We can never go beyond saying what we tentatively believe to be the case and we must always be prepared to accept counterarguments based on good data. The continuing dialogue that ensues has several components. We tentatively describe phenomena, tentatively conclude what things mean and how they are to be explained. We may also try to predict what is going to happen in the future or in other contexts. Models are central to this process. They are vehicles for summarizing, in as explicit a manner as possible, the various dialogues that are taking place.

Theories in the social sciences can be vague and general. Models tentatively specify what variables we believe are important, our current thinking about what their natures are, and how we believe they are related to other variables in context. Models are, therefore, more explicit than theories. They facilitate sense making by making explicit the alternative implications of different theories explicit, thus increasing the credibility of the remaining implications.

Nature of Reality

The last component of the set of assumptions that provides a supportive framework for the development and evaluation of models is assumptions regarding the nature of reality. We have already discussed the ways in which our observations of the world are shaped by our preconceived theories and implicit or explicit values. A more all-embracing position would argue that all reality is subjective and there are as many realities as there are people—or perhaps, cultures—creating them. Guba and Lincoln (1989) argued, for example, that " . . . there is no reality except that created by people" (pp. 12–13). Such a position is in stark contrast with the position that holds that there is a single underlying reality that we are more or less successful in our attempts to approximate. A more moderate critical realist position favors approximation at best. Critical realists do not assume, as positivists might, that there is an underlying reality that may be described and understood with precision and objectivity.

Events surely occur (particular people get elected to office, catastrophes take place, children graduate from or drop out of school, and so on). People and objects exist as well. Such tangible entities as events, people, and objects are "ontologically real" (Schwandt, 1994, p. 134) in that they do have an existence outside of our experience of them. Yet how we experience events, people, and objects (what Schwandt [1994, p. 134] calls "experiental reality") is a social construction. There may be multiple, often conflicting constructions that are all potentially meaningful (Schwandt, 1994). People in different power positions, for example, stratified by race, gender, or position in the class structure, may see things differently from one another and from social scientists who happen to be examining the same phenomena (Kincheloe & McLaren, 1994).

Does all of this create real problems, as it were, for modeling as an enterprise? It probably would if we believed, along with positivists, that our ability to only approximately describe and explain what is going on is solely a function of poor measurement tools, or if we believed that the only reason we combine methodological approaches is to capture as much of a single underlying reality as possible (Denzin & Lincoln, 1994). Such positions suggest there really is only one reality, but our tools are not good enough, precise enough, or error-free enough to get there. The solution is opting for a more complicated view of the nature of reality, as Miles and Huberman (1994) put it:

> . . . that social phenomena exist not only in the mind but also in the objective world and that some lawful, reasonably stable relationships are to be found among them. (p. 4)

Surely we may describe, interpret, and explain these relationships in different ways. We use multiple methods to provide richer—although still approximate—descriptions, interpretations, and explanations so as to weigh the conflicting understandings as best we can. Models should simply help us create and discipline these dialogues.

FROM FRAMEWORK TO DEFINITION OF MODELS

In sum, the definition of models that I have been working with empha-sizes that models are *organizing devices* that *facilitate* a *continuous, explicit dialogue* among *multiple sources* of *data* and *assumptions*. To end this introductory discussion, let me summarize how this definition relates to the emerging framework of assumptions that is shared by many qualitative and quantitative researchers.

Organizing devices are tentative summaries rather than definitive statements about what is to be considered the problem at hand, what things are important to consider in understanding the patterns that may exist, and what these patterns may be. All tentative; all subject to change and be reframed.

A *dialogue* denotes an exchange of information back and forth be-tween at least two parties.

The *continuous* nature of this dialogue refers to the iterative, tenta-tive nature of this process. Again, all tentative; all subject to reframing.

The *explicit* nature of this dialogue refers to the exposure of assump-tions and data to public scrutiny so that credibility, interpretation, and validity may be challenged.

The *multiple sources of data* used in the process refer to the possible use of both qualitative and quantitative data in the pursuit of a deeper understanding of variables and relationships.

Facilitation is a supportive process. Substitutes are possible, but models are one way of summarizing information in a manner that can make the exchange of ideas easier and more explicit.

Paraphrasing Tufte's (1983) thoughts about tabular data for models, we might do well to think of models as a vehicle for quickly and vividly giving the viewer a large number of ideas without using much space or ink.

EXERCISES

1. Get a logo set (yes, they still exist) and construct a small model of some social phenomenon. The fragility and simplicity of the model should be apparent. What are the implications of these properties for modeling in the social sciences?

2. Imagine trying to assess how well children are adapting to an elementary school classroom. What objective measures would you consider? What subjective assessments would you make? Are these two types of assessment compatible?

3. Thinking of these same children, how different are the assessments by you as researcher and the assessments of the teachers and the students?

4. For the children in this classroom, is there only one reality that is being assessed, or are there multiple realities?

5. Models are presented in this chapter as organizing devices that focus dialogue between data and assumptions. How does this position differ from some of the other ways of thinking about models presented early in the chapter?

6. House (1994) asked us to:

> . . . consider an evaluation of a reading program in which mixed methods are used. Standardized test scores are collected in a randomized, control group design, and students are interviewed after the program as to what they have learned. Suppose the test score comparison indicates that there is no learning gain, but the interviews indicate that the new-program students have a deeper understanding of the subject matter. (p. 17)

What does the evaluator do now?

SUGGESTIONS FOR FURTHER READING

To fully appreciate the historic gulf between qualitative and quantitative researchers, it should prove useful to examine alternative ways of thinking about the separation. Some of these are referred to in the text. There are other fine and interesting examples of similar distinctions between apparently different phenomena. The distinction between book and article sociology developed by Feagin, Orum, and Sjoberg (1991) touches on many of the same issues even though it appears to concern a separate phenomenon. Bryman's (1988) comparison of qualitative and quantitative research expands the number of dimensions on which comparisons between the two may thoughtfully be pursued. Hirsch, Michaels, and Friedman (1987) give a revealing account of the differences between dirty hands and clean model approaches to research. And Van Maanen's (1983) artfully constructed exchange between a qualitative and quantitative researcher captures the essence of researchers talking past one another. There is not a shortage of discussions of this problem. Much can be learned by reading broadly.

2

The Big Leap: Carving
Situations up Into Concepts

I been all over the world
To the Gulf of Mexico
I ain't never seen no milk cow
With a saddle on his back befo'[1]

In chapter 1, I suggested that concepts are analogous to the blocks in a logo set. This chapter is about those block-like concepts. Unlike blocks, however, we cannot take the nature of concepts for granted. Blocks are tangible and, barring active intervention of some kind, have a relatively constant shape and texture. Concepts are much more elusive, changeable, and tentative, but they help us manage the complexity of our observations by collapsing similar and dissimilar observations separately, as well as differentiating levels of intensity associated with the concepts.

This chapter is not a nuts-and-bolts discussion of measurement from qualitative, quantitative, or mixed-method points of view. There are excellent introductory and advanced discussions of these topics (see the suggestions for further reading at the end of the chapter). There are conceptual issues of particular relevance to modeling, however, that should be discussed. It is with concepts that we first come face to face with a continuing search for what things mean from different points of view. It is also the first time that we are able to observe at work the processes of convergence (grouping things that make some kind of sense together) and divergence (keeping things apart that make some kind of sense being apart) that propels the iterative cycles that we discussed in the last chapter. Keep in mind the idea that saddles do not belong on milk cows as we move forward in this treatment of conceptual issues. Having a saddle may be a great indicator of something, but it is not the concept *milk cow*.

To organize this chapter, I start with a brief discussion of why these building blocks should be called concepts—at least in this book on

---

[1] From "Cabbage Head," a song recorded by Dr. John on his 1992 Warner Brothers *Going Back to New Orleans* album (Byrd & Rebennack).

19

conceptual modeling. From there, I review the concept specification process and the general strategies for progressively clarifying and grounding concepts. I then introduce four overlapping forms of understanding, or making sense, and validity as they apply to concepts: description, interpretation, explanation, and prediction. The chapter ends with a brief discussion of traps and pitfalls in naming concepts.

WHAT'S IN A NAME?

Building blocks need to be called something. Why concepts, as opposed to *variables* or *conditions*? The answer lies in the implications and connotations of the terms as they are used by researchers in the field. Variable connotes precision and draws attention to what varies in situations. This places the term in the quantitative, variable-oriented tradition. Variables capture dimensionalized information about particular social phenomena. Examples would be years of education, level of maternal depression, or severity of visual-motor problems. In the process, however, there are some other unfortunate connotations: quick and overly superficial measurement, routinized and thoughtless application, and a tendency to be reified and/or taken for granted by those who use the term. The real problem may lie in the elementary software packages we train students to use. They are seductively easy and may lead to the conclusion that because a variable is developed by use of the computer it has some special properties associated with it. This is at the heart of what Abbott (1988, 1992) called *general linear reality*, a view of reality that he argued has been accepted as reasonable because it permits our unreflective use of the statistical routines collectively identified as the general linear model. As these packages have become more sophisticated, awareness (at least among those using such packages and reflecting on what they are doing) of the fragility of assumptions has increased and more attention is being placed on relationships between indicators and the latent variables with which they are associated (e.g., see Hoyle, 1995a). My sense, however, is that using the term *variable* without its more abstract companion would cut down on the potentially fruitful dialogue around modeling issues that can take place between quantitative and qualitative researchers. For qualitative researchers, there is simply too much negative baggage associated with the term.

Condition connotes more description than either concept or variable and the presence or absence of particular elements. Examples of conditions are conflict between older and younger military officials in Third World countries, or presence of a family support component in a preschool program. Because it represents a dichotomy, with elements being present or absent, condition also draws attention to nonvarying elements of a situation that may be of great importance in shaping outcomes. Because conditions are dichotomies, it is easier to examine the configurations of elements that may give cases their identity. The identity of a high school which sends 60% of its graduates on to college may vary considerably depending on the kind of neighborhood in which it is located. If such a high school serves a poor area of a city, that combination of poor neighborhood/high success rate has strong implications for the identity of the school in the minds of both insiders and outsiders.

Condition does not suffer from connotations of simplicity or reification (assuming that something is real just because we have a measure for it), although there is a sense of the tangible that is associated with the term, suggesting that there is a fixed reality that is being grappled with. The computer packages used in comparative research constantly force the researcher back to the data rather than separating the researcher from the data. As a general term for the construction of models, however, it is neither widely shared nor capable of easily being translated into the language of variables or concepts.

Concept is a somewhat more abstract term than either *condition* or *variable*, and it implies a richness, depth, and complexity that undermines any sense of oversimplification. Examples of concepts are role development, resource depletion, and aggressiveness. Software packages in the qualitative tradition make it easier to deal with larger amounts of data, but there seems to be less of a sense of separation from the data that may be experienced with some of the quantitative packages. Although most strongly identified with the qualitative tradition, concept is also fundamental to the quantitative tradition; concepts are assumed to be more abstract versions of variables and the building blocks of theories (e.g., Maxwell, 1992). The vagueness that is a connotation of the term *concept* serves it well because it implies a process of development that is never finished. This is an essential characteristic to me, for the tentativeness of specifying and respecifying concepts must be kept in mind if one is to avoid thinking of the process as settled. The nature of the phenomenon must not be studied being taken for granted. Consequently, I have oriented the following discussion around concepts because it is a more general term than *variable* and does not share the unfortunate connotations of the latter term. It also seems easier to translate concepts into the language of conditions than vice versa.

THE CONCEPT SPECIFICATION PROCESS

Specifying concepts—the process of enriching and strengthening the clarity and meaningfulness of concepts by iteratively grounding them in empirical indicators—helps us manage masses of data. This is one of three interrelated specification processes going on simultaneously. The other two, discussed in coming chapters, iteratively and tentatively decide which concepts are important for describing, explaining, and interpreting what is happening in a situation, and how concepts are related to one another. It is artificial to treat these as distinct specification processes, but doing so allows moving from the simpler aspects of modeling to the more complex. In the language of the metaphor I have been using, first the building blocks, then the structure.

The concept specification process has two important parts. A building block implies something discrete, so that one can separate one from another. One important part of the concept specification process, then, is grouping things together that have properties in common (convergence) and separating things that have different properties in common (differentiation, or *divergence*). The companion part of the process involves mapping things with common properties onto dimensions ranging from high to low, dimensions that permit discriminations about intensity, potency, extent of development; or, as a simple dichotomy, presence versus absence. These are dimensionalization strategies. Both sets of strategies are extremely important for the specification and respecification of concepts.

Both quantitative and qualitative researchers use convergent/discriminant and dimensionalization strategies in practice. Recall that one of the reasons for the possibility of building bridges between quantitative and qualitative work is that research in practice for many quantitative researchers does not proceed in the strictly linear, deductive path laid out in quantitative methods texts (Neuman, 1994). As Burawoy (1991) put it:

> In the social sciences the lore of objectivity relies on the separation of the intellectual product from its process of production. The false paths, the endless labors, the turns now this way and that, the theories abandoned, and the data collected but never presented—all lie concealed behind the finished product. The article, the book, the text is evaluated on its own merits, independent of how it emerged. We are taught not to confound the process of discovery with the process of justification. The latter is true science whereas the former is the realm of the intuitive, the tacit, the ineffable . . . (p. 8)

It should come as no surprise, then, that many of the activities that quantitative and qualitative researchers engage in to develop, refine, and ground their concepts in practice bear at least some similarity to one another. The similarities are usually missed because quantitative researchers spend more time manipulating numbers whereas qualitative researchers spend more time manipulating masses of words and pictures.

Examining qualitative and quantitative works that discuss the specification of concepts under various guises, one usually finds diagrams that look something like those represented in Figs. 2.1A, 2.1B, and 2.1C (e.g., see Hoyle & Smith, 1994; Kim & Mueller, 1978; Neuman, 1994; Strauss, 1987). Such diagrams depict the presumed relationship between a variety of indicators and an underlying concept. Qualitative

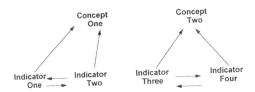

FIG. 2.1A. Alternative concept-indicator models and their assumptions. It is out of the pattern of association among indicators that the meaning of concepts emerges at the beginning of the specification process.

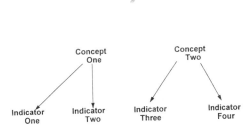

FIG. 2.1B. Alternative concept-indicator models and their assumptions. Concepts are responsible for any observed variation among indicators. Conceptual definition brings theoretical meaning to indicators.

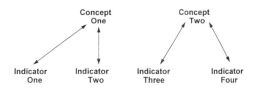

FIG. 2.1C. Alternative concept-indicator models and their assumptions. Concepts and indicators mutually inform one another, with concepts bringing theoretical input and indicators grounding concepts.

researchers are more likely to think of these as *concept-indicator models* (Strauss, 1987). Quantitative researchers are more likely to think of these as *measurement models* (Byrne, 1994).

The Qualitative Approach to Concept Specification

Quoting from Glaser (1978), Strauss (1987) described this relationship between concept and indicators for grounded theory as:

> Grounded theory is based on a concept-indicator model, which directs the conceptual coding of a set of empirical indicators . . . such as behavioral actions and events, observed or described in documents and in the words of interviewees and informants. These data are indicators of a concept the analyst derives from them, at first provisionally but later with more certainty. (p. 25)

There are four important elements in this passage. Glaser (1978) and Strauss (1987) treated such diagrams as models that related concepts to indicators. The model serves to summarize, make explicit, and inform—the loose meaning I take from "direct"—the iterative, continuing *conceptual specification process.* Such rhetoric underscores the tentativeness and iterativeness of the process of conceptual specification over time. Strauss' model use is also compatible with a definition that describes models as organizing devices for a continuing, explicit dialogue between multiple sources of data and assumptions.

As with all qualitative research, tentativeness and iterativeness are central components of the grounded-theory approach to concept specification. There is disagreement among qualitative researchers about how to assure these components. The grounded-theory approach argues that induction—letting the data speak without any preconceived notions of what they mean, or working from data to theory—is the appropriate posture (Fig. 2.1A). The use of the phrase "derives from them [the indicators]" reflects this particular bias. For grounded theorists, this posture is intended to assure that the conceptual specification process will proceed "at first provisionally but later with more certainty."

Other qualitative researchers feel equally strongly about the tentativeness and iterativeness of the research process, but argue that it is not possible to enter the field without theoretical expectations. Burawoy (1991b), for example, argued that theoretical expectations—a more deductive approach—should be encouraged before entering the field. Prior theoretical expectations should be encouraged, however, in the explicit normative context of uncovering surprises, contradictions, anomalies, things that do not fit, and counterinstances. In Burawoy's approach, theoretical expectations serve to heighten the sense of surprise so that field researchers become more sensitive to what is being observed in the field rather than blinded by their theoretical presuppositions (Fig. 2.1B). Similarly, Miles and Huberman (1994) believed that researchers should enter the field after examining prior theorizing and other empirical research so as to develop at least a provisional, tentative coding scheme.

Once the conceptual specification process has started, however, *how* the process began is irrelevant because it is cyclic. Both grounded theorists and other qualitative researchers imagine that the process of specifying concepts proceeds like a combination of Figs. 2.1A and 2.1B as represented in Fig. 2.1C. In Fig. 2.1C the arrows moving back and forth between concepts and indicators indicate a running exchange of ideas and evidence, a dialogue between what data say about the meaning of concepts, and what the summarized common meaning implies about each of the indicators. The reciprocal arrows among the indicators serve to remind researchers that the meaning of concepts is ultimately embedded in indicators and their relationship to one another. As confidence grows that the concept is robust and several indicators are interchangeable with one another, it would presumably be appropriate to drop these arrows as redundant.

The driving force behind the conceptual specification process in qualitative research is a continuing interrogation of data from all sources, both during and after immersion in the field. With such a continuing comparison:

> [T]he analyst is forced into confronting similarities and differences and degrees of consistency of meaning among indicators . . . concepts and their dimensions have earned their way into the theory by systematic generation from data. (Strauss, 1987, pp. 25–26, citing Glaser, 1978)

When analysts enter the field with few theoretical expectations, the initial comparisons are solely among indicators. As the analysis proceeds, the comparisons involve the concept that is being specified. When analysts enter the field with some theoretical expectations, the tentative meaning of indicators is defined by their relationship to the underlying concept.

The confrontation of similarities and differences has a double meaning. It refers, on the one hand to the convergence/discrimination process in that indicators that hang together are put into categories which minimize the overlap of indicators. It refers, on the other hand, to the dimensionalization process in which indicators are arrayed on dimensions from strong to weak, developed to undeveloped, intense to not intense, or high to low. In qualitative research, this dimensionalization process is driven primarily by looking for consistencies of meaning. It is *not* about assigning numbers or mapping particular data points. Precise estimates are deliberately traded for richness and for situating the indicators in a web of meaning that brings the fundamental nature of the concept to life.

There appears to be general agreement among qualitative researchers that the process of conceptual specification is cyclic, tentative and continuing. New observations are deliberately brought in to test the coherence of the emerging concept (Miles & Huberman, 1994) until *saturation* is achieved. Saturation is reflected in uncovering fewer and fewer anomalies, counterinstances, gaps, and ambiguities that could suggest that the nature of the emerging concept is not yet clear, that there is not sufficient separation from other concepts, or that dimensions of the concept have not yet been brought into focus.

The Quantitative Approach to Concept Specification

How similar is the conceptual specification process in quantitative research? The range of data brought to bear on the conceptual specification process is usually more narrow, owing to a need to be able to quantify everything and have it available for as many cases as possible. Richness of detail and in-depth analysis of the consistency of meaning among indicators is traded for much greater precision in two senses. Precision is gained both in terms of assessing how central an indicator is to the common meaning of a concept (through factor loadings) and in terms of the relative placement of cases on the concept dimensions.

Consider factor analysis, for example. Factor analysis is a statistical technique that assumes:

> . . . that some underlying factors [concepts] which are smaller in number than the number of observed variables [indicators], are responsible for the covariation among the observed variables [indicators]. (Kim & Mueller, 1978, p. 12)

This basic assumption imposes the model represented in Fig. 2.1B on the observed relationships among the indicators.[2] Technically, consistency of meaning has nothing to do with the procedures of factor analysis in the early stages. The argument proceeds solely on statistical terms. Any empirical relationships among the indicators that could not be attributed to measurement or sampling errors is assumed to be due to

---

[2]This model is oversimplified in that it does not show the impact of error terms. Quantitative analysis is much more probabilistic—as opposed to deterministic—than qualitative analysis. For factor analysis, this means that the underlying factor is the presumed major influence on explaining variation in the indicator, but there might be random components to the explanation of each as well. If there were systematic components explaining variation in more than one of the indicators, that would indicate the presence of another factor. Kim and Mueller's (1978) first volume is a good introduction to what factor analysis is and how to do it.

the influence of the underlying factors. To represent this situation, the only arrows in the diagram indicating influence and relationship flow from the concept to the indicators. Each of the observed variables is assumed to reflect a linear combination of the underlying factors. In the cleanest cases, there is either only one factor or else the underlying factors are not associated with one another.

What factor analysis and similar techniques provide is a tool for the researcher to dig under the surface of observations to examine what indicators may empirically have in common with different underlying factors. The argument proceeds according to statistical principles, and it is limited by the quality of the indicators that are available for all of the cases of interest. It would be a mistake to believe that the process is a mechanical one, however, with the researcher blindly following the dictates of the statistical programs that generate the output. Quantitative researchers pretest their instruments to assure the quality of their data. They ransack other researchers' scales and theories to inform their theoretical understanding of the underlying factors that may be present. They do long interviews and focus groups to try to get into the points of view of those living through the situations they are analyzing.

Factor analysis is far from being the only quantitative technique conceptual specification by showing how some indicators converge with one concept and diverge from others. Simpler forms exist for trying to evaluate the internal consistency of a set of indicators on a scale (Bernard, 1994). An internally consistent scale (summarized as a high-coefficient alpha) is one in which all of the items may be thought of as falling on the same dimension. More complicated assessments, using what are termed *multitrait-multimethod matrices*, attempt to not only differentiate concepts from one another but also to separate out associations among the indicators that are attributable to the data-gathering method (Althauser, Heberlein, & Scott, 1971). By removing such method variance (shared variance attributable to the common way of gathering data), the remaining variance among the indicators may be considered to be more substantively meaningful.

The leverage that is available with advanced quantitative concept specification comes at a cost. Marsh and Grayson (1995), for example, argued that to do latent-variable models of multitrait, multimethod data, one should have at least four different traits, three different methods, and a sample size of more than 250 observations. Those are huge constraints. But if the indicators available for these observations are well-measured, common-sensical, and transparent, such techniques can serve as a powerful ally to more qualitative forms of concept specification.

Both quantitative and qualitative approaches to conceptual respecification examine and reexamine indicators until they hang together in ways that converge and make sense. They are also both concerned with differentiating concepts to foster a more analytic approach. Finally, they both use dimensionalization strategies, although the mechanics and procedures in the two approaches are quite different. Having established some common ground, it remains to tease out the varieties of meaning that making sense has.

OVERLAPPING FORMS
OF UNDERSTANDING AND VALIDITY

To this point, I have described the specification process in qualitative and quantitative analysis as if the understanding yielded by the process were one-dimensional. It is not. There are many interrelated aspects of understanding and sense-making involved. Associated with each is a form of validity.

Researchers interrogate their data so as to describe the patterns and regularities that exist. In many forms of qualitative research, the search for meaning occurs so closely in conjunction with the struggle to provide a factually accurate description that it is hard to separate the two. Tesch (1990) suggested part of this collapsing of description and interpretation is due to the types of computer programs used for qualitative analysis. Many others would argue that for qualitative analysis at least, the embedding of what is being described in the lived experience of participants is so important that it is coincident with description (Miles & Huberman, 1994). So, for example, when Bernard (1988) made the following distinction, he implicitly collapsed description and interpretation,

> Qualitative analysis—in fact, all analysis—is the search for patterns in the data and for ideas that help explain the existence of those patterns. (p. 319)

Quantitative researchers, on the other hand, usually plead for theoretically informed and commonsensical approaches to the use of statistical description, as in Marsh and Grayson (1995),

> . . . researchers should evaluate results in relation to technical [i.e., statistically descriptive] considerations . . . but they should also place more emphasis on substantive interpretations and theoretical considerations. (p. 198)

Many researchers make analytic distinctions involving more than two kinds of sense-making. Hammersley (1991, 1992) and Wolcutt (1994) distinguished among description, interpretation, and explanation. Maxwell (1992) distinguished among five types of understanding:

description, interpretation, theory, generalizeability, and evaluation (an ethical compass). Four types may be derived from the analyses of Maxwell (1992) and Cook and Campbell (1979): description, interpretation, explanation, and prediction. These four are used in this book because they capture the important alternative dialogues that are essential in the development and evaluation of models. To highlight the cyclic nature of the dialogues, however, the next sections are organized around how models make it easier to engage in these dialogues.

USING MODELS TO MAKE DESCRIPTIVE SENSE
OF CONCEPTS

Making *descriptive* sense of concepts entails being as explicit as possible about procedures used to gather and organize data. Qualitative researchers tend to think in terms of leaving an audit trail from data gathering (Miles & Huberman, 1994). Quantitative researchers emphasize being as explicit as possible about how samples are drawn and how data are gathered and analyzed to uncover patterns (Babbie, 1992). Factual accuracy is the goal. When we ask how good a job a researcher is doing, these matters become questions of validity. The more credible the claim to factual accuracy, the more descriptively valid the research.

Descriptive validity is often termed *reliability* (Bernard, 1994; Kerlinger, 1986; Neuman, 1994). For example, interchangeable indicators are sometimes used in the form of a split-half reliability test. Split-half reliability tests split a sample of items in two parts and construct separate scales on each subset. If the scores are highly correlated, the test is said to be reliable. Similarly, when two coders or raters categorize the same set of events or actions, this is often referred to as *interrater reliability*. The extent of the reliability of the coding scheme is reflected in the size of the correlation among the different coders' judgments. I treat these not as matters of reliability, but as matters of descriptive validity. Where two coders give the same result, the claim of descriptive validity is increased because one can eliminate the possibility that the person making the judgment is making factually inaccurate decisions as to what to report and how to report it. When two versions of a test give the same result, the researcher is on firmer ground in claiming that the indicators are interchangeable.

Because, as we have seen, facts are theory-laden and values cannot be excluded from the research process, claims to descriptive validity are inextricably bound up with claims of theoretical and interpretive validity. Where the methods of testing are different or the training, values, and theoretical background of the coders are different, the claim to descriptive validity of concepts is even stronger. Different biases are presumably involved as training and method vary. Such claims are also buttressed when different researchers working within different perspectives describe a concept the same way or accept the same indicators as grounding. In practice, however, there are ceiling effects on how much agreement across perspectives there can really be. As Maxwell (1992) pointed out, for the categories we use to describe things to be descriptively valid, these categories have to be part of our "taken for granted ideas about space, time, physical objects and our perception of these." (p. 287).

An extended example may be useful at this point. In some recent work, a colleague and I have been trying to capture some of the important elements of a home-based, preschool program called HIPPY (Home Instructional Program for Preschool Youngsters). A central goal of the program is working with parents to prepare children for school. Parents are taught to play the role of teacher to their children in a series of graded lessons over a 2-year period. Because role playing and role development were at the heart of how the participants and providers conceptualized the program, and because role playing is a process that is central to a variety of theories, we decided to see if we could empirically describe roles for parents-as-teachers and children-as-students and use this information to assess the impact of the program.

To increase our openness to possibilities, we brainstormed with the paraprofessionals who were delivering the program, engaged in role playing ourselves, made videotapes of trainers and paraprofessionals role playing, videotaped parents and children doing lessons, and argued among ourselves about what to concentrate on.

It became apparent to us that if we were going to try to work with program providers to help them evaluate the potential impact of the program as it was being delivered, we had to balance two competing objectives. On the one hand, we had to examine aspects of the program's potential impact and gather these data for most, if not all, of the children and parents passing through the program. On the other hand, we had to try to not examine only what was easy or convenient to measure, thereby oversimplifying the richness and complexity of the process by which parents and children come to act and think in ways that may be described as parent-as-teacher and child-as-student role behavior.

This dilemma points to a fundamental problem with much quantitative measurement: It is superficial and thin (Denzin, 1989). This is true even for multiple indicators if all of the indicators come from the same sources (as with items from a questionnaire asked by the same people from the same point of reference). More qualitative researchers use phrases such as "lifting the veil," "getting close to," "digging deep," and "intimate contact" to describe the continuing effort to get close to and capture the essence of what they are trying to understand.

Much quantitative work uses scales that may be internally consistent (as represented by a high alpha coefficient, for example). Such efforts inevitably involve selecting aspects of the situation that are easier to observe and/or record so that more subtle and intangible information gets shunted aside. The risk is that those things that are easier to scale may chase out those things that are more richly descriptive. In the student role commitment work, we have been able to use observations from parents, program paraprofessionals, and external evaluators, each coming at the child from a different relationship and different frame of reference, to construct simple role development scales. These scales draw on experiences from sessions in which the child interacts with the parent or other adults who are playing the role of teacher. There are items dealing with how much fun the child seems to be having during the HIPPY sessions, how helpful the child is in getting the sessions started, how quickly the child responds to the questions, how distracted they are when other children come in the room or the TV is on, and so on. On average, these scales have alpha coefficients of at least .85, considered good in most circles.

There is a lot going on in these sessions that we cannot easily access and for which these items may be an only marginally successful proxy. Using the student-role example, I have tried to graphically represent the tradeoff between thinner but more numerically precise variable assessments, and richer but more difficult to quantify assessments in Fig. 2.2. The observations of children during role-playing sessions have been made by at least two, and often three, observers (parents, paraprofessionals, and evaluators) using different frames of reference.

The parents, for example, have the most intimate understanding of what is happening between the family and the program, and they have the most rich and dense relationships among themselves. Parents and children also have the most experience working together on the program's lesson plans, with the former deliberately playing the role of

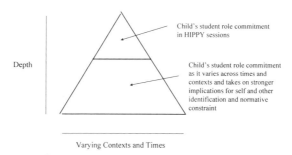

FIG. 2.2. Comparing thinness and richness.

teacher and the latter learning and playing at what it is to be a student. The parents' perspective on what is happening in these lesson-plan sessions is shaped by these factors and others that have to do with their own personal experiences and background. The external evaluator's perspective on these lesson plans, the program and the family is much different. They have met the child only once or twice during the year, have little if anything to do with program operations, and have only limited familiarity with the lesson plans. The evaluators will also have had more education in their backgrounds than either the parents or the paraprofessionals, and their organizational allegiances will involve evaluation rather than program operations. Somewhere in the middle are the paraprofessionals who work with the parents every week but who may only see and work with the child twice a year. As the primary representative of the program, they have a vested interest and more intimate knowledge of the program than either the parents or the evaluators.

These three different frames of reference are a limited form of triangulation (Denzin, 1978). This triangulation gives us a somewhat richer understanding of where the children are in their program-specific role commitment. At the very least, the alternative viewpoints help us reduce the possibility that our observations of the children during these role-play sessions are an artifact of a particular way of gathering data on how the children are acting. Even so, looking only at what is happening to the children in the context of these lesson-plan sessions as they may become more committed to the student role is inevitably thinner and more superficial than it might be.

Descriptively, this thinness manifests itself as only a slice of the data available in the upper part of the triangle represented in Fig. 2.2. There are other, more subtle ways of capturing what is going on in those sessions. For example, there are several nonverbal cues that could in part be captured with a more sophisticated observer-coding system. Eye contact, facial expression, posture, and body angle could contribute to our descriptive understanding of what is actually happening. Additionally, these sessions could be videotaped, providing even more potential descriptive indicators of what is happening in those role-play sessions.

There is much to say for explicitly displaying, on a single page, the tentative assumptions one is making about the nature of a concept (cf. Miles & Huberman, 1994). It organizes and compresses information so that one can get it on the table and talk about it. Fig. 2.3 is a particular form of display, one that grounded theorists would call a concept-indicator model, and what more quantitative researchers would call a simplified measurement model.

Concept-indicator models explicitly show just what indicators are being used and what are taken to be the underlying commonalities, represented as concepts. As with other models, they are of interest *both*

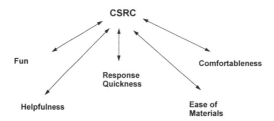

FIG. 2.3. Concept-indicator model for child-as-student role commitment (CSRC).

for what they have in them and for what is left out. In this instance, Fig. 2.3 contains the indicators that survived the brainstorming, pretesting, and discussion that led to the first wave of analysis (Britt & Wilson, 1995). What the indicators stated earlier share is a common concern with how a child is acting and feeling during the sessions. Imposing the tentative organizing label of *child-as-student role commitment* on a scale developed from these items is a deliberate shorthand and simplified reference.

This model was a working model in the sense that it served as a vehicle for talking with the program director and paraprofessionals working in the home and, as well as for discussions among the members of the research team. It served to sensitize us to what we were actually measuring and to the extent to which we were examining only a subset of potentially interchangeable indicators. Not included are observations and questions about how the child uses, talks about, or plays with the HIPPY materials outside of the HIPPY sessions, the extent to which the child might think of the HIPPY lessons as homework, or even more subtle gestures that might be taking place in the sessions themselves.

These surviving indicators were the things we felt we could accurately record using a variety of modestly-trained individuals in a language that could be understood and shared by parents, program personnel, and researchers. Enhancing the descriptive validity of these simple measures could not proceed quantitatively without an enormous expenditure of time, effort, and money. Such efforts might also cost the good will of parents and program personnel. Instead, when we had analyzed the data, we sat down again with the paraprofessionals and other program staff at the local and national levels, presented them with our summary diagrams, and asked them (among other things) how good a job these scales did of describing how children acted during the role-play sessions, and what else typically went on that these scales were not picking up. This is a standard device (Miles & Huberman, 1994) for assessing the validity of a descriptive account. We merely substituted a diagram for the written word.

Such sessions are usually very revealing of empirical regularities as well as their interpretation and explanation. We were surprised that a child's thinking of doing the lesson plans as homework did not scale for the parents. It turns out that the way we asked the question—"Does your child ever refer to engaging in the HIPPY lessons as homework?"—permitted over 90% of the parents to respond affirmatively. With no variation, an item cannot scale well—even if it seems to get at the very essence of what becoming committed to the student role is all about in the eyes of students, parents, teachers, and researchers. The importance of homework was reaffirmed by the paraprofessionals with whom we talked at length about our results.

USING MODELS TO MAKE INTERPRETIVE SENSE OF CONCEPTS

Interpretive sense making starts from a different position than making sense descriptively. For descriptive purposes, it would be enough to note that milk cows have a lot of distinguishing characteristics that hang together—but that saddles is not one of them. The co-occurrence of indicators gives descriptive meaning to milk cows. Interpretive sense-making implicates the experience of those in the situation who have some familiarity with milk cows, how they are used, how they react to petting, how you milk them, and so on. Interactions and experiences with milk cows are the source of interpretive sense-making.

Interpretive sense-making involves trying to get into the shoes of those who have lived, or who are living, through the situation being analyzed, trying to comprehend how they see, define and understand what is going on around them. It goes beyond trying to capture the voice of participants for a variety of reasons, however. Maxwell (1992) summarized some of these as:

> The development of accounts of participants' meanings is usually based to a large extent on the participants' own accounts, but it is essential not to treat these accounts as incorrigible: participants may be unaware of their own feelings or views, may recall these inaccurately, and may consciously or unconsciously distort or conceal their views. (p. 290)

Some people have a better memory than others. Some things are better recorded than others. Biases certainly occur because of memory lapses, but a more certain form of bias occurs because of positional differences that exist in situations.

Recall the old saw, "Where you sit determines what you see." Males often see things differently from females. Adults often have a different version of events than children or adolescents. Those who lived through the Depression have a different interpretation of some events than those who did not. Engineers in manufacturing divisions of companies see the world differently from those in sales. Different ethnic groups may interpret what happened in a situation very differently. Somewhat more generally, those closer to the center of a society or those who have more power in a situation usually see things differently from those who are on the periphery or who have less power. The more heterogeneous the situation along any of these lines of cleavage, the more incredible it is to argue that there is only one story, one account, one reality.

The researcher is not committed to "any old story," as Altheide and Johnson (1994, p. 496) put it, but wants to communicate the "truth about the setting and the situation" as it is viewed by the participants. In light of the problems that may be encountered because of forgetfulness or distortion, telling the actual story requires active intervention on the part of researchers.

In this chapter, the focus is on concepts and indicators. The questions become: How do the individuals and groups who are living through the situation I am analyzing interpret the events that are going on around them? How do they organize that information into more abstract categories and make sense out of it? Different research traditions have different ways of attacking these questions.

Qualitative researchers use the term *emic* codes to refer to how participants name, define, and think about what is going on around them. Such codes are in contrast to *etic* codes that the researcher might use to define and code what is going on from the point of view of a particular theory. Ethnographers, who share the grounded-theory bias toward minimizing one's own theoretical organization before going into the field, embrace emic codes from the start of an investigation. Those who share Burawoy (1991b) or Miles and Huberman's (1994) qualitative preferences for trying to provide some preliminary theoretical organization open themselves to the possibility of surprises, and actively look for counterinstances. This posture assures emic grounding as well.

Quantitative researchers have had to struggle to a greater extent to make plausible claims for interpretive validity. Pretest procedures refine questions until they are worded in such a way that they are at least transparent to those being interviewed. Smith (1982) suggested developing a tentative understanding of how people make sense out of complicated issues by drawing on interviews published in newspapers before attempting to develop questions for surveys. Seiber (1973) suggested several procedures for combining survey data with qualitative analysis to build more sound analyses. Most, if not all, discussions of the development of interpretive sense-making from a quantitative point of view seem derived from Campbell's (1979) observation that our ability to do good quantitative work is based on an implicit understanding of what we are studying.

Drawing again by way of example from the work with preschool children, making interpretive sense of this phenomenon requires, at a minimum, documenting that the role of student, for example, is transparent both to those who are participating in the program and to those who are delivering it. Beyond transparency, however, making a credible claim to interpretive validity requires further documentation. Does being a student mean the same thing to those participating in the program and those delivering it? What do participants and providers rely on to indicate how "into being a student" a child is, as one of our paraprofessionals phrased it? And finally, how much overlap is there between the concept-indicator models we develop and the way providers and participants organize information?

One strategy that we relied on a lot was simply immersing ourselves in the situation, allowing the national trainer from HIPPY, the program director, the paraprofessionals, and the parents to tell us in the language they were using what was going on in the program in general, and what they thought was happening to the children in particular. This assures at least an emic origin for the indicators and concepts that are developed. The repeated references to role playing—with parents being asked to be the first and most important teacher to their children—combined with the delivery of the lessons through role playing and frequent references among parents and providers to getting children ready for school led us to believe that conceptualizing how the program operated in terms of role development would not violate how the participants thought about and understood the program and their varied involvement in it. Our sense that we were on the right track was reinforced by the fact that it did not seem to make a difference whether we were talking to well-educated parents or poorly educated parents, to program staff with masters degrees or those who were marginally literate themselves. We kept getting the same answers: Everyone seemed to think of the program as a vehicle for getting children ready for school.

Choosing names for concepts that resemble those used by participants does not serve as any sort of guarantor of interpretive validity, but it is a start. To increase the chances that we were attending to the same things as parents and providers, we asked paraprofessionals how good sessions differed from bad sessions and what they thought children were getting out of the program. As they started giving us things they attended to, we started organizing these as indicators. Good/bad session discussions were useful probes because they generated a lot of stories and detail without predisposing the paraprofessionals to what we thought was going on. The helpfulness of children in getting lessons started, for example, came through in stories about children bringing materials to their parents without being asked, dropping what they were doing in order to participate in the lessons when asked, and reminding the parent it was time to do their HIPPY homework. Long interviews with some of the parents generated similar stories, boosting our confidence that we were interpreting what was going on through the eyes of the parents and staff.

Dialogue between researchers and participants profits greatly from concept-indicator models. Being able to point to concepts and say, "This is what we think you are telling us about good sessions in terms of their impact on the child," or point to the indicators and say, " . . . and these are the things you are telling us that you use in deciding when sessions are good" is helpful in a couple respects. It minimizes the status differences between researchers and participants by confining all the research summary to a single page, a simple diagram—something that can be controlled, put on the table, drawn on, or even wadded up. Such models also make it easier to ask respecification questions in deceptively simple ways: "What are we leaving out?" or, "What are we missing here?"

Most importantly for interpretive sense making, concept-indicator models made it easier to probe what things meant. "How do you know when a child is being helpful in getting a lesson started?" or, "What does having fun in the lessons have to do with learning how to be a student?" are questions that are a lot easier to ask—and hear—when you can point to a sheet of paper. Models transform such questions from abstract discussions of epistemic correlations between concepts and indicators into shared, solvable puzzles.

It would be misleading to argue, however, that after a period of time, we did not alter how program providers organized how they thought about the impact of the program on children. For example, in a few of these exchanges and discussions things that happened in sessions came up that the paraprofessionals had not at first realized the significance of, as in this exchange regarding homework:

> Yeah, [Florence] mentioned that [Tommy] kept wanting to do his homework [by which he meant that he wanted to do the HIPPY lesson]. I just passed it off and didn't think twice about it, but yeah, I see now how that means he's getting into being ready to go to school.

Nor would it be accurate to claim that all parents and paraprofessionals were equally adept at talking about, organizing and understanding what it meant for their children to be getting ready to go to school. In our study, there was a systematic bias toward greater understanding among those parents who either had more than a high-school education and/or were going to school themselves. This bias has less to do with power than with the ability to verbally express some of the things that are happening to children as they go through the program.

Power, education, and experience differentials could lead to different interpretations that work against one another rather than blending into shared, solvable puzzles. For example, although it is true that all parents talked about the program as a vehicle for *getting children ready for school*, the meaning of getting children ready for school differed quite a bit depending on how educated the parents were. The more-educated parents emphasized intangible indicators like taking lessons seriously and learning to sit still. Less educated parents—even with considerable probing—emphasized learning colors, learning to connect dots, and other concrete skills. These divergent interpretations of getting ready for school cannot simply be ironed out. They must be incorporated as variations in the analysis.

Interpretive validity, then, is very concerned with the meanings people associate with the phenomena they and researchers observe. Models may help organize these meanings by making it possible to sit down and discuss them as equals in a puzzle-solving task. The puzzle, however, may not fit together the same way for everyone. Some people may define the situation one way. Some may define it in other ways. The points of divergence must be respected.

USING MODELS TO MAKE EXPLANATORY SENSE OF CONCEPTS

For concepts, issues of theoretical or explanatory sense making involve linking our grounded-in-indicators concepts into higher-order, theoretical concepts that are the basic building blocks of theories. Quantitative research is usually seen as being more deductive, with the higher-order constructs dictating what the concepts-as-indicated should be. Qualitative research, on the other hand, is usually seen as emphasizing induction, with the indicators dictating what the eventual concepts should look like. In actual practice, induction and deduction occur as a continuing cycle of respecification, and there are parallels between how quantitative and qualitative researchers view the process of making theoretical sense.

Consider the way Cook and Campbell (1979) defined the process of increasing the credibility of their claims to construct validity:

> . . . we shall use the term construct validity . . . to refer to the approximate validity with which we can make generalizations about higher-order constructs from research operations. (p. 38)

Cook and Campbell's book on quasi-experimentation is a landmark in the quantitative tradition. In spite of that, there is a strong emphasis on moving from indicators (research operations) to constructs. Lower-level indicators are not enough: For Cook and Campbell, these individual and research operations must make sense in terms of the more abstract concepts that have relevance and theoretical meaning outside of the quasi-experimental situation.

Maxwell (1992), working within a somewhat more liberal critical realist perspective as an ethnographer, seemed to emphasize the reverse dialogue:

> Any theory has two components: the concept or categories that the theory employs, and the relationships that are thought to exist among these concepts. Corresponding to these two aspects of a theory are two aspects of theoretical validity: the validity of the concepts themselves as they are applied to the phenomenon, and the validity of the postulated relationships among the concepts. (p. 291)

Here, the emphasis seems to be on the extent to which the higher-level concepts inform and give theoretical meaning to the indicators.

In actual practice, again, the process is cyclic, with the process of establishing indicators refining the theoretical meaning of concepts as they apply in the situation being studied, and the essential nature of the higher-order concepts focusing attention on particular indicators.

The tentativeness of the process stands out in a critical realist perspective, but because of the explicitness of this refinement of *etic*, researcher-derived concepts should be appreciated as well. It is in the explicitness of this dialogue that I believe the major utility of using concept-indicator models is found. Arguments among research colleagues do not have such great status differences that there is an appreciable leveling effect from using models in talking to one another. Models do, however, force researchers to be explicit about what it is that they are assuming about the nature of a concept as it applies to a particular situation. Models do make it easier to bring up what one believes should be attended to in a particular situation and, by implication, what one believes should not be attended to.

The chastening process of examining things that do not fit—and questioning those things that do appear to fit—may be focused and given form by drawing them on a sheet of paper. *Things* has a double meaning in this process: It may refer either to indicators or concepts. We make continuing decisions about which indicators are relevant and irrelevant. Simultaneously, we continue to discuss whether these indicators have what is conveyed by the definition of the higher-order construct in common.

To go back to our role-commitment example, I have talked about the handful of indicators that were selected to represent student-role commitment as it was expressed in the lesson delivery sessions (Fig. 2.3). With theoretical validity, interest shifts to the specification of concepts and indicators that are meaningful in terms of the theories that researchers either bring with them or find emerging from the analysis.

Theoretical validity claims are made more credible by eliminating alternative interpretations of the tentative set of indicators. For the role development concept that emerged from our interactions with providers and participants in the program, there are alternative interpretations that might have fit the tentatively selected indicators if somewhat different combinations were chosen. So, for example, had we chosen to ask about fun during sessions, happy when it is time to do HIPPY, helpfulness getting session started, helpfulness putting materials away, or playfulness, an interpretation in terms of enjoyment or attachment to the HIPPY sessions might have made better sense not only from a theoretical point of view but also from interpretive and descriptive points of view. Alternatively, had we focused more on skillfulness, easiness of materials, speed of response, drawing ability, or word recognition, this cognitive-skill dimension would have stood out more and challenged for a conceptual definition that emphasized indicators drawn from such a theoretical category.

The point of this exercise is to suggest that concepts are very dependent on the tentatively selected indicators for their theoretical meaning. Altering the kinds of things that are considered indicators has strong implications for the theoretical definition that is tied to those indicators. On the other hand, conceptual definitions firmly rooted in a theoretical tradition guide us in the selection of indicators. So, for example, *if* we are going to credibly claim that student role development is involved, should we not be trying to assess, for example, how long a child is able to work at a task without supervision, how successfully HIPPY lessons compete for time with other interesting activities in the child's life, how much fun the HIPPY lesson plans are against other parent–child activities, or whether the child uses the word *homework* to refer to the emerging sense of obligation for engaging in the HIPPY lessons?

Each of these potential "gaps" (Burawoy, 1991b, p. 10) or "inadequacies" (Ragin, 1987, p. 164) adds a somewhat different element to the picture of what the student role might be. Their exclusion represents judgments about the possibility of such an indicator occurring in the delivery of lesson plans, how interchangeable the indicators would be with indicators already included, how difficult the those would be to assess, and how varied the meaning of the indicator might be.[3]

Modeling in this context becomes a way of disciplining the interrogation of field notes, documents, questionnaires, videotapes, and other sources of data. Modeling becomes a way of embedding the results of various dimensional scaling techniques in a meaningful set of theoretical alternatives so as to not reify the results as guarantors of conceptual validity. Modeling also becomes a convenient way of *explicitly* summarizing, in a small space, the implications of the brainstorming search for counterinstances so that they can be discussed with colleagues and other interested parties.

---

[3] We were surprised, for example, that talking about homework was so prevalent that almost all children, parents, and providers used the term. Hence, thinking of the use of the term homework as an indicator that a child is beginning to develop a sense of responsibility for doing the HIPPY lessons appeared to be unlikely—especially at age four!

MAKING PREDICTIVE SENSE OF CONCEPTS
THROUGH MODELING

Prediction may sound like a strange term to use with concepts. We are not, after all, trying to predict who will win the World Series or how many votes will be cast for a particular candidate in the next Presidential election. Yet, making predictions about concepts is an integral part of both qualitative and quantitative research. Predictions force us to look at the limits of our descriptive, interpretive, and explanatory sense making. When we describe the indicators that hang together and label them as a *concept*, their hanging together may be *context dependent* (meaning that we may only observe this particular configuration in a particular context). When we come to understand what the people living in a particular context mean when they talk about a concept, that interpretive understanding may also be context dependent. And when we engage a dialogue between theory and concepts, that explanatory sense making may be context dependent as well.

If these various forms of sense making are context dependent, what happens when the context changes? Do the same concepts grounded in the same indicators help us make sense of what is going on in other contexts and at other times? Do different indicators that may be linked conceptually help us make sense of what is going on as contexts and times change? These are questions that make us push the limits of our understanding.

Prediction is, first of all, an essential part of the specification of concepts *across* groups, times, institutions, settings or, most generally, context. Can we adequately describe the extent of family violence in Bermuda with a scale that was developed in Bangladesh? Can we understand the theoretical meaning of job burnout in a small, traditionally run, low-tech textile mill in rural Georgia using a scale developed in a large, progressively run, high-tech software developer in the urban Northeast? Does the meaning of computers in classrooms characterized by teamwork, self-guided inquiry, and a non-authoritative leadership style on the part of the teacher help us to interpret how students and teachers in more traditional classrooms will understand computers and their use?

These are powerful questions regarding what is usually termed *generalizeability*: the extent to which what we learn descriptively, interpretively, and theoretically in one context can inform our descriptions, interpretations, and theories in others. Most qualitative researchers would probably agree with the general rule of thumb stated by Miles and Huberman (1994):

Focusing solely on individual behavior without attending to contexts runs a serious risk of misunderstanding the meaning of events. (p. 102)

I believe the risks are broader and deeper than that. We risk misunderstanding how events may be described, interpreted, and explained. At the same time, I believe generalization is a challenge that must be met by social scientists if their work is to be treated as credible by policy makers. In the process, however, we are going to need to be sensitive to the multiple issues involved in understanding a phenomenon from the three viewpoints I have discussed (description, interpretation, and explanation). At that point, social scientists may not be able to generalize very well, but we should be able to understand the surprises, inconsistencies, differences, and gaps more quickly than we would going into a situation cold.

These are risks to which both quantitative and qualitative researchers are sensitive. Consider, for example, how Bernard (1994) cautioned the reader about too quickly generalizing the results of a Guttman-scaling effort:

> DeWalt (1979) used Guttman scaling to test his index of material style of life in a Mexican farming community. He scored 54 respondents on whether they possessed eight material items (a radio, a stove, a sewing machine, etc.) and achieved a remarkable [Coefficient of Reproducibility] of .95. This means that, for his data, the index of material style of life is highly reliable and differentiates among informants. . . . An index must be checked . . . each time it is used on a population. My hunch is that DeWalt's material-style-of-life scale has its analog in nearly all societies. The particular list of items that DeWalt used in Mexico may not scale for a village in Cameroon, but some list of material items will scale there. You just have to find them. (p. 296)

Contexts change, and as they change, the way things may be described, interpreted, and explained will almost inevitably change.

The elements of context to which we need to be sensitive are many. Anything that has implications for how things are described, interpreted, and explained is fair game. It may be as simple as other things that are immediately relevant in the situation (Miles & Huberman, 1994). It may be as complex as events and actions that mutually define one another:

> . . . the whole is composed of inseparable aspects that simultaneously and conjointly define the whole . . . the root metaphor . . . is the historical event—a spatial and temporal confluence of people, settings and activities that constitutes a complex organized unit . . . the aspects of a system, that is, person and context, coexist jointly and define one another and contribute to the meaning and nature of . . . the event (Altman & Rogoff, 1987, p. 24, cited in Salomon, 1991, p. 13)

Salomon (1991) built an argument for the impossibility of understanding the meaning of the introduction of computers in classrooms without understanding the other properties of the organized system of a classroom. Although different in scale and approach, note how similar the underlying reasoning is in Isaac and Griffin's (1989) argument for differences in meaning of union membership in different historical periods. In the following passage, for example, they criticized some longitudinal studies that purported to explain union membership as if it meant the same thing over long periods of time, through

> ... war and peace, depression and prosperity, the passage of the Wagner Act and its partial dismemberment by the Taft-Hartley Amendment, legal and employ [sic] repression of unions and legislative and employer tolerance or even encouragement, waves of immigration and alien quotas, and times of labor insurgency and quiescence. (p. 876)

Sociocultural systems of any size, as well as all simpler contingencies, need to be considered before predictions may be made explicit.

Returning to the role-commitment example, consider how the student-role concept would have to change as the child grows older. Changing age is more than a simple ticking off of chronological time. Isaac and Griffin (1989) reminded us that such an approach would be *ahistorical*. Rather, as the child grows older, many things in his or her environment (and person) are changing and reconfiguring as well. With these changes come the necessity of changing the nature of the student role concept. For example, as soon as the child and parent stop the HIPPY program, assessing student role development in the context of the lesson plans makes no sense at all, theoretical or otherwise. The context has changed. School classrooms become relevant (Pietrkowski & Baker, 1993) and interactions between student and classroom teacher become salient. Much broader interactions between parent and child become relevant (such as shared understandings of homework), but these have only loose ties to the materials used in the HIPPY program lesson-plan sessions. These contexts must be mapped. As Bernard (1994) might have said, analogs to the student role exist in these contexts; we just have to find them.

The pursuit of analogs proceeds by imagining how the indicators, which are useful in constructing descriptive, interpretive, and explanatory dialogues might become appropriate to other contexts. This imagination process is made easier by starting with the concept-indicator model *explicitly framed and labeled* for the HIPPY-lesson context, then starting a new, explicitly framed and labeled concept-indicator model for the new context, such as an elementary-school classroom. At this point, descriptive, interpretive, and theoretical questions may be asked as they refer to the specific indicators. For example, is an indicator that relates to the child having fun potentially useful in describing attitude in the classroom? Why or why not? Does having fun as a student in the classroom mean the same thing to students as having fun in the HIPPY lessons? What theoretical meaning does having fun have in the classroom environment? How is it the same and different from the theoretical meaning of having fun in the HIPPY lessons?

The devil is in these sorts of details. Mapping them on a piece of paper is a good way of keeping track of them and grounding these dialogues in regards to how, why, and why not particular indicators might be transferable in some form to the new environment. A parallel set of dialogues should be taking place for indicators that appear to be relevant in the classroom that had no analog in the HIPPY-lesson context. Working by oneself on a task, for example, has no analog in the HIPPY-lesson environment: The delivery of the lessons is through continuing interaction between the parent and child; there are no possibilities for self-monitored work—at least as far as the HIPPY program is concerned. Working through why it was not a viable indicator in the HIPPY-lesson context and why it might be in the classroom enriches the understanding of both environments. Such a dialogue may also have implications for the delivery of the HIPPY program. If the delivery mechanism could be altered somewhat to permit some time for the child to work on a task by herself, then the transfer of the student role from the HIPPY-lesson context to the classroom context might be stronger.

Drawing and redrawing, specifying and respecifying, discussing and rediscussing are not to be private activities. Teachers, parents, and students should be involved in regrounding the interpretive and descriptive dialogues. Colleagues, teachers, and the work of others should be integrated to reground the theoretical and descriptive dialogues. Model drawing is a useful vehicle for conducting all of these dialogues.

Recall that the descriptive-validity task was to select a set of indicators that was factually accurate and so common-sensical and simply worded that it did not require either explanation or interpretation. Words like *fun*, *helpful*, and *easy* are appropriate here *if* they appear to be interchangeable with the factors that account for most of what is going on in the situation. With interpretive validity, the task shifts toward assessing the extent to which those indicators may claim an emic status, and the extent to which they are considered meaningful by the variety of individuals and groups acting in the situation being analyzed. With theoretical validity claims, the task shifts again, this time toward indicators that are most meaningful in terms of the theory or theories that inform a more general understanding or accounting of the situation. Predictive-validity concerns refocus all of these dialogues by sensitizing the researcher to the importance of context. All description, interpretation, and explanation are forms of local knowledge, confined to the context being studied until challenged and examined as a set of dialogues that bear on questions of description, interpretation, and expla-nation from one context to another. Predictive validity questions push our ability to make sense by making us confront how concepts might change as contexts change. A parallel set of challenges that we must confront involves changes of a different sort: changes in intensity, seriousness, potency, level of development, or some other way of describ-ing changes in a vertical direction.

DIMENSIONALIZATION OF CONCEPTS: TESTING LIMITS IN A DIFFERENT DIRECTION

Left to be discussed are some simple guidelines for developing variable names that can be easily manipulated within the rhetoric of causation. Underneath and driving this discussion is a need for concepts that differentiate individuals, groups, classrooms, organizations, communi-ties, and so on in terms of how intensely the qualities associated with the concept are manifested. This pushes us to test limits in a manner analogous to generalization: It makes us confront how classrooms with a lot of vitality, for example, might differ from classrooms with not much vitality at all. In our research on role commitment, it is important to be able to differentiate those children with higher levels of commitment from those with lower levels. Similarly, communities with greater de-grees of economic development need to be separated from communities with lesser degrees if the nature of economic development in the context being studied is to become clear.

Table 2.1 has some common traps and problems in naming variables and their resolution. There must be a specific and communicable sense of just what is varying and a sense of the continuum—or parallel continua—it is presumed to vary along. Rather than referring to some-thing vague like *economic situation*, for example, specifying what factor of the economic situation that is presumed to vary is important. Eco-nomic situations can vary in their harshness, stability, credentials and training required, as well as the type of industry or discrimination—and probably a host of other factors. The more complex the constructs involved, the more likely there are to be multiple dimensions that could vary, and the more necessary it is to carefully specify just what is varying.

A frequent and serious problem involves collapsing the polarity in regards to the relationship between variables into the name of the variable. For example, one might refer to higher income or higher education to try to be more precise about the implications of movement in the concept of interest. One might be predicting that higher income would lead to lower anomie, but collapsing the direction of movement of both variables into

TABLE 2.1
Concept Definitions: Common Problems and Suggested Resolutions

Problem	Resolution
Using Adjectival Concept Names	*Create Nouns*
Religious	Religiosity
Smart	Intelligence
Impulsive	Impulsivity
Collapsing Polarity and Concept Names	*Leave Polarity out of Concept Names*
Higher Income	Income
Less Anomie	Anomie
High Assistance	Assistance
Leaving Concept Dimensions Vague	*Specify Concept dimensions*
Economic Situation	Harshness of Economic Situation
Education	Years of Education
Collapsing Complex Dimensions and Concept Names	*Make Dimension a Part of the Definition*
Positive Self-esteem	Positiveness of Self-esteem
Demanding Responsibilities	Responsibility Press

definitions only makes the analysis of relationships more complicated. There are conventions for assessing and symbolizing the nature of the relationship between concepts. I discuss these in the next chapter. Suffice it to say at this point that concept names should not include information about relationships.

SUMMARY

This chapter has introduced concepts as one of the building blocks of models. Concepts are a necessary component of both models and theories because they keep us from drowning in a sea of detail. We group together indicators that belong and separate things that seem not to. Concepts are not static in how we define and understand them or in how we ground them with indicators of varying kinds. There is a continuing, tentative respecification going on. Concept-indicator or measurement models are useful for keeping track of the process.

Conceptual respecification is essentially a reexamination process of how we make sense of the concepts included in our models. In this chapter, we examined descriptive, interpretive, and explanatory sense-making. Predictive validity questions make us confront the limits of these forms of understanding across contexts and time. For example, what does our description of a concept in one context tell us about what to expect in another context? Dimensionalization makes us confront the limits of these forms of understanding on a vertical dimension. For example, how can we describe the differences between communities that are economically underdeveloped from communities that are economically developed in a post-industrial economy?

All of these questions are concerned with conceptual respecification. The next chapter examines a second building block of models: relationships between concepts.

EXERCISES

1. Take three or four observations that you think hang together descriptively, arranging them loosely within a triangle. Then extend this small triangle downward on both sides so as to form a larger triangle, as in Fig. 2.2. The empty space in both the smaller and larger triangles represents alternative indicators that vary in depth and contextual richness. Fill in some of the blank spaces, asking the following questions:

- Do different combinations of indicators skew the meaning of the emerging concept in different ways (see Fig. 2.1A)?
- Does the name and meaning you have given to the initial combination of indicators alter where you look for additional indicators, how you look for them, and how you think about them (Fig. 2.1C)?
- Is it apparent that you are always faced with looking at a sample of situations, actions, rationalizations, tactics, and so on, in developing concepts?

2. Sit down with another student, decide on a concept you would like to know about, and after separately creating two laundry lists of indicators for this concept, discuss how you might simplify the process by focusing only on a smaller number of indicators.

a. How interchangeable are the indicators you have chosen with the indicators you have left out? Do the indicators you have chosen seem to provide a factually accurate description of the concept and its dimensions for the situation in which you are interested?

b. From an interpretive point of view, do you have emic indicators? Is their meaning transparent? If not transparent, is the meaning such that participants in the situation you are studying will not only understand but be likely to use them in their everyday discourse? Might some of your participants disagree with one another regarding the meaning of the terms you are using? Can you map subsets of presumably more and less interpretively valid indicators? Will the participants in the situation you are studying agree on the common meaning and name you have given to this concept?

c. From an explanatory point of view, do the indicators you have chosen bear a straightforward relationship to a theoretical perspective? How do they overlap with other efforts to theoretically ground this concept? Are there any gaps or surprises in your concept-indicator model relative to what literature has to say about this concept?

d. From a predictive validity point of view, imagine trying to use your concept and its indicators in a situation that differs fundamentally in some contextual characteristic, such as the age of the participants, the extent of technological sophistication, or a cluster of contextual characteristics that create an identifiable era or classroom. How would your concept and its indicators change if you were to alter the situation you are analyzing? Does the meaning of the concept change to the participants? Does the theoretical meaning change? How do the indicators change, and why?

3. What are the differences among descriptive, interpretive, explanatory, and predictive validity claims?

4. Both quantitative and qualitative approaches to concept specification have strong sources of leverage. What are they?

5. What are the ways in which using models facilitate the descriptive, interpretive, explanatory, and predictive dialogues taking place in concept specification?

6. In this chapter, I have artificially simplified the discussion by assuming that there are unobserved or unmeasured concepts on the one hand, and indicators on the other. The actual state of affairs is more like a continuum. Van Maanan (1983) reminded us that the indicators we discover are already the products of interpretation and might well be called *first-order concepts*. On the other end of the continuum, it is possible to combine concepts together to make still higher-order concepts. For the concept you have been using in these exercises, try stretching your concept-indicator model in both directions. What is the most appropriate level for the analysis you have in mind?

7. It is important to practice the various aspects of modeling with respect to something you are sufficiently interested in to immerse yourself in the investigation.

- With immersion comes a continuing theoretical dialogue with the various literatures that may inform your investigation;
- With immersion comes increased opportunities for dialogue between yourself as researcher and the diverse people and groups that lived or are living through the situation being investigated;
- With immersion comes a continuing descriptive dialogue among aspects of the situation that may hang together as alternate indicators of an emerging concept;
- With immersion comes a continuing dialogue regarding the nature of the context(s) within which your investigation is taking place.

SUGGESTIONS FOR FURTHER READING

There are a couple of mixed-method texts that discuss issues relating to measurement and concept specification from alternate perspectives. Bernard (1994), Brewer and Hunter (1989), Neuman (1994), and Ragin (1994) are useful starting points.

Denzin, N. K., & Lincoln, Y. S. (1994). *Handbook of qualitative research*. Thousand Oaks, CA: Sage.

This collection of chapters draws on authors and their work in a variety of fields. The chapter by Altheide and Johnson specifically addresses criteria for assessing interpretive validity. There are several other chapters in the sections on strategies of inquiry, methods of collecting and analyzing and the act of interpretation that are also relevant to questions of reliability and validity in qualitative research.

Hammersley, M. (1992). *What's wrong with ethnography? Methodological explorations*. London: Routledge.

This is an excellent extended analysis of problems in establishing reliability and validity in ethnographic research.

Maxwell, J. A. (1992). Understanding and validity in qualitative research. *Harvard Educational Review*, *62*, 279–300.

Validity is seen as a key issue in establishing the credibility of qualitative research: Where valid results are not possible, policies, programs, and predictions based on such analyses cannot be relied on. Five types of validity in qualitative analysis are presented.

Miles, M. B., & Huberman, A. M. (1994). *Qualitative data analysis*. Thousand Oaks, CA: Sage.

This is a major reference work in qualitative analysis packed with techniques for generating meaning.

Hoyle, R. H. (Ed). (1995a). *Structural equation modeling*. Thousand Oaks, CA: Sage.

This is a good reference for how quantitative researchers using structural equation modeling talk about and understand issues of specification.

Kim, J., & Mueller, C. W. (1978). *Introduction to factor analysis*. Newbury Park, CA: Sage.

3

Sticks and Spaces: Relationships Between Concepts

"Well, he kept getting up so I kept on hitting him."

"Did your hitting him cause him to get up, or is that too strong? . . ."

"Naw, he kept getting up cause I wasn't strong enough to hit him harder."

In the last chapter, I focused on the ways in which the complexity of our observations and data-gathering efforts may be managed by reducing large numbers of indicators into a smaller number of concepts. Convergence/discrimination and dimensionalization were discussed as major strategies for making sense of concepts in four areas: description, interpretation, explanation, and prediction. The varied ways of thinking about concept-indicator models that I discussed all had one thing in common: They all were based on the assumption that what was important about relationships among indicators was what their association told us about the underlying concepts. All of the dialogues taking place are based on the assumption that the empirical associations that these indicators have in common derive from or define the underlying concept. These dialogues include how factually accurate indicators of concepts are, what they mean to the people living through situations, what they mean in terms of the emerging or existing theoretical perspectives we favor, or how limited they are to the context in which they are occurring.

This chapter treats associations among concepts, those abstract collections of indicators that help us manage complexity (Fig. 3.1). It is not simply assessing what concepts are associated with one another that is of interest, however. Rather, it is presumed patterns of influence between concepts that is of interest. This is an important distinction. Were the logic of the last chapter to be followed, nondirectional associations among concepts would be examined to assess what they had in common so that still more abstract concepts could be formed. This is a legitimate

FIG. 3.1. Non-directional and directional associations between concepts.

exercise, but it is part of the continuing process of conceptual respecification to ask what the appropriate level of abstraction is for the concepts in which we are interested (see exercise 5, chapter 2). Looking for patterns of influence (i.e., directional relationships) assumes that the concepts of interest are conceptually distinct and begins to ask questions like, "If this concept occurs in a particular context, does it influence the chances of other concepts being present?"

To argue that one social phenomenon influences another without considering other contributing factors or the conditions under which a relationship operates is very unrealistic. The quote that starts this chapter is an example of that. Even this brief exchange suggests a very complicated situation, and it would take awhile to disentangle the multiple aspects that are influencing one another. Focusing on only two concepts, however, gets us started and allows us to discuss the assumptions regarding the linking of those concepts. Following this, I turn to the question of how strong the language should be in discussing flows of influence among social science concepts. The chapter ends with a discussion of the interpenetration of specification processes. Once these issues have been discussed and conventions developed where appropriate, subsequent chapters treat more complex configurations of concepts.

DIMENSIONS OF RELATIONSHIPS

There are several aspects or dimensions of describing the flow of influence between two concepts. In this section, I discuss six dimensions that capture much of the complexity that should frame a set of dialogues about how social phenomena are related to one another. These dimensions are listed with sets of illustrative questions that should be asked in considering each dimension:

1. Temporality
   What is the relative time order of the two concepts?
   How should expectations and goal-oriented behavior be treated?

How should uneven starting and stopping points of concepts be handled?

Can lagged (delayed) effects be fairly incorporated in relationships?

2. Direction

Does influence flow in one direction only or in both directions?

3. Polarity

Do the linked concepts change in the same or opposite directions?

4. Symmetry

Are the polarities that are believed to exist contingent on the direction of change in the concept exerting the influence?

5. Strength

How strong or important are the relationships between the linked concepts?

6. Linearity

May the relationship(s) between the linked concepts be assumed to be linear?

This section is devoted to the consideration of these dimensions of relationships in somewhat greater detail.

Temporality

Temporality involves making several assumptions about how time enters into the relationships between two concepts. In a later chapter, the concept of historical contingency—that the relationship between two concepts differs from one time period to another—will be introduced. There time becomes context rather than other things regarding the order in which phenomena start and stop. In this section, we discuss the relative time order of concepts, the problem of goal-oriented behavior, the problem of different starting and stopping times, and the pace of the process by which one concept is thought to affect another. These are questions that we should be sensitive to as we begin to cluster concepts together in ways we believe are associated with the process by which some phenomena influence others.

Time Order. Davis (1988) reduced some of what is important to understand about time to the simple phrase, "Something afterwards can't cause something before it" (p. 8). All who have discussed the nature of causation (Marini & Singer, 1988, for example) agree that this is an indispensable component. Miles and Huberman (1994) suggested a variety of displays to sensitize the researcher to the time-ordering of effects. In some cases, the assignment of time order is unambiguous; in other cases, it is not. How committed parents are to the first year of a program designed to help their children be prepared for school most assuredly comes before the achievement of their children on stand-ardized academic tests the following year. We may not have a sense of what the mechanism is by which parental commitment affects subsequent achievement, but we can at least unambiguously assign causal order to the two variables. Whether it is unambiguous or not should not blind us to the fact that one cannot escape making some assumptions about time.

Goal-Orientedness. The realities and phenomena we are seeking to model, however, are inherently richer than any of the models we construct. This is why the construction of models represents several simplifying assumptions. Much of the behavior of individuals is—or at least appears—*to be* goal directed: People do things because they expect something to happen—although there is sufficient irrationality, conflicting goals, and unexpected outcomes to make this assumption difficult at times. Because people are imagining a future state of affairs, does this violate a strict interpretation of temporal order? We could argue about this for some time, but a simple answer is, "No, not if you include expectations in the model, or postulate them as part of the mechanism." Including expectations in models or postulated mechanisms is a reasonable simplifying assumption to the extent that we do not lose too much of the richness of the phenomena by making this assumption. Managers may institute new policies because they expect certain consequences to flow. Including the managers' evolving expectations regarding what is going to happen in the future makes explicit the goal-orientedness of their actions. In chapter 5, we will see that the inclusion of expectations is only a partial solution because of the tendency for such expectations to become self-fulfilling.

Demographic Attributes. Reality is also temporally richer than we can comfortably deal with when we are trying to examine how attributes (like race and sex) are conducive to the development of certain patterns of behavior and attitude. Holland (1986) claimed that attributes cannot be causes, although most of the quantitatively competent reviewers of this assertion disagree (Marini & Singer, 1988). Blalock (1966) argued a more modest position in his lectures on modeling: that attributes like race and sex summarize our ignorance regarding causal processes. Consequently, we should never be too comfortable that we are actually explaining anything when we find such associations. Attributes are certainly legitimate contenders for representation in causal models, but they do represent real problems when it comes to time order.

We can unambiguously assign an arrow from sex to math achievement—but in doing so, we should not feel comfortable that we have done very much. Males tend to do better at math than females (at least, and perhaps *only*, for the present, in our culture). One is certainly a biological male or female before math competence is assessed. And it is nonsensical to think that being competent at math makes one more male—at least biologically. The association of maleness and math competence says nothing about the mechanism, of course, but the specific point I am driving at is that maleness is something that is carried into thousands of environmental interactions over the course of many years before math competence is assessed. It may even be relevant at the time that math competence is assessed. When does the effect actually occur? Did it occur when genes were being combined and replicated, at some time early in the socialization of boys and girls, at some point when school becomes part of the everyday life of boys and girls, at the time of the assessment, or some combination of all of these? This ambiguity was what Blalock was referring to when he argued that demographic attributes summarize our ignorance.

Ambiguity of Start/Stop Times. A similar problem arises when we are dealing with events. When does a divorce start and stop? When does it start and stop having an effect on the adults and children involved? Does it have different short and longer-term effects (Miles & Huberman, 1994)? Does it start or end as an event when a piece of paper is signed by a judge? Or do we say that it is a discrete event while consensually hushing up that it is an amorphous kind of important happening (Abbott, 1992) that has an almost indeterminate beginning and ending point?

Lagged or Delayed Effects. Once we get as comfortable as we feel we can with the temporal ordering of concepts, we also need to understand that the mechanisms by which concepts affect one another do not always take place at the same pace. When one concept changes, how long does it take the other concept to be affected? Blalock's (1964) early treatment of this problem asked the reader to suspend judgment and simply assume that the impact of one variable on another was almost simultaneous.[1] That is rarely an easy or even appropriate assumption to make. When we believe there is a delay or a lag, we should try to be explicit about how long the delay is before the effect occurs, or how the effect is distributed across time. When the government passes legislation, it takes time for it to begin having effects because it takes awhile for individuals and corporations to become aware of the change and understand what it is that they are supposed to do. Including a concept like the extent of awareness of the legislation in the model may make the operation of the impact of the legislation clearer. It does not resolve the lag problem, however. It simply makes it explicit. It may be, for example, that we expect that there will be a lag of two months before word gets out on what the legislation is and what it means. Symbolically,

---

[1]The actual simplifying assumption involved more than two variables: Blalock (1964) simplified the analysis by assuming that when one variable changed, the effects rippled through the whole system very quickly. Hence, this is even more stringent and potentially artificial than dealing with only two variables.

lags may be represented by writing the word delay across the arrow connecting the two variables.

Let me go back to the Davis (1985) quote I started this section with: "Something afterwards can't cause something before it" (p. 8). The actual state of affairs is more complicated than this useful rule of thumb would indicate. Uncritically adhering to Davis' rule of thumb runs the risk that we take for granted the way time influences the causal dynamics of what we are trying to understand. The social sciences have been guilty of not thinking critically and substantively about the meaning of time. Speaking of sociohistorical research in particular, Griffin and Isaac (1992) argued:

> Simply put, time is neither theorized nor historicized in most time-series research because it is not understood to have a theoretical or historical meaning or function. (p. 167)

Some of the issues that must be addressed in considering time appear to be reduced to convention, as in the representation of delays and lags by a slashed line and a delay notation. This is misleading in at least one respect. Recipes and conventions *cannot*—and probably should not—be given.

Several strategies exist for solidifying and making more plausible our conceptions of time in the construction and use of models. One is to treat Davis' rule of thumb with the same tentativeness that he did: *not* as a simple, definitive decision rule, but as the beginning of a quest for information. The consequences of not treating such a rule of thumb as the beginning of a quest for information are stark. For quantitative researchers, it means uncritically accepting statistical output at face value and treating the precise size of coefficients with more respect than they usually deserve. This is a component of the quantitative posture that Firestone (1987) characterized in Table 3.1. For qualitative researchers, such blind acceptance of time ordering would mean becoming comfortable and treating the simple chronological exposition of events as sufficiently compelling and informative.

Neither an unthinking or mechanical qualitative or quantitative approach is acceptable, but there is more to do than simply feel uncomfortable or defensive. The different ways of making sense of situations through description, interpretation, and explanation are important here. These different ways of making sense have the specification and/or elimination of alternative possibilities in common as a vehicle for establishing credibility. Where alternatives cannot be eliminated, they can at least be made explicit so that any simplifying assumptions may be put in context.

TABLE 3.1
Quantitative and Qualitative Differences in Rhetoric in Two Studies of the Impact of Principal Leadership and Environment of Student Outcomes (Adapted from Firestone, 1987)

	Quantitative	*Qualitative*
Variables versus Actions	A world of variables and static states. The rhetoric involves levels of centralization or principal support, but what a principal does to centralize or how s/he provides support remains an inference.	A world of events in which actors act. An informant, for example, talks of political battles that led to important legislation for the school system. The state or level of entrepreneurism is assessed through discussion of a dispute between an agency's board and its top leadership over outside funding tactics.
Hydraulic Determinism Versus Limits and Opportunities	A decontextualized portrait of one variable creating pressure on another variable to change is presented. Regression coefficients are used to express precise expectations for amount of expected change. The language of percent of variance explained reinforces the almost physical linkages which are presumed to exist between variables.	A complex portrait of limits and opportunities which create a context of action for agents. There are, for example, required budget-approval procedures and external funding competitions must be dealt with. Rather than determining action in a probabilistic sense, the language implies shaping action by agents.
Randomness and Error versus Choice	Attempts are made through study design and instruments to reduce error as much as possible, and then use randomness to remove form consideration any other possible confounding variables. "Once as much error is eliminated as possible, two alternatives remain—randomness and the causal forces of the measured variables—and statistical tests are used to choose between them (19)."	Choice rather than causality is emphasized in the qualitative study. Constraints, opportunities and other aspects of the environment are seen as being real and requiring decision and action. Strategies must be developed and adapted as decisions are made, actions ensue, and consequences follow.

With all of the time-related problems discussed in this section, there are several strategies that provide an immense amount of material to work with when making greater sense out of these relationships. We should gather as much descriptive information as possible. We should ground that information in the varied perspectives of those living through the situation. We should be cyclically engaging in dialogue with relevant theoretical perspectives. And we should be assessing the nature of changes across situations.

In many cases, the harder we look at relationships, the more complicated and potentially convoluted their effects become so that the real extent of our ignorance, as Blalock (1966) would have it, becomes apparent. In the process, however, a few more relevant concepts may unexpectedly come to light. If more concepts do appear, we are immediately pushed beyond the artificiality of two variables to a more elaborated model—the subject of the next few chapters. If more concepts do not become present, at least there is a greater richness of detail regarding the relationship of interest. For example, more education does not lead simply to more income after a lag period. As we look more closely at this relationship, we learn more about other concepts that are empirically associated with education and income. We also learn more about the processes by which educational gains are translated into income gains in the shorter and longer term through a host of choices and actions. The resulting model is a lot more complicated, but it is also a lot more realistic.

Direction

A second area in which assumptions need to be made, and symbolic conventions need to be stated, concern the flow of influence. Flows of influence, a deliberately weak term, are intended to capture two things at once: the deductive, downward part of the relationship specification process: the impact of some concepts on others that should exist if the causal mechanisms that we believe to be operating actually are; and the inductive, upward part of the relationship specification process: field observations about which concepts seem to be affecting which, no matter what the causal dynamics actually are. These should be recognizable as the split between deduction and induction, or between the hypothetico-deductive method and grounded theory (Glaser & Straus, 1967). By giving them equal status, the emphasis is on an ongoing theory reconstruction process (Burawoy, 1991a) and gives credence to the use of models as organizing devices for summarizing what we know about relationships.

Direction of influence flow is indicated in modeling terms as an arrow. The head of the arrow points toward the concept that is thought of as being *dependent* (the thing being influenced). The tail of the arrow is placed next to the concept that is thought of as being *independent* (the thing doing the influencing). Influence flows along the arrow from tail to head.

The simpler case involving two concepts exists when one concept is thought to influence the other, but not vice versa (Fig. 3.2). When

FIG. 3.2. Recursive model.

concepts are assumed to not ever be affected by anything else, they are considered *exogenous*; they cannot, in other words, receive influence. They can only influence. *Endogenous* concepts, on the other hand, may either receive influence or they may influence other concepts.[2] Where the concepts in a model may be unambiguously ordered in terms of their flow of influence, the resulting model is called a *recursive model*.

Consider this brief discussion from Brown and Warner (1992):

> Although the presence of a long-standing merit system is no guarantee of its efficacy, we hypothesize that the introduction of merit considerations limited the role of machine politics and increased the influence of middle and upper classes on the policies of the police on issues like intemperance. If so, arrest rates for cities "reformed" for a longer period of time should be higher than those for cities that only recently had adopted a merit system or had no merit system at all. (pp. 296–297)

Two observable concepts involving the flow of influence that may be drawn from this discussion are the length of time a city has been reformed (reform date) and arrest rate. The symbolic representation of this unidirectional flow of influence is presented in Figure 3.2 as an arrow flowing from reform date to arrest rate. Note that this is all that is captured in the model. The causal mechanism that is actually presumed by Brown and Warner (1992) to be operating is specifically not captured in the model—but it is specified in the text.

If each concept is thought of as influencing the other, for theoretical or observational reasons, there should be two arrows, one going in each direction (Fig. 3.3). Such relationships are called *reciprocal relationships* or *feedback loops* and the resulting model is said to be *nonrecursive* because the variables cannot be unambiguously ordered (in one direction) in their flow of influence. Such relationships are more difficult to

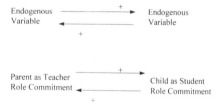

FIG. 3.3. Nonrecursive model.

---

[2]In the language of variables, *independent variables* may be either exogenous or endogenous. If they influence some things and do not receive any influence, they are exogenous. If they both give and receive influence, they are endogenous. *Dependent variables* can only be endogenous.

estimate using purely statistical methods, but much of the more exciting and provocative theorizing in the social sciences deals with such relationships. Dialectical relationships are feedback relationships, for example. Actions that have consequences that then have implications for the social entities originally engaging in the action are feedback relationships.

By way of example, the bottom part of Fig. 3.3 represents a reciprocal relationship that we believe operates between parental commitment to the role of teacher, and child commitment to the role of student. Role theory suggests that roles have dialectical relationships with complementary roles. The arrows going in each direction are symbolic ways of capturing the idea that the role of parent as teacher and child as student are mutually dependent on one another for their development.

Developing conventions for how to represent the direction of presumed influence flows is the easy part. The more challenging part is enriching the descriptive, interpretive, explanatory, and predictive understanding of the relationship in question. Making sense of things from these different points of view entails making explicit, and eliminating where possible, alternative descriptions, interpretations, explanations, and predictions. As I indicated in the brief discussion of temporal problems, it is difficult to discuss these processes without incorporating new concepts. These begin to impress themselves on our analyses as we continue to engage in a dialogue with ourselves and others as to what is going on. These are questions for the next few chapters. Here it will have to be sufficient to reiterate that arguing that influence flows in only one direction between concepts should be repeatedly questioned because most social lives involve feedback and dialectical processes. For some years, standard statistical packages required the imposition of an overly simplistic, recursive pattern among concepts in order for the analysis to proceed. In the process, the indefensibility of this assumption, in many cases, got swept under the rug. Now that statistical procedures are more flexible in the combinations of assumptions they can tolerate, direction of influence flow has become a legitimate topic of discussion again, with explicit discussion of the problems involved. In a recent discussion of reasoning and objectivity in structural equation modeling, for example, Mulaik and James (1995) discussed the major problem in a straightforward manner:

> It is quite possible to fit models with different directions of causation to the same correlational data, and even achieve comparable fit. . . . Specifying causal direction will be difficult and even problematic when cross-sectional data involving variables measured essentially at the same time are studied, less of a problem when selected causes clearly precede effects in time. (p. 133)

The straightforwardness should be applauded, but one gets the impression that underneath this discussion is a recognition on the part of Mulaik and James that they implicitly share Campbell's (1974) dictum that our ability to specify and make sense out of many quantitative relationships is dependent on our achieving a more qualitatively rich understanding of the processes involved.

Qualitative researchers are somewhat ambivalent about the representation of feedback and other dialectical processes. On the one hand, they understand the artificiality of imposing a recursive order on fundamentally dialectical social processes. These are simplifying assumptions, after all, and qualitative researchers usually have a richer vocabulary for describing properties of relationships than quantitative researchers do (e.g., Strauss & Corbin, 1990). As the next few chapters show, however, the power of feedback processes cannot be denied and therefore must be confronted. The trick, of course, is to find a way of doing so that enlightens rather than bewilders (Miles & Huberman, 1994), and focuses attention on the processes that are driving the observations made of surface phenomena.

Direction of influence, then, is a complicated matter. It is easy to assume that the direction of influence flows only in one direction because that is what is easy or convenient to believe—or because we do not get an error message from our computer packages when we oversimplify the direction of influence. Beware of packages that do not make you think about the reasonableness of your assumptions.

Polarity

Polarity reflects a crude distinction between what happens when the more influential concept (independent or exogenous) increases or decreases in value. If the dependent concept is thought to move in the same direction, this is symbolized by a plus sign (+) or same sign (s) near the head of the arrow. It is movement of both concepts in the same direction that is represented by an s or + (Fig. 3.4).

When the independent and dependent concepts move in opposite directions, a negative sign (–) or opposite sign (o) is used to represent this. When

FIG. 3.4. Polarity examples.

the independent concept increases, either an *o* or a – near the head of the arrow is used to indicate that the dependent concept is thought to decrease.

A convenient tactic for keeping the assignment of polarities from becoming confusing is to imagine that you are standing on the independent concept asking the question, "What would happen to the dependent concept, if the concept I am standing on were to increase in value?"[3] If the answer is, "The dependent variable should (on the basis of theoretical [deductive] and/or emerging data [inductive] expectations) also increase in value," then a + or s should be placed near the head of the arrow connecting the two concepts. On the other hand, if the answer comes back that the dependent variable is expected to decrease, then a – or *o* should be placed near the head of the arrow. Such a procedure has the side benefit of reminding us of the impact of human agency on the construction and maintenance of the realities in which we live.

Polarities assume an even greater importance in models where reciprocal relationships are present. The mutual influence of variables on each other defines a *feedback loop*. The loop as a whole may be assigned a polarity by multiplying the existing polarities of the individual relationships together. The polarity of the loop is critically important for understanding the pattern of observations that will occur across time.

Where the polarities of the component relationships are opposite in sign, so that multiplying them together yields a negative relationship, a *negative feedback loop* exists. Such loops are self-correcting, with a result that observations tend to oscillate across time. Where the component relationships are of the same sign—or more simply, when there are an even number of negative (–) relationships—a *positive feedback loop* exists. Such loops are characterized by an escalating pattern of observations across time.[4]

The relationship between the DWI arrest rate for a community and its alcohol-related accident rate (Fig. 3.5) illustrates a typical negative feedback loop.[5] The negative relationship between the DWI arrest rate

---

[3]Blalock (1966) used to exhort his students to imagine being in the models they were developing, standing on each of the variables and asking from that vantage point what was expected to happen to the other variables. System dynamics aficionados talk about walking through a model. We come back to the double entendres or layers of meaning that could be associated with such a process of bringing people back into their models. For the moment, however, think of this tactic as simply one that is useful in minimizing confusion in the assignment of polarities.

[4]A short introduction to systems thinking is available in Kaufman (1980). A management-related discussion based on frequently found feedback loops is Senge (1990). A more extended treatment of assumptions and applications is found in Randers (1980).

[5]Bear in mind two points. There are other variables that will affect both of the variables in this loop and the strength of their mutual influence. And the explanations for the links between these variables may be elaborated to increase our understanding of the mechanics involved.

FIG. 3.5. Negative feedback loop.

and the alcohol-related accident rate reflects the presumed operation of combined deterrent and incapacitation effects: The more people who are arrested for driving while intoxicated are a percentage of the total population, the fewer accidents involving alcohol there will be. Some at-risk drivers are in treatment or in jail; others are perhaps being more careful, and servers of alcohol may be taking more steps to keep inebriates off the road. Collectively, these things reduce the chances of further accidents. When alcohol-related accidents go down, pressure is reduced for vigilant enforcement of these laws. Should accidents start increasing again, however, public pressure will increase the chances of greater enforcement of DWI laws—and so on across time.

The positive feedback loop represented by the mutual relationship between the extent to which a parent is committed to playing the role of teacher to their children and their child's commitment to playing the role of student (Fig. 3.3) should yield a substantially different pattern of observations across time. These two roles mutually reinforce one another, so that as the commitment of one person increases, the other increases also. As before in the case of the intoxicated driver/enforcement loop, there may be several reasons—both explanatory and interpretive—for the mutual reinforcement of these concepts, and this mutual reinforcement might be stronger in some situations than others. But unlike the implications of the negative feedback loop, this positive feedback loop should result in a pattern of each role's becoming stronger and more embellished across time.

The convention and strategies for assigning polarities are straightforward. Assessment of polarity helps flesh out the nature of the relationship(s) specified between variables. Together with direction in a recursive model, polarity helps paint a denser picture of the relationship. With feedback introduced, so that each concept affects the other in ways prescribed by the combined polarities, the density of information available becomes even greater.

Density of information is, of course, a relative term. Diagramming a relationship is the easy part; it simply summarizes the claim being made about one aspect of the relationship. For it to be meaningful, it must be tied to descriptive, interpretive, explanatory, and predictive evidence that enriches and makes credible the sense we are trying to make of the patterns of change associated with the variables and concepts in question (Hammersley, 1991).

Symmetry

Lieberson (1985) sensitized us to a substantively interesting simplifying assumption that we may sometimes inadvertently make when dealing with polarities. He distinguishes between symmetric and asymmetric relationships. *Symmetric* relationships are those in which changes in the independent variable or concept result in parallel changes in the dependent variable or concept whether the independent variable increases or decreases. Two cases are possible. *Symmetric same-direction relationships* would be those in which increases in the independent variable are followed by increases in the dependent variable, and decreases in the independent variable are followed by decreases in the dependent variable. *Symmetric opposite-direction relationships* are those in which increases in the independent variable are followed by decreases in the dependent variable or decreases in the independent variable are followed by increases in the dependent variable.

Lieberson cited Homans' (1950) discussion of the relationship between the frequency of interaction among individuals, and their liking for one another. This is a nonrecursive, positive relationship, meaning that each variable affects the other, and when either goes up or down, the other changes in the same direction. Lieberson asked us to not take for granted that changes of variables will have corresponding effects on the other associated variables. We can plausibly do so in this interactional frequency/liking example, but we may not be able to—or at least should not take for granted that we will be able to—in others.

Asymmetric relationships are those in which the impact of changes in the independent on the dependent variable is different depending on how the independent variable is changing. Asymmetric relationships may, for example, have increases in the independent variable, followed by decreases in the dependent, but decreases in the independent variable may not have any effect on the dependent variable. This would be the case, say, when an irreversible change is set in motion by the initial change in the independent variable, as in the case of Weber's discussion of the Protestant ethic on the spirit of capitalism, cited by Lieberson (1985):

> In Weber's classic essay on the role of the Protestant ethic in the development of capitalism, for example, he argued that the Protestant ethic was a prerequisite for legitimating and encouraging certain attitudes toward the acquisition of material goods and worldly signs of success. However, once such attitudes are established as acceptable, then these crucial

dispositions will prevail even if the religious beliefs were to disappear. (pp. 67–68)

There are probably many more asymmetric relationships in social life than we have been willing to admit. Any changes at the individual, group, or more aggregated level of analysis that come about for one set of reasons may become self-sustaining, create their own nurturing ideologies and support structures, or be taken over by independently derived ideologies and support structures. The consequences of failing to heed Lieberson's caveat have a wide range. At one end, we may merely be embarrassed as we are unable to account for events failing to respond to the diminution of the variables that presumably brought them into being in the first place. On a larger scale, if we do not heed his advice, we may be frightfully wrong in our estimates of the long-term implications of policy shifts.

Complications such as potential asymmetry, however, should be welcomed if we develop the habit of not assuming that the relationships in which we are interested are always symmetric. Just as Isaac et al. (1994) treated patterns of relationships that change over time into new configurations to be explained, so complications such as asymmetric relationships should be treated as additional pieces of data to be explained. Uncovering asymmetric relationships should also reinforce our posture toward learning as much as possible from all sources about the nature of relationships we are seeking to understand.

There are no modeling conventions established for representing symmetric and asymmetric relations. An unobtrusive way of symbolically representing such relationships would be to preface the name of the independent variable with a parenthetically-enclosed A, as in Fig. 3.6. As with the other dimensions of relationships I have been discussing in this chapter, however, remember that the diagram is only a summary of ideas. For it to be meaningful, the conventions and the symbolic representation must be embedded in a solid evidentiary base.

Strength

The discussion of polarity to this point has assumed that the pluses and minuses that indicate direction are of sufficient substantive importance to be worth paying attention to. How big or strong does a relationship have to be in order to be substantively important? Coefficients can be statistically significant because of large sample sizes and small standard errors while still being small in terms of the actual impact that the

(A)X ⟶ Y

FIG. 3.6. Representing asymmetric relationships.

coefficients represent. Estimates of how strong relationships are, and the conditions under which they hold, are very important, but as Achen (1991) and others have reminded us, too great an emphasis on the estimation of coefficients can displace effort away from the rich nature of relationships. Precise estimates of the strength of relationships symbolize the danger of using a scalpel where a machete is more appropriate. We need to know whether effects are large or small, or significant in some greater sense that does not depend so much on the sheer size of samples. We need to focus on what Freedman (1985) called the "main empirical regularities." Quantitative methods may be one route to assessing how important different effects are, but they should be supplemented with more qualitative data because of how fragile the required assumptions are and how thin and potentially superficial the description of process is with most quantitative data.[6]

The question of importance comes through in other continuing discussions. One of these focuses on the question of rhetoric. Reichardt and Gollub (1987) provided an interesting set of comparisons between language that focuses on the size or strength of relationships, and language that focuses on the direction of relationships. To follow the spirit of one of their comparisons, it might be reported that one school was 40% more effective in helping students master cognitive skills. The percentage difference is a relatively low-level way of describing the strength of relationships. Yet, it does convey more information than reporting that one school was more effective than another school. Similar comparisons could be made that draw on progressively more elegant statistical comparisons. The important point is that the degree of quantification and precision reported should not outstrip the capacity of assumptions to support the claim. In this, there is remarkable agreement among both qualitative researchers such as Hammersley (1991) and more quantitatively-oriented researchers like Achen (1991) and Freedman (1985).

There is also a darker side of the relative importance question that was brought to light by Lieberson (1985). He draws a distinction between basic and superficial causes:

> A *basic cause* is one that in a given context actually does affect the dependent variable such that changes in its level will alter the dependent variable . . . Within a given context, a *superficial cause* is one that appears to affect causally the dependent variable in a symmetrical or asymmetrical way. But in practice, shifts in either direction have no actual consequence for the dependent variable. (pp. 186–187)

---

[6]Any statistical text on multiple regression analysis will have a discussion of the factors that affect the characteristics of coefficient estimates, including the chances of coefficients being considered statistically significant.

In some respects, this is similar to what qualitative researchers refer to when they talk about getting it right, or as Wolcutt (1994) re-phrased it, "at least not getting everything wrong" (p. 24). There can hardly be a more important statement regarding the tentativeness of our conclusions and the models we construct to summarize them. Quantitative researchers are given pause because as Lieberson (1985) pointed out, conventional statistical analyses cannot separate basic from superficial causes. Consequently, the observed strength of association between variables and concepts—a descriptive form of sense making—does not tell us whether a basic or superficial cause is operating. Qualitative researchers (e.g., Douglas, 1976) may take for granted that what people tell them is self-serving and/or distorted, so even though their descriptive sense-making is closely allied with interpretive sense making, they are not content to accept statements too quickly (Hammersley, 1991). What seems to save researchers in both camps is the nagging sense that there are deeper realities than what meets even the well-trained eye or well-programmed computer. Consequently, trying to make sense of things in a variety of ways is a common posture.

Several options are available (Fig. 3.7) for representing how strong and/or substantively meaningful relationships are. In Detroit, we have t-shirts that read "Detroit, where only the strong survive." When exam-ining the relationship between two variables, this t-shirt phrase may be paraphrased as "Models, where only the strong survive." If a relation-ship is not considered strong, robust, or important, one option is to leave it out on the principle that only relationships that have survived re-peated reality testing with different sources of data should make their way into the models being developed.

The second and third options recognize that weaker relationships may still be theoretically and/or practically meaningful. Lines of varying thickness are often used to suggest more important relationships or those that are considered stronger in some sense. Less intrusive is the

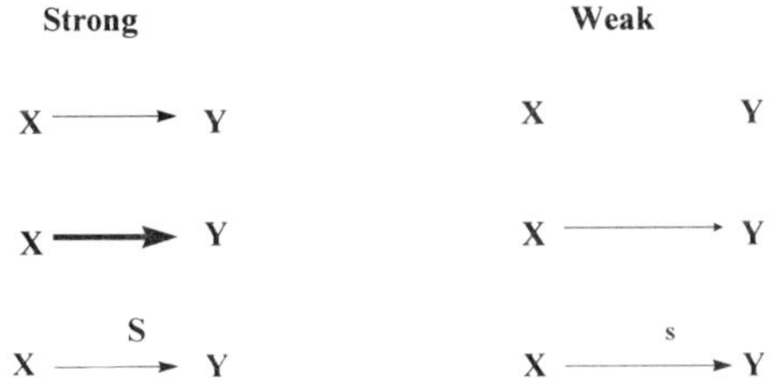

FIG. 3.7. Representing relationships of varying strength.

option of using upper- and lower-case letters to represent stronger and weaker relationships, respectively. My own preference, however, is to simply leave out relationships that are so weak that they are significant only because of the size of one's sample. Substantive arguments, in my mind, should drive what we present in our models.

Linearity

Imposing a requirement of linearity between variables has been a hallmark of the quantitative approach to modeling (Abbott, 1988; Mulaik & James, 1995). When relationships are not expected to be linear, there are standard ways of transforming them so that they become approximately linear. Without such transformations, assumptions become even more complex and more fragile.

Suppose, however, that rather than having to satisfy the linearity assumption, we relax it and permit the introduction of more qualitative or quantitative data to show its form (Babbie, 1992)? The tradeoff in some cases is in allowing the assumptions on which a quantitative estimate is based to be violated, in return for a much richer description of varying combinations of pairings of the independent and dependent variables and concepts. As long as the richer description is compatible with an approximately linear relationship, the signs indicating polarity will serve to represent the assumption of linearity for the relationships. So, where a relationship is assumed to be positive, a + or *s* sign will serve to indicate that the relationship is linear and positive, for example.

We frequently encounter situations in which the relationships that are being described are curvilinear rather than linear. Mechanically, we need to be able to represent such relationships (Fig. 3.8). Where the relationships are non-linear, two more standard possibilities will be recognized: *U* and *Inverted-U* shapes, symbolized as in Fig. 3.8. An inverted-*U* shape will permit description of relationships that start off positive, reach a maximum, then become negative. The relationship between stress and ability to make complex decisions has often been referred to as having a curvilinear, inverted-*U* shape. At lower levels of stress, the more stress (*eustress* in some formulations), the greater the awareness of and sensitivity to the environment. Because these factors increase the chances of being able to decide amongst complex options, stress is temporarily positively related to such a decision capability. Beyond a certain point, however, the ability to focus on what is happen-

FIG. 3.8. Representing curvilinear relationships.

ing in the environment begins to diminish. Consequently, beyond that level, for even greater increases in stress, the ability to make complex decisions becomes sharply negative. The overall relationship may be summarized as an inverted-U shape.

Again, summarizing these possibilities in symbolic form by convention is the easy part. The more difficult part is making descriptive, interpretive, explanatory, and descriptive sense of the relationship in question. Linearity should not be accepted automatically—especially because it is the default option on a computer program. As with the other assumptions that I have been discussing, the show me attitude expressed by Hammersley (1991) should be adopted.

THE RHETORIC OF RELATIONSHIPS:
HOW STRONG SHOULD OUR LANGUAGE BE?

The process of modeling is complicated enough with two concepts. Moving from logo blocks to concepts is problematic because of how much cannot be taken for granted. There is a similar problem in moving from logo sticks and spaces to relationships, and we must be sensitive to the language that we use to talk about how concepts are related to one another. Clues to the difficulty of this enterprise are contained in the language of relationships. In the abstract, we are likely to run into the following kinds of expressions of influence:

A causes B
A increases (decreases) B
A increases the chances of or leads to B
A is conducive to the development of B
A creates B
A produces B
A one-standard deviation increase in A causes B to change by .35 in a positive (negative) direction.

The rhetoric for expressing the influence of one concept on another varies across disciplines, with harder disciplines using more precise, deterministic, and stronger language than softer disciplines (Hirsch et al, 1987). To a certain extent, these differences seem to flow from the kinds of methods used to study social phenomena. Where manipulation of variables is involved, for example, stronger language is expected and used, as in the following passage from Cook (1993):

> Causal connections are implicit in such statements as "External threat causes in-group cohesion," "HeadStart increases achievement," "Aspirin reduces headaches," and "School segregation causes white flight." These examples are characterized by a manipulable treatment specified in

general language, a response specified in the same type of language, and a causal connection that describes the nature of the link between the two; if one is made to vary, the other varies with it and would not have varied had the cause not been present. (p. 40)

Some rhetorical differences fall along a quantitative qualitative split. Table 3.1 summarizes a somewhat extreme portrait drawn by Firestone (1987) concerning alternative approaches to understanding the impact that principals have on the nature of student outcomes. Qualitative researchers tend to describe events and actions. They talk of limits, possibilities, and choices. Quantitative researchers, on the other hand, tend to emphasize a quasi-experimental, statistical approach. They talk in terms of variance explained and an almost physical linkage—what has pejoratively been called a billiard-ball approach—between concepts.

Firestone's presentation may be factually accurate for the studies involved, but it is hard to generalize to all qualitative and quantitative studies because there is a lot of variation regarding how members of both traditions talk about their work. On the one hand, many quantitative researchers think of their techniques as tools to be used to bring patterns to life, not as machines that dictate how processes must be discussed. Blalock, one of the important early proponents of quantitative causal modeling in the social sciences, used to urge his students to imagine people standing in the middle of models making decisions about how to act. And even among those using sophisticated quantitative packages like LISREL, a nonmechanical approach seems the norm. Consider the following short passage from an article describing factors associated with environmental concern and action in Canada:

The evidence indicates that, for the Canadian setting at least . . . the greater the impact one feels ecological problems have on one's health, and the more "cognitively mobilized" [aware and ready to act] one is, the more likely one is to be concerned about the environment. Notice here that the explanatory importance of cognitive mobilization (.52) far outweighs that of health consciousness (.31) and one possible reason for this finding may have to do with the conceptual reach of the two explanations. (Nevitte & Kanji, 1995, p. 91)

On the other hand, some qualitative work is deterministic [as opposed to probabilistic] in nature, but it builds in the importance of context and meaning. In spite of that, there is always the chance that some qualitative work will be both implausible and convoluted (Amenta & Poulson, 1994). Qualitative comparative analysis is unabashedly deterministic, for example, yet there is little that is implausible or convoluted in rhetoric like the following:

At first glance, the equation for the presence of ethnic political mobilization . . . offers greatest support for the ethnic competition perspective.

Although neither term reproduces the core prediction of this perspective . . . both terms are compatible with this perspective because the images they evoke are those of powerful subnations with the resources necessary for challenging the core cultural group. (Ragin, 1987, p. 144)

In sum, there are some problems with using overly strong language to express influence in the social sciences. With strong language, concepts are considered to be straightforward functions of one another. Especially if the term *variable* is used, there is no hint in strong causal language that the variables themselves may be surface traces or proxies for deeper, more complex, and hidden latent variables. With strong language, one loses the sense that there are causal mechanisms that are not explicitly incorporated in the model. And with strong causal language, there is not a sense of human agency. The lack of recognition of these aspects explanatory of social phenomena in the language of causal reasoning can perpetuate a natural-science-biased logic that does not accurately reflect how social science is thought to be practiced (Little, 1991):

> . . . an important point about causal reasoning in connection with social phenomena: The *mechanisms* that link cause and effect are typically *grounded in the meaningful, intentional behavior of individuals.* These mechanisms include the features of rational choice, the operation of norms and values in agents' decision making, the effects of symbolic structures on individuals' behavior, the ways in which social and economic structures constrain individual choice, and so on. The point follows from the circumstance that distinguishes social science from natural science: *Social phenomena are constituted by individuals whose behavior is the result of their rational decision making and nonrational psychological processes that sometimes are at work...* In each case [of the sorts of things that have causal properties that affect social phenomena], it is *plain how the relevant factor acquires its causal powers through the actions and beliefs of the individuals who embody it.* [italics added] (p. 16)

Little's fundamental message here is that variables and concepts acquire causal power through the actions and beliefs of individuals and other social entities. Strong language cannot and should not be imposed from outside in an effort to borrow credibility from the natural and physical sciences. We cannot be seduced into focusing only on "small chunks of social life" (Feagin, Orum, & Sjoberg, 1991, p. 272) because those are the phenomena that lend themselves most easily to large-scale sample surveys and subsequently to description in strong language. The strength of the language we use to talk about relationships must be earned and derived from the confidence with which we believe patterns may be described and understood.

THE INTERPENETRATION
OF SPECIFICATION PROCESSES

In the last chapter I talked about the iterative, cyclic concept specification process as if it were self-contained. If the concept specification process was totally self-contained, the only information that would be examined in the progressive clarification and grounding of a concept would be potential indicators, how they hang together descriptively, their meaning in the eyes of individuals living through the situation, the dialogue regarding their theoretical meaning, and how sensitive all of these criteria are to changes in context.

The concept specification process is not self-contained, however. The relationship specification process described in this chapter and the concept specification process described in the last chapter are interdependent. How a concept is specified has implications for the nature of its relationship with other concepts, and how concepts are related to one another has implications for the specification of concepts.

Cook (1993) gave an example of how the latter form of interdependence of specification processes works in practice. He and his colleagues originally evaluated a patient education program that had combinations of pre- and post-surgical education components (Original Model in Fig. 3.9). They suspected that patient education had an impact on the speed of surgical recovery. Their initial analyses suggested that only postsurgical education components had an appreciable impact on the speed of surgical recovery, *not* presurgical education. Consequently, they revised their simple model of the impact of education to reflect this change (Revised Model in Fig. 3.9).

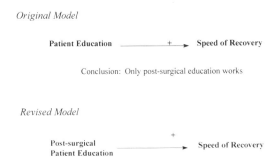

FIG. 3.9. Concept respecification as an iterative process
(Cook, 1993).

The results of their analysis of the relationship—the *relationship specification process*—suggested that they could make better sense of the empirical regularities present in the situation being analyzed by revising the specification of the patient education concept—a *concept respecification process*.

This interpenetration of specification processes is similar to the manner in which analytic induction takes place (Bryman, 1988; Hicks, 1994). Problems are first defined and hypothesis is advanced to explain the problem. Cases are examined one at a time to determine the fit with the hypothesis. If there is a lack of fit, *either* the hypothesis is reformulated *or* the problem is redefined. Hypothesis reformulation is equivalent to relationship respecification. Problem redefinition is equivalent to concept respecification.

Where multiple cases and statistical comparisons are involved for the small number of concepts being considered, the same logic may be applied. Quantitative researchers are concerned with being able to disconfirm the hypotheses they advance. They do this by having a lot more factual information than assumptions that they make about concepts and indicators and their interrelationship (Hoyle, 1995a; Mulaik & James, 1995). Hypotheses are confirmed or disconfirmed with a certain level of confidence. If they are disconfirmed, the hypothesis (a simple model involving two concepts) may be respecified, or the concepts may be respecified.

The joint processes of concept and relationship respecification go on simultaneously. Disconfirmation—or tentative confirmation—may occur, but this is not the end of the processes involved. Testing is not the goal in such a process; rather reformulation and theory building is (Burawoy, 1991b; Hicks, 1994) with a strong commitment to deepening our understanding of phenomena rather than weakening or watering down the power of the analysis. The model serves simply as a vehicle for summarizing the end result of these respecifications.

What keeps these processes honest is the continuing questioning of the sense that is emerging along the descriptive, interpretive, explanatory, and predictive dimensions that I have laid out. Discussing these with reference to only two concepts that influence is presumed to occur between is constraining. In the next chapter, I turn to the process of elaborating models to more closely mirror—albeit in simplified form—the realities that are demanding an accounting.

SUMMARY

This chapter has been a dramatic oversimplification of the modeling enterprise in order to concentrate on the mechanics of describing the relationship between two variables. Maxwell (1992) reminded us that theories consist of two building blocks: concepts and relationships. The same is true for models. In the last two chapters we have considered these basic building blocks and reviewed some of the problems associated with the rhetoric of causation. In the coming chapters, we attempt to make the modeling process more realistic, powerful, insightful, and useful.

Several dimensions of relationships have been reviewed: temporality, direction, polarity, linearity, strength, and symmetry. Conventions for symbolically representing these dimensions and increasing the density of information available for consideration have been presented as well. It is easy to draw arrows between concepts. Bear in mind that there is a lot that must be considered in describing and understanding relationships. When we make claims about the polarity, linearity, strength, and other aspects of relationships, these must be justified. Justification requires eliminating, as best one can, the alternative possibility. So, for example, when we argue that a relationship is linear, it is important to be able to show that it is not nonlinear. Several of the exercises at the end of this chapter provide practice in confronting claims with supportive evidence.

Bear in mind as well that there are now two cyclic, iterative respecification processes that are going on simultaneously: concept respecification (deciding what concepts are and are not) and relationship respecification (deciding what relationships are and are not). As our models become more complicated with the addition of other concepts, a critical third respecification is taking place: deciding what concepts are important and unimportant.

SUGGESTIONS FOR FURTHER READING

Hammersley (1991) is an excellent extended discussion to the nature of ethnographic claims regarding description, interpretation, and explanation and the need for challenging the data that support the claims. Achen (1991) is an excellent example of quantitative analysis thoughtfully applied to an important social phenomenon in a way that allows the credibility of the analysis to emerge from the elimination of alternative interpretations. Richardson (1986) approached the question of rhetoric strength from a system dynamics perspective. It is a useful reminder of the generality of the strong-language problem.

EXERCISES

1. Firestone's (1987) discussion of how principals act when confronted with events that was examined in this chapter is reminiscent of Abbott's (1988) metaphor of a fish swimming through a pool filled with things that need to be negotiated—a metaphor drawn as an alternative to

general-linear-model reasoning. One complex dimension along which the rhetoric of cause varies is its strength. Strong causal language is more mechanical, more precise, less attuned to process and less storied. For a relationship between two concepts in which you are interested, briefly discuss the relationship using alternative stronger and weaker rhetoric.

2. Compare Firestone's (1987) discussion with two paragraphs from Achen (1991) and Freedman (1985) in chapter 1 that talk about the potential for over-emphasis on precision. With this discussion, where do your rhetorical discussions from Exercise 1 fall, relative to Achen and Feedman's comments?

3. Arguing that influence flows from one concept to another is a complicated claim (Hammersley, 1991) about direction that becomes more credible as more evidence compatible with the claim is found. For two concepts in which you are interested, what examples of quantitative and qualitative information can you imagine bringing to bear to make your claims regarding influence more credible?

4. Counterinstances bring richness and opportunities for respecification in three areas: the nature of the concepts being related, new concepts that might help make sense out of the situation, and rethinking how the concepts are related to one another. For the relationships you are interested in, are you encountering counterinstances that do not fit? How can you use this information as leverage for respecifying your emerging model?

5. Claims regarding linearity may be buttressed by using a variety of quantitative and qualitative information. Plotting more precisely-measured variables against one another may be revealing, and there are a variety of transformational techniques available for increasing the linearity of relationships. Such transformational techniques should never be used mechanically, so it is a good idea to try to understand both theoretically and interpretively what is going on with your relationships both before and after transformation. Qualitative information may be helpful as well as you compare instances in which there are varying intensities of one concept and another. For a pair of concepts in which you are interested, what sort of information could you bring to bear regarding linearity?

6. Claims regarding polarity and strength of relationships are subject to the same sorts of credibility-building techniques as other aspects of relationships. Combining qualitative and quantitative information reminds us that our attempts to make those aspects of specification more credible are a continuing dialogue rather than something to be assessed once and taken for granted. As before, for a pair of concepts in which you are interested, how can you bring multiple sources of information to bear on issues of strength and polarity?

4

Elaboration Within
the Constraints
of an Additive Model

Why do I have to, Daddy?

Do it because I said so. That's all you need to know.[1]

Most of us have been in the position of the child and/or the parent in this exchange. From the child's perspective, the situation seems complicated and actions require some justification. From the father's perspective, time, safety, and drained emotional resources may be intruding on his response, but even he might admit that the child eventually needs to know more about what is going on and why it is happening. Two-concept models share the simplicity of the father's initial response. Claiming with any confidence that a two-concept model captures the essence of a phenomenon is presumptuous at best and foolhardy or dangerous at worst. More information is needed, and that information may come in the form of more concepts and more complicated relationships among these concepts. Adding concepts to models is a form of respecification usually called elaboration.

This chapter focuses on elaboration within the constraints of an additive model. I discuss additivity in greater detail shortly, but for now go back to the little exchange I overheard on a subway platform recently. If you believe that the son's reaction is going to be the same on a busy subway platform as it would be in the family's kitchen, that is additivity. If you believe the reaction might be different in the two contexts, then you are arguing for a reaction that is at least partially context-dependent. Chapter 6 focuses on context-dependent models. After discussing the nature of additivity more formally, this chapter goes on to talk about adding additional concepts to models to gain more leverage in digging under the surface of our initial observations.

---

[1] This was an exchange between a child and parent overheard on a New York subway platform.

THE ADDITIVITY CONSTRAINT

This respecification process of adding and subtracting concepts to models parallels and complements the other two forms of specification that I have discussed. By the end of this chapter you will be in a position to continually rethink what concepts you think are important, what the nature of each of these concepts is, and how each of the concepts is related to the others, at least within the constraints of an additive model. In the process, you will also be making decisions about which concepts are not important, what their nature is not, and how these concepts are unrelated to one another. Together, these three complementary, interpenetrating forms of specification help us gain greater understanding of the situations being analyzed.

The important qualifier is buried in the last paragraph: " . . . at least within the constraints of an additive model." An additive model is one in which the researcher believes that each concept is free to take on a range of values (present versus absent in the most limiting case) no matter what the values of the other concepts (in the most limiting case, whether any other concept is present or absent in the situation). There are no contingencies assumed to be operating. Nothing else must be present for indicators to adequately describe a particular concept. Nothing else must be present for a particular concept to have a predictable impact on another; the assumption is, in effect, that looking at average effects in different contexts is legitimate because the effects are relatively constant. The meaning of concepts and how their relationships are interpreted by those living through the situations of interest is assumed to be the same for all contexts considered. And the theoretical assumptions from which causal mechanisms might be woven are assumed to hold in all contexts being analyzed.

Such is the nature of the additivity simplifying assumption: all questions of descriptive, interpretive, and theoretical understanding involving the nature of concepts, their relationships and which ones are important may be answered *without regard to context(s) within which these matters are being analyzed*. Additivity is, to be blunt, a simplifying assumption of the first order, and it is a dominating simplifying assumption in much quantitative work. Jaccard, Turrisi, and Wan (1990), for example, reviewed 116 structural-equation-analysis articles in major sociological and psychological journals over the previous 5 years: only eight included interaction effects (a formal term for the dependence of an effect of one concept on another being contingent on the presence of a third).

In practice, quantitative researchers often frame their analyses so that relatively constant meanings, explanatory mechanisms, and effect sizes—the varying meanings of additivity—become more tolerable assumptions. Consequently, the very modest percentage of studies that

Jaccard et al. (1990) found that formally considered interaction effects *may* be a bit misleading. On the other hand, such an apparent lack of concern with interaction effects strongly suggests that if something does not vary, quantitative researchers are less likely to pay attention to it. These researchers seem, on occasion, to be seduced by the rhetoric of variation and explained variance. If something does not vary and does not by itself explain any variance of note, it is suspect as a concept of importance.

Qualitative researchers are usually very sensitive to the context dependence of their studies (Miles & Huberman, 1994) and the local nature of the knowledge that they derive from these analyses. This sensitivity breaks down when qualitative researchers presume that they have captured something so fundamental and essential that it has universal applicability (Burawoy, 1991b).

Framing an argument or study is a way of emphasizing the importance of context. So, for example, researchers may carefully describe the boundaries of a study of classroom dynamics as one conducted in an urban, predominantly minority, English-speaking area that possesses a poorly resourced school system characterized by conflicts between the superintendent and the Board of Education, and a strong teachers' union. Notice that there are several elements of context here that are operating at different levels. They may have some influence on classroom dynamics. By limiting the analysis to this situation, the collection of descriptive, interpretive, and explanatory simplifying assumptions embraced by additivity becomes more reasonable. Only the good judgment of researchers (and possibly the reviewers of their work) ensure that such background details are not mechanical, tedious, and irrelevant to questions of description, interpretation, and explanation for the context(s) that remain after the imposition of this frame.

At a minimum, the introduction of additional concepts is justified to the extent that they expose patterns that are not simply common sense. Both Merton (1967) and Collins (1982), for example, have argued that it is the capacity to take us beyond what is revealed by common sense that gives the social sciences their promise to expand our knowledge of the world and helps keep us from merely restating the obvious. Making sense beyond common sense is, however, a multidimensional affair. It involves creating more detailed, factually accurate descriptions of the dynamics of situations. It requires those living through the situation to provide thicker descriptions of the meanings imposed on concepts and their relationships. And it involves establishing a more thoughtful dialogue with alternate theoretical perspectives that may inform a situation's dynamics. Elaboration should be thought of as a tool that helps us move toward greater understanding in these areas. I move from simpler elaborations that do not appear to alter the nature of the original relationship to more complex elaborations in which the nature of the original relationship does change.

ELABORATIONS THAT DO NOT APPEAR
TO ALTER THE NATURE OF THE
ORIGINAL RELATIONSHIP

Let us start with a simple, ordered two-concept model:

$(A \xrightarrow{+} B)$. Figure 4.1 displays some simple elaborations that do not appear to change the nature of the relationship between the two concepts in the original model. To highlight this fact, the original relationship is enclosed in a rectangle. The distinguishing feature of these elaborations is that the added concepts (C, where C is understood to represent several potential concepts) are *related to only one* of the original concepts. This is a more strict criterion than might at first be apparent. As we see later in the chapter, concepts that are related to both of the originals might be introduced, and they may or may not cause the original relationship to disappear. What I am suggesting is not really an empirical argument, however, but a theoretical one. The nature of a relationship is more complex than its apparent strength and direction. The nature of a relationship is dependent for its meaning on the descriptive and interpretive context, and on the theoretical structure within which the relationship is embedded. The introduction of third concepts that are related to both of the original concepts inevitably change that nature even if the empirical size of the relationship stays strong enough to be considered descriptively important.

The introduction of such third concepts is not trivial even though the nature of the original relationship is apparently unchanged. Staying abstract for the moment, in two of the cases (I and IV) represented in Fig. 4.1, the added concepts increase the chances of *either A or B occurring*, becoming more prevalent, or more pronounced. Consequently, the additional concepts represent alternative sources of understanding why A or B occurs to a greater extent in some situations than others, or fluctuates in the same situation across time.

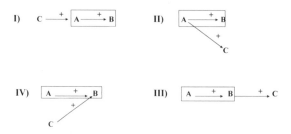

FIG. 4.1. Elaborations that do not alter the nature
of the relationship between two concepts.

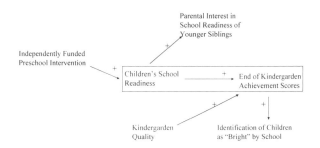

FIG. 4.2. Elaboration where additional variables do not technically alter the nature of the original relationship.

In the other two cases represented in Fig. 4.1 (II and III), changes in *either A or B increase the chances of C's occurring*. The richness of our understanding of what happens when one or the other of the original concepts changes is thus increased. From this, a reformulation of the problem, reevaluation of what it is important to understand, or simply interesting insights, may occur. If nothing else, such elaboration precludes our focusing our attention too narrowly to realistically reflect the situation being investigated.

Figure 4.2 grounds this discussion in a concrete example that has all of the types of relationships specified in Fig. 4.1. We start with an assumed association between school readiness and subsequent scores on kindergarten achievement test scores: The greater the readiness of children for school at the time they enter kindergarten, the higher their test scores will be at the end of their kindergarten year. As much intuitive sense as this relationship may make to us, it may make sense only because we are providing context for the relationship or fleshing out the definition of the situation within which we believe this relationship occurs. We may, for example, be making implicit assumptions about how school readiness comes about, or what the consequences of high test scores are for children.[2]

One way of elaborating the relationship between school readiness and kindergarten test scores is to ask what the *prior conditions* are that increase the chances that children will be ready for school at the time they enter kindergarten. Several concepts come to mind, including the education and income of parents. Such concepts might have a cumula-

---

[2]We might also be making some assumptions about why school readiness affects kindergarten test scores, but that gets us ahead of our discussion. Such inquiries lead ineluctably to alterations in the original relationship. That may be the source of a lot of excitement, but we are not there yet.

tive positive influence on other concepts in the model through time. For example, wealthier parents might be more likely to buy their children computers, expose them to interesting educational materials in the home, or simply increase the chances that the children will be exposed to people who have achieved career success by becoming educated. An example of a prior concept that might have a more limited impact is the presence of an independently funded preschool intervention.[3] Such a program may have an impact on how ready children are for kindergarten without directly affecting how well the children do on their achievement tests at the end. Hence, it does not alter the original relationship but our understanding of what is going on has become enriched.

Similarly, we might make some of the *consequences* of having higher test scores at the end of kindergarten more explicit. There may be consequences for the children, the parents of the children, the relationships between the children and their parents, the school system's formal and informal organization, and so on. Without making some of these assumptions explicit, we may quickly come to believe that looking only at the relationship between how ready children are for school and how well they test in kindergarten is either too small a piece of the important action or very naive. Of the many things that might be a consequence of higher test scores, one may be the extent to which the higher-scoring children are identified by the school system as being bright. The initial assessments that kindergarten teachers make of children's intelligence may also influence the extent to which they are considered bright at the end of the kindergarten year. This does not violate the constraint that we not alter the original relationship as long as the test scores of the children in kindergarten are responsible for the labeling of some of the children as being smart. But note what making this concept explicit does. It gives us a richer understanding of the importance of the original relationship. It may provoke us to ask what else might be important to consider in general, or to redefine what we should be looking at concerning how schools come to form impressions regarding the relative intelligence of children.

To carry the argument further, we could add the other concepts represented in Fig. 4.2. These concepts do not alter the original relationship in a descriptive sense, but at the very least, they increase our understanding of what appears to be happening on in terms of alternate sources influencing the concepts in the original relationship and alternate consequences.

---

[3]It is important that the preschool intervention be independently funded for this example so that the relationship between the preschool intervention and the quality of the kindergarten is minimized. Because the quality of the kindergarten is also assumed to have an effect on the other concept in the original (test scores), to have a relationship between the preschool intervention and the kindergarten would violate the constraint that the new concepts do not alter the original relationship.

At another level, we may see the relevance of theoretical perspectives that may not have been so apparent when examining only two concepts. The relationship itself may be unchanged, but how we look at it, what we see, and how we understand it will change as the perspectives that we are using to inform our understanding changes.

ELABORATIONS THAT ALTER THE NATURE
OF THE RELATIONSHIP BETWEEN CONCEPTS

The constraint of adding concepts that are related to only one of the original concepts becomes highly artificial. In predominantly additive models, much of the interest in the introduction of additional concepts to two-concept models has focused on concepts that either are related to both of the two originals or that specify the conditions under which they are related. Such concepts make it possible to go develop a richer understanding of some of the complexities in the original situation of interest. They offer a completely different source of leverage for revealing more about how and why concepts affect one another.

There are two straightforward ways in which added concepts can change the nature of the relationship between two concepts of interest in additive models: spurious effects and indirect or mediating effects. We call such concepts by a variety of names. *Spurious relationships* are those in which the added concepts plausibly account for whatever relationship appears between the concepts in the original relationship, thus making the original relationship noncausal. *Indirect effects* occur when the added concept(s) absorbs at least one of the specified mechanisms by which the independent concept affects the dependent concept. Any other influence of the first concept on the second is referred to as a *direct effect*. Where indirect effects are more complicated by virtue of being more numerous, they may be further divided into those that have *mutually reinforcing paths* and those that have *mutually antagonistic paths*.

Spurious Relationships

Spurious relationships are, by definition, concerned with things that are misleading and false. Relationships are observed among concepts. Cause is imputed to one or the other, or confusion ensues. But are the described relationships real? Or are they attributable to the operation of other concepts? Spurious relationships have a parallel in the concept respecification process when certain indicators appear to give one meaning to an emerging concept, but, on closer examination, give a false or at least misleading meaning. Bringing additional indicators to bear on the argument turned out to be the best strategy for deepening our understanding of how quickly patients were recovering from surgery. A similar resolution is appropriate when considering relationships. And just as with the concept respecification process, we want to examine what the relationships mean to those involved in the situation and how the relationships may be understood theoretically.

Meeker and Hage (1991) present the case of an observed positive relationship between two routinely-kept transportation indicators: gasoline consumption and the incidence of traffic fatalities (Fig. 4.3A). But what does this association mean? A common element appears to be that both of these indicators are related to driving speed. Those who drive more slowly are less likely to have fatal traffic accidents. Those who drive more slowly also consume less gas. Because this common element (Fig. 4.3B) plausibly influences both of the other concepts, the relationship between the original concepts is said to be spurious.

Descriptively, this means, for both quantitative and qualitative researchers (Miles & Huberman, 1994, for example), that the empirical association between the two concepts is illusory. Quantitative researchers see the measures of association being used reduced to zero when the third concept is statistically controlled. Qualitative researchers question the association between these two concepts in context, and tentatively decide on the basis of observations that whenever the two original concepts are present, a third concept that appears to influence both is also present.

Formally, a third concept must satisfy two criteria to be considered as a generator of spuriousness: It must be related to both of the other variables with polarities that, when multiplied together, yield the same polarity as the original relationship; it must be exogenous with respect to the original two concepts.

For the examples diagrammed in Fig. 4.3, the observed positive relationship between gas consumption and fatalities is attributable to

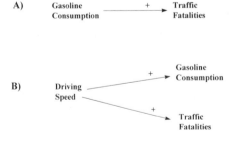

FIG. 4.3. Simple spuriousness examples.

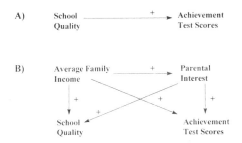

FIG 4.4. Exploring noncausal mechanisms.

the fact that driving speed, as a concept exogenous to both of the original concepts, is positively related to both. We would have had the same result if it had been negatively associated with both of the original concepts because such a pattern creates a positive relationship between the original variables. Had it been positively related to one and negatively related to the other, we would have ended up with a spurious inverse or negative relationship.

Potential spuriousness provides an ever-present source of alternative noncausal mechanisms by which concepts might be related. Checking for spuriousness has become a standard operating procedure in much research, although the real value of such procedures (until they become routine) is that they force us to not take for granted the mechanisms that are most immediately plausible and with which we are most comfortable. Suppose we observed a relationship between the quality of elementary schools and the achievement-test scores of its students (Fig. 4.4A). Before we get carried away with the obviousness of the mechanisms involved, consider the alternative interpretation presented in Fig. 4.4B (adapted from Fig. 8.5 in Langbein, 1980). Here the relationship between the quality of the schools and the achievement-test results of their students is attributable to two other concepts: the social class of families living in the area served by the school, and the extent of parental interest in the education of their children. Langbein (1980) suggested that these factors present a plausible alternative, noncausal mechanism by which the original concepts might be related. Extending this logic, such concepts provide a baseline set of mechanisms against which the impact of interventions to improve the quality of schools would have to be judged (see, for example, Yancey & Saporito, 1995).

There are two lessons to be drawn from Langbein's example of the potentially spurious influence of average family income and family interest variables on the relationship between school quality and achievement test scores. One should not mistakenly conclude that spuriousness is of only occasional importance in multivariate (predominantly additive, complex) models, with only single relationships at risk of being considered spurious. In the Langbein example, there are other characteristics of schools, teachers, and children across time and in different contexts whose relationships would be at risk of being considered spurious. The first lesson, then, is that spuriousness is potentially rampant in multivariate models. The second lesson ties the consideration of spuriousness back to our earlier discussion of elaborations that do not alter the original relationship between two variables. In that section, we discussed how adding variables enriches the understanding of the situation that is being examined and fosters alternative ways of capturing the essence of the dynamics of the situation. Considering spuriousness moves us beyond simple enrichment by pointing to alternative mechanisms that may be responsible for the association we are observing. The mechanisms are captured in shortened form by the additional aggregated family characteristics of the areas in which the schools are found, but it is the mechanisms that are of prime importance in this exercise, not simply the variables. Alternative mechanisms are of prime importance in the move toward greater descriptive, interpretive, and explanatory understanding. The credibility of claims in all three areas is increased to the extent that alternative interpretations are eliminated (Cook & Campbell, 1979; Maxwell, 1992).

We observe that good-quality schools are associated with good test outcomes for the children in those schools. We may be all too quick to impose a sense of *why* such associations exist and so we place the driving force for these relationships on the school. We may gloss over the fact that schools exist in different environments and that these environments are much less conducive to the fostering of good students and good schools. When we routinely look for spuriousness, or some standard recipe of things to control, we lose sight of the real reason for such exercises: looking for intellectually exciting and practically relevant alternative ways of understanding what is going on in a situation being studied. (For more practice with spuriousness, do exercises 2 through 4 at the end of this chapter.)

Indirect or Mediating Effects

The primary utility of indirect effects is that they help us develop a more specific understanding of the causal mechanics that relate changes in independent variables with changes in dependent variables.[4] On many occasions, these represent elaborations of relatively obvious causal

---

[4]I use the terms *mediating effect* and *indirect effect* interchangeably. The language of mediation is somewhat more popular in psychology and social psychology (Baron & Kenny, 1986). Indirect effect is a more popular term in sociology.

mechanisms. Their utility increases the more nonobvious or ironic and nonsensical the original relationships appear to be. Wainer (1986) cited an example in which the no-nonsense approach of the Reagan administration toward limiting the funds available for college education appeared to be tightening up the system and making for more efficient use of resources in education. The presumed relationship, as represented in Fig. 4.5A, suggests that limiting the federal expenditure of funds for college tuition expenses actually improves the average SAT test scores among high school students. What actually appears to have happened is that the reduction in funds caused many high school students from poorer families to not take the SAT, resulting in a smaller (and better prepared) percentage of all eligible students taking the exam (Fig. 4.5B). Introducing the percentage of students taking the SAT test into the analysis makes greater interpretive and theoretical sense of an apparently nonsensical relationship.

Descriptively, mediating or intervening concepts have much in common with concepts that generate spuriousness. Like the latter, the mediating concept must be empirically related to both of the original concepts. The crucial difference is one that is imposed by the researchers and/or the people living through the situation. Rather than coming before (strictly speaking, exogenous) with respect to both of the original concepts (as with spuriousness), mediating concepts come between the two original concepts. The mediating concept is affected or influenced by one of the original concepts and affects or influences the other. Hence, such concepts offer the prospect of making explicit how and or why one concept influences another. In the Wainer (1986) example, increases in federal funds available for college decreased average scores *because* a larger and less well-prepared percentage of high school students took the exam when more funds were available. The percentage of high school

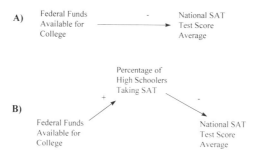

FIG. 4.5. Penetrating nonsensical relationships.

students taking the SAT is a mediating variable. It mediates between or interprets the relationship between federal funding and SAT averages for the nation as a whole. In this case, the mediating variable helps us understand why the original relationship was nonsensical.

The identification of mediating concepts *specifies* particular paths through which influence may flow. This specification process organizes and summarizes in a small space—on a sheet of paper or computer screen—the specific, explicit assumptions one is making to increase the descriptive, interpretive, and explanatory understanding of influence flows. Sometimes this process can get enormously complicated, as with Miles and Huberman's (1994) introduction of almost 20 mediating variables and concepts to understand the relationships among a set of four antecedent concepts and six outcomes in their school improvement study. A later chapter considers strategies for dealing with such complexity. So, for example, it might be possible to conceptually respecify the problem by collapsing together concepts that are empirically or theoretically closely associated with one another. For the moment, let me discuss a couple of examples of how researchers can dig under the surface to get at causal dynamics, the hows and whys of influence processes.

Mutually Reinforcing, Complementary Indirect Effects

The specification of causal mechanisms—the hows and whys of studying influence—becomes somewhat more interesting and challenging when there are multiple paths of influence between independent and dependent variables and concepts. As in some of the previous examples, however, the relationships may not be obvious. It has been observed, for example, that there is an association between the amount of TV a child watches and how elevated his or her cholesterol levels are (Fig. 4.6A). What accounts for this relationship? What is it about watching TV that influences cholesterol levels? There's no immediately apparent mechanism that would seem to credibly account for this relationship.

As it turns out, watching TV increases the chances that a child will consume large quantities of saturated-fat-laden junk food, and decreases the chances that a child will be engaging in exercise (Fig. 4.6B). Exercise and saturated-fat consumption have credible and understandable links with cholesterol levels, so the addition of these variables helps us uncover some plausible and mutually reinforcing mechanisms by which TV viewing has an impact on cholesterol levels.

Now let's take a closer look at what is actually happening when we introduce additional variables. The different causal mechanisms show up as different paths of influence between TV viewing and cholesterol levels that detail *how* the former has an impact on the latter. One path goes through fast food consumption. In the language of causal modeling,

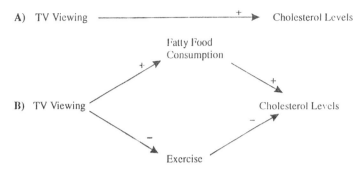

FIG. 4.6. Mutually reinforcing indirect effects.

we say that part of the influence of TV viewing on cholesterol levels is mediated by increased consumption of fast food: As TV watching increases, the chances of consuming more fast food go up (note the + sign), and as more fast food is consumed, cholesterol levels go up. Because both of the arrows in this path are positive, multiplying them together yields a positive sign as well, so the overall influence of this path is expected to be positive, meaning that TV hours and cholesterol levels move in the same direction.

The second path suggests that some of the influence of TV viewing on cholesterol levels is mediated by exercise levels: As more TV is watched, the amount and intensity of exercise may decrease (note the − sign on this arrow). Following the path along, as exercise levels go up, cholesterol levels are expected to go down (another − sign). This path with the same sign as the first, has a complementary impact. The second path has two negative signs associated with it; multiplying them together to get the expected influence of the path yields an expected + impact for the path as a whole.

Notice that Fig. 4.6B does not have an arrow going directly from hours of TV/day and cholesterol levels, as in Fig. 4.6A. By leaving this arrow out, we are indicating that we tentatively believe that all of the impact of TV viewing on cholesterol levels may be understood by examining the relative influence of the two paths of influence specified in Fig. 4.6. To argue that one or more variables mediate the impact of an independent variable on a dependent variable is to argue that the causal impact of the independent variable is absorbed by the intervening variables. The specific example that we have been discussing posits that the impact of TV viewing on cholesterol levels may be understood as involving two complementary, mutually reinforcing paths of influence, and that these paths absorb all of the impact of the former variable on the latter.

To the extent that these paths of influence are embedded in a theoretical perspective, they should reveal insights regarding the mechanism(s) by which TV viewing has an impact on cholesterol levels. Even in this relatively simple example, however, these theoretical perspectives involve at least two or three levels of analysis. On the one hand, we would need some psychological or sociological theorizing about the place of TV watching in the lives of children. And on the other hand, we would need some assumptions from physiological psychology, sports medicine, or nutrition to explain the impact of exercise and fatty-food consumption on cholesterol levels. Social scientists might be less interested in the precise mechanics by which exercise and fatty-food consumption effect changes in cholesterol levels, and might therefore be more willing to take those on faith. They would demand a greater degree of coherence and plausibility regarding the explanation of the impact of TV viewing on exercise levels and fatty-food consumption (cf. Hammersley, 1991).

It is a rare model that would have much coherence and plausibility independent of the theoretical perspectives in which it is embedded (Burawoy, 1991a; Freedman, 1985). Coherence and plausibility must be accessed by elaborating models so that as mechanisms become more theoretically interpretable and coherent, the theoretical perspectives themselves become more accessible and useable. In the example we have been working with, a feel for how this process works is obtained when a fuller sense of the implications of what happens when children watch a lot of TV is provided. When there is a better understanding of how lifestyle choices tie together and have implications for children's health status, that feel for the process increases. These are contextual considerations. Further, just as considering spuriousness moved elaboration to a different level beyond enriching our understanding of the larger situation, examining these mediating links becomes a strong tool for moving us closer to the heart of the real factors and mechanisms that are responsible for the observations we make.

Mutually Antagonistic Indirect Effects

Although the impact of TV-watching on cholesterol levels may not be particularly self-evident, the mechanisms by which it works are mutually reinforcing (complementary). Mutual reinforcement occurs when a variable launches processes or mechanisms that work in the same direction. In this case, TV viewing increases the chances of fatty-food consumption and decreases the chances of exercise. But the direction that is important here is the overall direction of each path of influence from TV viewing to cholesterol level. By each of these separate paths, the result of increased TV viewing should be elevated cholesterol levels. This need not always be the case. Indeed, the leverage available from modeling might be greater in those cases where there are inconsistent or mutually antagonistic mechanisms at work.

Consider the relationship between how educated a person is and how liberal their political philosophy is (Fig. 4.7). Becoming more educated usually entails being exposed to different cultures and different ways of thinking about the world and how it could reasonably be organized and understood. Being challenged to think critically about the assumptions and premises that underlie one's own social life is another part of education. Such experiences should theoretically leave one less inclined to accept the legitimacy of the status quo, and more inclined to believe that there is more than one way do something or organize a society. These processes—which may plausibly hang together as a mechanism—result, in short, in a greater degree of liberalism. We should expect a positive, direct effect of increasing education on liberal attitudes. What we are considering here as a direct effect could easily become an indirect effect if we were to include concepts that captured some of the aspects of the supposed mechanism. We could, for example, try to assess the extent to which one is challenged to think critically or the extent of exposure to other cultures and ways of organizing social life. When we do not elaborate further, we are essentially saying that we are comfortable with the theoretical explanation of the linkage between the two variables. More simply, we are saying that we do not believe further elaboration helps us understand any more about what is going on.

Becoming educated also has very tangible effects on expected income. Increasing education to achieve a college degree alters one's expected lifetime earnings by several hundred thousand dollars, for example. As income increases, however, one result may be a greater degree of attachment to the organization of social life within which this attainment was possible (the status quo). Hence, although education may directly increase the chances of more liberal attitudes to the extent that it results in more income, it may have an indirect result that works in the opposite direction, thus suppressing the extent of liberalism which would result.

FIG. 4.7. In praise of inconsistency: Suppressor effects that mask dynamics.

Such *suppressor effects* (Davis, 1985) are intriguing because they reveal something more of the richness, potential ironies, inconsistencies, and potentially unanticipated consequences of what happens when variables change either naturally or because they have been manipulated in some way. As before, we could further elaborate the relationship between education and income or between income and liberalism. Not doing so suggests that we are content with the credibility of the mechanism that has been introduced to explain the indirect effect, and with the evidence that has been brought together to support those claims.

SUMMARY AND CONCLUSIONS

This chapter has considered several different forms of elaboration, where elaboration is understood to be a specification process in which variables and concepts are added to a model. In some cases, such additions do not appear to alter the polarity or strength of the original relationship, but merely introduce variables that are related to either the original independent or dependent variable. Such elaborations present a baseline for subsequent discussions because they help to enrich our understanding of alternative influences on and consequences of the variables in the original relationship in context. From such exercises, alternative theoretical perspectives may become more relevant. A sense of what is really important to understand about a situation may emerge or become further clarified.

Another class of evaluations that move us to a qualitatively different level are those that alter the nature of the originally described relationship. The two original-relationship-altering elaborations that have been considered are spuriousness and mediation or indirect effects. Both types are similar in that they provide alternative ways of accounting for how and why the original relationship in which we are interested exists. Spuriousness looks for sources of influence that are exogenous with respect to both variables in the original relationship. Mediation looks for variables that come between the original independent and dependent variables, laying out the paths by which different mechanisms might be operating.

The single most important lesson to learn from this examination is that elaboration is a tool for digging under the surface of what is observed in order to construct alternative ways of thinking about how and why the original variables and concepts are empirically associated with one another. As such, the process of elaboration serves as a corrective for too-quickly believing that what we observe has some immediately plausible explanation, or that we should accept as self-evident the mechanisms by that what we observe is produced. Think of this as adopting a skeptical posture regarding your own and others' understanding of what is happening in the situations being studied, especially when the dynamics of a situation appear to be explained by common sense. Moving beyond common sense to appreciate the fragile and complicated nature of what we are observing, then, is the larger lesson that should be learned here.

In the next chapter, a more specific form of elaboration appears: feedback relationships. Feedback may alter both the concepts that are considered important, and how they are related. Appreciating feedback makes social phenomena more understandable and helps us see things we might not have seen before. Hence, like elaboration, feedback provides a source of powerful leverage for digging under the surface of social phenomena.

EXERCISES

1. It has been established that people who drink are more likely to get lung cancer than people who do not drink. What variables might be introduced to help make sense of this relationship? Do the variables and concepts that you are introducing complement one another in terms of having consistent effects on the relationship between drinking and lung cancer?

2. The relationship between age and earnings for adults appears problematic. What variables might be introduced to help make sense of this relationship? If you are puzzled by what is happening between these two, consult Davis (1985, pp. 58–59).

3. Consider Fig. 4.E1, which is an elaboration of Fig. 4.1 in the text. How is the nature of the relationship between children's school readiness and test scores changed by the introduction of these other variables. Why is it changed?

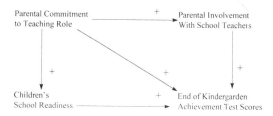

FIG. 4.E1. Elaboration where additional concepts do alter the nature of the original relations.

4. Miles and Huberman (1994) use this example to convey the risk of prematurely concluding that influence exists between two concepts:

> Researchers noted that polio patients who traveled longer distances [for treatment] were more likely to die sooner [than those who traveled shorter distances]. (pp. 272–273)

Is this observed association attributable (descriptively) to the effects of long transportation on mortality chances, or is there a spurious relationship here? What else might be involved. Note how they set up a 2X2 table to organize their observations.

5. For the polio patient example just examined, how might those who transported the patients interpret the original association? What about the relatives of the patients who died? What about the attending doctors and nurses? Are these alternate realities competing for credibility? How does one decide among them?

6. Not taking an association for granted often starts with asking why an association exists or how one variable or concept affects another. The Miles and Huberman (1994) example is a good one to consider because there is at least a plausible explanation for why transportation might affect the mortality risk of polio patients. What is it? Where no plausible explanations exist, looking for spuriousness is easier, but never should be taken for granted.

7. Figures 4.E2 and 4.E3 reflect a discussion by Cook (1993) of confounded meanings in the case of length of hospital stay as an indicator of speediness of recovery from surgery. Does it reflect variation in how well people are after surgery, or something about the pressure that some hospitals may feel to release patients early in order to better recoup their costs? What does elaboration do for us in descriptive, interpretive, predictive, and theoretical terms?

SUGGESTED READINGS

Blalock's (1992) *Encyclopedia of Sociology* presentation of causal infer-ence models from a quantitative perspective helps bring home the leverage that is available in model building and assessment if quanti-tative assumptions appear appropriate. More extended treatments are available from many sources in a variety of disciplines. Berry's (1993) presentation of regression assumptions falls squarely within the critical realist tradition.

Miles and Humberman (1994) contains numerous examples of model elaboration from a qualitative perspective. The importance of contextual specification to frame analysis in a way of examining patterns of influ-ence among the remaining concepts and variables is an important theme. Hammersley's (1991) discussion of the descriptive and explanatory aspects of claims regarding complex relationships among concepts and the challenges that must be made to the evidence supporting such claims should not be missed.

It is also interesting to consider how researchers trying to embrace both qualitative and quantitative methods discuss problems of mediation and spuriousness. Both Bernard (1994) and Neuman (1994) offer useful discussions of these problems at an elementary level.

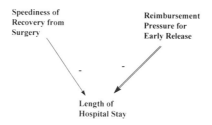

FIG. 4.E2. Panel one.

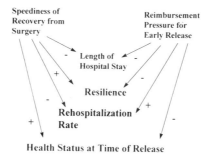

FIG. 4.E3. Panel two.

5

Closing Circles
and Uncovering Dynamics:
Feedback in Social Life

Feedback exists when the changes that take place in a concept have effects that in turn, have implications for the status of the original concept. In an earlier chapter, I considered a simple feedback loop in which there were only two concepts that either mutually reinforced or balanced one another. In this chapter, I consider more complicated examples in which concepts have been added to the model that specify indirect effects. Expanding the discussion of elaboration to consider feedback loops—a closed sequence of causes and effects—and their connections to one another to form feedback systems opens the door to much more realistic and powerful analyses of social phenomena. As one text in systems dynamics put it:

> We assert that organizations, economies, societies—in fact, all human systems—are feedback systems. Viewing them as such provides great leverage for understanding societal problems. (Richardson & Pugh, 1981, p. 2)

By the end of this chapter you should have an appreciation of the leverage that is available from examining feedback loops that may be present among the variables and concepts you have considered sufficiently important to put in your emerging model.

Practical examples of unanticipated consequences that create feedback loops abound in problems that we have as individuals, families, organizations, communities, or societies. When there is too much traffic congestion, for example, we may respond by building more highways on the assumption that that will take care of the problem. When insects devastate our crops, we may increase the amount of pesticide we use, forgetting about or not being sensitive to the unintended consequences of such actions and the extent to which these policies may unleash feedback loops that come back to haunt us.

Problems generate attempts to control the individuals or situations that appear to be associated with the problems. Often, we are confused by the fact that those who have the most problems are the best at coping.

Their repertoires of tactics and strategies may be deeper and broader, they may be more practiced at implementing them, and they may have been through it all before so that they may have a better understanding of the potential impact of their actions. But just because people and groups are trying to cope does not mean that they are successful at coping, that their coping skills are up to meeting the level of trauma and stress in their lives, or that the kinds of things they are doing to cope is having the effect of reducing their problems. The relationships are nonobvious; the results may be unanticipated, and the problems may get worse rather than better. Examining indirect effects and the implications of feedback loops is a method of teasing out the different implications of these events, and it may offer some insight at a variety of levels of analysis.

Consider the set of three models in Figs. 5.1. 5.2, and 5.3. The models examine how the industrial competitiveness of Japan may have changed in response to increasing labor costs—Japan no longer has a relative advantage because of cheap labor—and the increasingly strong yen, which has gained greatly at the expense of the dollar over the last few years. These models have been simplified by removing any feedback effects, both to simplify the analysis even further and to show the utility of focusing on part of the larger analysis. The direct effects of these threats to competitiveness have been to undermine—or at least threaten to undermine—the future competitiveness of Japan. The Japanese stock market has lost ground for some years, as their blue chip stocks are selling at much lower multiples than has been the case for the last decade or so. If the Japanese were not to try to offset the implications of increasing labor costs and a strengthening yen, their long-term competitive position would erode. The direct effects in Fig. 5.1 represent the continuing pressure that threatens to undermine competitiveness.

In point of fact, however, the Japanese have systematically been trying to neutralize the implications of increasing labor costs and a strengthening yen by implementing two broad-scale strategies. They have a coherent economic policy that has permitted large corporations to borrow money for capitalization at very low interest rates. The result has been heavy investment in newer labor-saving technologies that increase Japan's relative competitiveness. The Japanese have also created a climate favorable to the capitalization of manufacturing ventures in the rest of the Pacific Rim countries (Thailand, Malaysia, the Philippines, etc.) where the cost of labor is much cheaper. No doubt this has been facilitated politically by the fact that unemployment is quite low in Japan and the unions are relatively weak. By offshoring labor-intensive, low-wage manufacturing, the Japanese have also been able to improve their competitive posture. These indirect effects are represented in Fig. 5.2. Again, the potential problems posed by labor costs and the strength of the yen have stimulated strategies for coping with these problems.

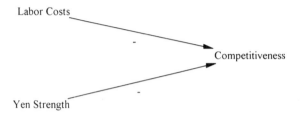

FIG. 5.1. Factors undermining Japanese competitiveness.

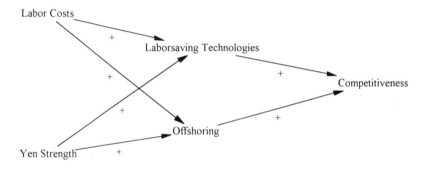

FIG. 5.2. Coping mechanisms reinforcing Japanese competitiveness.

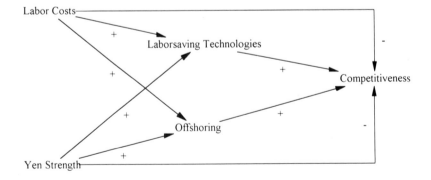

FIG. 5.3. Direct and indirect effects in Japanese competitiveness.

Fig. 5.3 brings the direct and indirect effects together in a more complete model. The relative success of the Japanese remaining competitive will depend on their ability to implement strategies that offset the competitive-threatening implications of higher labor costs and a strengthening yen. The direct effects represent the pressure exerted by these threats to competitiveness. The indirect effects reflect the influence of the strategies Japan has implemented to adapt to the pressure generated by rising labor costs and a strengthening Yen. The total effect of labor costs and yen strength depends on the relative effectiveness of the coping mechanisms and the magnitude of the problems created by rising the labor costs and the strengthened yen.

The effectiveness of these strategies should be enhanced if they mutually reinforce one another instead of working against one another (see chapter 4). For example, if investing in offshore manufacturing activities reduced the chances or degree of investment in new and/or labor-saving technologies, the overall picture would be less sanguine. Figure 5.3 shows no relationship between these two coping strategies. The extent to which there are mutually reinforcing or mutually undermining relationships needs to be evaluated. By specifying the concepts and the strategies they represent, a large first step has been taken in creating an understanding of the implications of the threats to economic competitiveness.

The general implications should not be missed here. A model that represents the relationships between incidence and/or prevalence of problems and the mechanisms used to cope with them may be elaborated on to examine the extent of the implementation of different coping strategies and the implications of doing so. Specifying what these strategies are and what their impact should be can help simplify a potentially confusing set of assumptions and observations.

The feedback loops between competitiveness and coping mechanisms were deliberately left out of the Japanese competitiveness example so that the shorter-term indirect effects could be explored. The insight and understanding gained from examining the contrary processes set in motion by increases in labor costs and yen strength through the direct and indirect effects is valuable. But it is less valuable than it could be, were feedback effects to be considered. The analysis of feedback potentially brings a whole new level of understanding the nature and implications of interconnected social phenomena across time.

Looking again at Fig. 5.3, for example, try putting yourself in the collective shoes of Japanese workers and imagining some other implications of the paired strategies of offshoring and investing in labor-saving technologies. As workers become displaced by machines and begin to lose the safety of lifetime employment—one of the earlier hallmarks of the Japanese model of labor relations—would you not expect the development of resentment, anger, and frustration among workers? And might not this be reflected in increased absenteeism, less company loyalty, and (more collectively) labor strife—even in a culture where individualism is less pronounced than in the United States?

If these are plausible longer-term side effects of the implementation of offshoring and investment in labor-saving technologies, the possibility for a positive feedback loop going from both of these concepts to labor costs is strong. Consequently, even though these paired strategies might increase competitiveness via one route, they may also create higher total labor costs and undermine competitiveness through a different one. These unintended consequences created by feedback between strategies and labor costs are a prime example of unintended consequences on a large scale. Notice that such a line of thought also requires rethinking the nature of what labor costs are, as well as being sensitive to unintended consequences of actions. Labor costs might have been originally conceptualized as being driven mostly by hourly wages. After becoming sensitive to the implications of unintended consequences of investment in labor-saving technologies and offshoring, however, the nature of what constitutes labor costs is considerably expanded.

Recall from earlier discussions that specification processes are interdependent. The more complicated the model, the more important it is not to let the mass of data and complexity of understanding overwhelm this interpenetration. In the Japanese competitiveness example, several of the concepts (competitiveness, offshoring, etc.) are very complex. The indicators that are used to infer the relative value or presence of these concepts may be enriched or altered *either* because of new insights that have been uncovered through concept respecification (chapter 2) *or* because of analysis of the relationships present in the model. Being sensitive to the potential for feedback among variables and concepts is a powerful form of leverage in this regard.

MODELING UNINTENDED CONSEQUENCES WITH FEEDBACK

It seems almost inevitable that some of our actions, some of the ways we use to cope with things, and some of the policies we pass to confront problems that arise will have consequences that we did not expect. Some of these unintended consequences are probably trivial, may not last very long, or are dampened in their effects by other factors. But sometimes, the consequences feed back in ways that counteract the intentions of our actions. The critical importance of feedback in generating these consequences is suggested in the Japanese competitiveness example. Let us look now at a smaller-scale situation in which the implications of feedback dominate.

In organizational settings, managers frequently concentrate on short-term performance and short-term resolutions to performance problems. Focusing on indirect effects—especially when they feed back on the intensity, prevalence, and definition of problems for which solutions are being sought—lengthens the time horizon to which we are sensitive. Box 5.1 briefly outlines an illustrative case in which a hospital-laboratory manager decided that overtime was beginning to be a problem that needed to be curtailed.[1]

In this hospital-laboratory case, the persistent overtime level of 7% had been identified as a problem that needed attention and resolution. The manager initially reacted[2] by instituting the no-break policy, an instance of a reactive management style. This had the short-term effect of reducing the amount of overtime. But it had a longer-term effect of reducing morale, which further resulted in increasing the chances of people quitting or being excessively tardy, engaging in sabotage of some form or another, becoming sick and staying away from work, or simply working more inefficiently. All of these possible indicators of workers' oppositional tactics created more overtime in the longer term because the work had to get done somehow.

Figure 5.4 organizes some of what can be learned from the vignette. To help trace out some of the implications of these dynamics, I have broken Fig. 5.4 down into its component feedback loops. After working through these to get at the practical implications of the structure of the model, the limitations and tradeoffs contained in the model will be discussed.

The first loop (Fig. 5.5) reflects the short-term feedback between the amount of overtime in the lab and how reactively the manager responds to the use of overtime. Mr. Smith's first response was to restrict breaks so that the lab technicians would have to spend more time with their equipment. This decreased overtime for a short

---

Box 5.1
Beware the Short-term Fix

John Smith is a department supervisor who oversees 21 professionals in a hospital lab. Since the introduction of new equipment three months ago, the overtime in the department has averaged 8%.

Defining overtime as a problem that needed to be corrected, Mr. Smith decided to reduce overtime abuse by instituting a "no break" policy. His intervention reduced overtime to 3% for the succeeding 9 weeks—despite grumbling from the professionals who worked in the lab.

At the end of the 9 weeks one of the lab technicians resigns and overtime rose to 6.4% to compensate for the lost position. Mr. Smith reacted to the surge in overtime by not allowing employees to go to training and development sessions except on their own time.

Overtime surged to 10% as morale plummeted among the lab workers. At this point, the lab workers and the manager were so mad at one another that almost anything each of them did was interpreted in the worst possible light. The situation exploded when the lab workers marched en masse to the office of the manager's supervisor and the manager was suspended.

---

[1] I am indebted to Ms. Linda Schlepp for permission to use this unpublished case.

[2] The distinctions between reactive and proactive styles of management are laid out in Britt (1991).

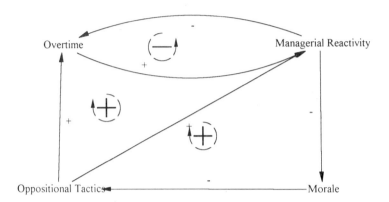

FIG. 5.4. Modeling the overtime problem in a hospital lab.
Reprinted with permission.

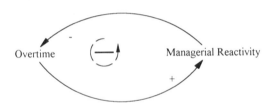

FIG. 5.5. Short-term balancing loop in the hospital lab overtime case.
Reprinted with permission.

period, but when overtime shot back up, Mr. Smith subsequently re-
sorted to reducing privileges, threatening firings, looking over the lab
technician's shoulders, and hassling workers who were taking sick
leave. Following each of these, there were moderate short-term reduc-
tions in overtime use.[3] One pattern that is observable and traceable,
then, is an association between each of the disciplinary actions of the
laboratory manager and a modest, temporary reduction in the amount
of overtime being used. The structure of this feedback loop—summarized by convention as a curved arrow that looks much like a snake

[3]Note that while overtime is an apparently simple thing to measure, to collect John's
several reactions together is to impose some more abstract category on these reactions. The
abstraction should reflect what the reactions have in common either as he, the workers, or
some theoretical perspective defines these commonalities. In the model presented in Fig. 5.4,
the category Managerial Reactivity was chosen because both were very close to the description of John's reactions provided by John's boss, and because the proactivity/reactivity
distinction enjoys some currency in the organizational behavior and development literatures.
It should be noted, however, that this represents a bias toward etic (externally imposed)
definitions that may be skewed toward understandings of the situation by the upper echelon
in the lab. An emic (participant defined) clustering provided by the workers might contain a
somewhat different cluster of responses and somewhat stronger wording.

eating its tail enclosing a minus sign—is such that the relationships between the two concepts serve to balance one another: Increases in overtime increase the chances of reactive responses on the manager's part; the reactive responses temporarily bring the overtime back under control.

The implications of feedback loops may be roughly assessed by multiplying the polarities of the relationships involved in the loop. If the multiplied polarities are negative, the loop is negative. If the multiplied polarities are positive, the loop is positive. Alternatively, if there are an odd number of negative polarities, the loop will be negative. If there are an even number of negative polarities, the loop will be positive.

The temporary drops in overtime use observed after disciplinary actions by the hospital manager do not describe all of the fluctuations in overtime use that are observable during the period being investigated. The temporary drops are a short-term pattern. From the vignette summarized in Box 5.1, it is clear that there are also longer-term patterns that have a very different character and trend to them. Graphing overtime usage across time merges the various short- and longer-term trends together and provides some reference for judging the adequacy of models that are constructed to help understand the situation. Those who study system dynamics refer to such longitudinal graphs of major, observable variables as reference modes (Richardson & Pugh, 1981). One way of judging the descriptive adequacy of a model is the extent to which it can replicate the reference modes of variables and concepts considered to be important.

Getting back to the particular case, we might find it credible that the lab technicians would comply with the authority or power of the manager—but to do so only reluctantly and for a short period of time. Figure 5.6 presents a second feedback loop. Its structure has different implications for the behavior of the participants involved in the lab. Rather than serving to balance and dampen one another, the concepts in this feedback loop serve to positively reinforce one another's effects. The result is more aptly described as escalation across time. Combined with the short-term balancing feedback presented in Fig. 5.5, this second, some-

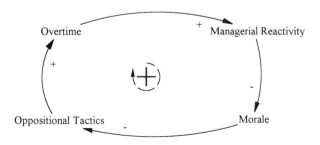

FIG. 5.6. Mid-term escalating loop. Reprinted with permission.

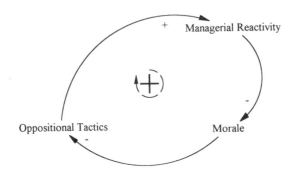

FIG. 5.7. Long-term escalating loop. Reprinted with permission.

what longer-term loop suggests a vicious cycle in which overtime goes up, Mr. Smith acts more reactively so as to bring overtime down in the short term, morale deteriorates further, workers become even more oppositional in how they are coping with the situation, and further upward pressure on overtime is created.

There is even more to be learned from this model, however. Just as we may speak of individuals being an accident waiting to happen, the longer-term prospects of this situation in the lab might be described as an explosion waiting to happen. As the workers and management become mutually alienated from one another, almost any issue that comes up can—and probably will—be transmuted into a problem over which they can fight. Consider the feedback loop represented in Fig. 5.7. Overtime can become functionally irrelevant to the increasing conflict present between management and workers. Mr. Smith could very easily begin reacting to how the workers seem to be working rather than their actual productivity, creating a source of increasing pressure even if overtime were to stay within some reasonable bounds. In point of fact, the situation did explode. The lab technicians wrote a letter of complaint to Mr. Smith's boss and marched en masse to her office.

For some, the interest in such a model may be in making sense of the evolution of what may be a contextually-dependent reactive management style. Each time the manager in this case study reacted to increased overtime, new instances of managerial reactivity were observable. Together, these instances mutually define one another and take shape as a more abstract concept of managerial reactivity. The primary importance of the models used to make sense of this case study may, for others, lie in the practical description of the implications of unintended consequences. Still others may wish to focus on the extent of mutual alienation that escalates across time—an exercise that may lead to different concepts being brought to bear for categorizing what is being observed. For still others, the main importance of such an analysis may lie in the subtle but powerful transmutation of even trivial events into opportunities for the expression of individual and collective resentment.

A lot may be learned from models that hold some combination of practical and theoretical value. But there are tradeoffs in almost all kinds of analyses. The model presented in Fig. 5.4, for example, may capture some of the essential dynamics present in the situation of the lab. There are few hints as to the theoretical perspectives or more formal theories in which this model might be embedded—and there are a lot to choose from, going back to some of the original Hawthorne Studies. And there are only thin descriptions of how the participants interpret what is going on, feel the impact of the situation as it evolves through time, and justify their actions toward one another and to people outside the immediate situation. Let us turn to a situation in which the analysis of feedback is especially helpful in making sense of the development of situational definitions, actions, and justifications for action across time.

SELF-FULFILLING PROPHECIES

Self-fulfilling prophecies first came to the notice of most social scientists in Merton's (1967) analysis. There are three necessary components that must exist before a self-fulfilling prophecy can be said to be operating. Prior expectations regarding differential performance, behavior, or other outcomes must be in place. These expectations shape the actions of those holding them, and these actions then have consequences. The feedback cycle is completed if the outcomes may be interpreted as a confirmation of the expectations with which the cycle started.

Self-fulfilling prophecies may operate at the individual level or at a higher, policy-oriented level. Suppose, for example, that a dominant group believed that a minority group was inferior (Fig. 5.8). As a consequence, the amount of money spent on educating minority children was one-tenth the money spent on educating majority children. These minority children would be likely to grow up with much higher rates of marginal literacy than members of the majority group. These differential outcomes could be used by members of the majority group to validate their own expectations and justify discriminatory policies regarding educational expenditures.

Self-fulfilling prophecies achieved a wide audience with the dissemination of Rosenthal's analysis of interaction between White, middle-class school teachers and poor, minority students (Rosenthal & Jacobson, 1968). In brief, they found that the teachers expected the poor, minority students to do poorly and the better-off White students to do better. As a partial consequence, they (often unknowingly) allocated their time, effort and praise accordingly, and when the minority students did more poorly than the White students, it reinforced their initial expectations.

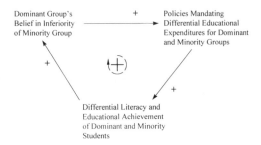

FIG. 5.8.   Educational resource discrimination as an example of
a self-fulfilling prophecy.

Since the publication of this famous study, a fair amount of work
has been done on self-fulfilling prophecies in school settings (Eder,
1981). Murphy (1974), for example, suggested that the operation of a
self-fulfilling prophecy works better under conditions where teachers
are the exclusive decision makers in classrooms, where their apprais-
als are relatively intransigent, and where the pupils are passive.
Violate some of these conditions, and the effect deteriorates or does
not show up at all. One could add to that list that respecification has
also taken place regarding the nature of the expectations involved.
Farkas et al. (1990) showed, for example, that such demographically
based expectations are proxies for a more complex picture formed by
teachers about students' seriousness about learning, as indicated by
observations on attentiveness, willingness to do homework, and so
on. When such expectations are controlled, the effect of the demographic factors on grade-point averages drops out.

The empirical work on self-fulfilling prophecies yet again brings home
the interpenetration of the various forms of specification with which we
have been dealing. How we think about the concepts we consider important
may change over time as we encounter instances that enrich, challenge,
and extend our understanding of what things mean. The patterns we
observe may also be contextually dependent in the sense that they are much
stronger in some circumstances than others. This is a form of respecification that is taken up in greater detail in the next chapter. The empirical
work that has been done here and on other phenomena is also a reminder
of the leverage obtainable from examining feedback loops when there are
documentable traces of major variables across time that may serve as
reference modes. The leverage afforded from examining feedback loops is
not limited to situations in which there are lots of data points across time,
however. Increasing our ability to make sense of situations is the most
fundamental claim, whether there is a lot of data available through time

or not. Let's turn to a situation in which the exploration of feedback helps extend the logic of a descriptive qualitative report.

PUSHING A QUALITATIVE DESCRIPTION

The process of specifying and respecifying the nature of the concepts, which ones appear to be important and how they might be related to one another, pushes the researcher to increasingly ask about different descriptive and interpretive aspects of the situation and demand more and more specificity from the theoretical perspectives being used to make sense of what is going on in particular situations. Considering the role that feedback may play in creating a plausible model of a situation is often a useful approach to organizing apparently disparate unrelated observations.

The short article by Cornford et al. (1993) summarized in Box 5.2 is illustrative of descriptive reports that convey a strong sense of the lived

---

Box 5.2
Making Sense of Mother/Doctor Interactions When Their Children Cough[*]

Mothers and doctors usually do not share the same "disease-oriented conception of biomedicine." The authors argue that it is important for general practitioners—the first point of medical contact for many patients—to understand the beliefs mothers have toward illness in order to successfully treat their child patients. Using tape-recorded, semi-structured interviews conducted in the homes of 30 Middlesbrough.

Twenty-two of the mothers expressed concern that their child was going to die. Although commonly mentioned, there was considerable variation in how worried the mothers were. They wanted treatment to prevent death, some reassurance that it was not going to happen, or both. In the words of one of the mothers quoted in the article:

I wasn't sleeping, I was sleeping but I kept waking up, sort of every hour, every half hour, just thinking just the thoughts, but it was just I couldn't rest, I was worried and it was affecting my sleep, yes, even though he [the child] wasn't awake. Yes, it was just a constant worry and it's, you know, you feel a bit foolish going to the doctor and saying you know I'm not really saying to the doctor how you really feel, you know I sort of went in quite blasé, "Oh by the way, he's got a bit of a cough, is he all right?" where in fairness I'm thinking "Is my child going to live?" Basically that's what I want to know, is he going to survive this?"

The authors felt that the mothers varied in how seriously they believed their child was at risk, and, from this mother's quote, perhaps in their willingness to talk to the doctor about their fears.

The authors go on to elaborate the potential consequences by pointing out that the combination of disturbed sleep and a cough that sounded as if it were in the child's chest was particularly worrisome. In their words: "There appeared to be some link in mothers' perceptions between disturbed sleep and fear of death, and between a chesty cough and the fear of permanent chest damage or dying from choking on phlegm." The chestiness of the cough was something mothers attended to, and often noted ("sometimes with disbelief and even sarcasm") that the doctor thought the chest was clear after listening with a stethoscope. (p. 194)

[*]Adapted from Cornford, Morgan, & Ridsdale, 1993

experience of individuals confronting a particular source of threat in their lives. It is not a complicated piece drawing on multiple sources of information across time that focuses on how women cope with the illnesses of their children. Not is it descriptions of interactions between mothers and general practitioners. It does convey the fears of the mothers, the variety of symptoms to which they are sensitive, and the kinds of things they want out of the consultation with the doctor. What it does *not* convey is a sense of how the various aspects of this scenario are linked to one another, what the driving forces are, what the longer-term consequences of these relationships are, and what the doctor needs to understand about these dynamics in order to more successfully interact with mothers of coughing children.

To push a descriptive account to a tentative model requires making decisions about what the most important variables are, what the nature of the variables and concepts are, and how they may be related. A theoretical perspective could help guide these assessments, but a posture of openness to what the data say must be preserved. In this case of mothers with coughing children, the descriptive account of the mothers' concerns suggests that mothers may become particularly sensitive to sleep disturbances and to coughs that appear to be lodged in the chest. There are also statements indicating that the mothers link these symptoms to the potential for long-term damage and/or death of their children.

The descriptive account by Cornford et al. (1993) suggests that it is these perceptions of risk to their children that motivates mothers to consult their doctors. But what mediates between contact with the doctor and the perception of these risks, and are there any other consequences that might be expected? The article summary in Box 5.2 contains a clue. The mother quoted here talks about not being able to rest, waking up on the hour or worse, and being worried about how her sleep might be affected. These are face-valid symptoms of anxiety on the mother's part. Adding her level of anxiety to the model brings some additional possibilities into focus. Anxiety may drive more than contact with the doctor, as the model in Fig. 5.9 reflects. It may drive greater sensitivity to children's symptoms, increasing the chances that the mothers will see more serious symptoms, believe that there is a greater chance of serious consequences, and even create even greater anxiety. It may, in short, be part of a positive feedback loop that may lead to spiraling anxiety over time.

It may be this spiraling anxiety that increases the chances that mothers will contact the doctor and subsequently press for both reassurance and treatment—specifically a treatment that they believe (on the basis of descriptive accounts) to be a guarantor of reducing their children's risk. To the extent that these requests are met with treatment and reassurances, the mother's anxiety should go down along with the seriousness of the children's symptoms. Such a pattern has the makings of a negative feedback loop, leading to a moderation of the mothers' anxiety.

The model reflected in Fig. 5.9 is speculative and open to alteration on the basis of more information. Without access to the raw data, there is no way of exposing the tentative model to more of a test. If it were possible to do so, we could examine the extent to which, for example, mothers who perceived more serious symptoms also perceived more serious consequences, or whether mothers who perceived greater potential damage were also more likely to be expressing feelings of anxiety. Even then, however, it would be a partial test because data were gathered only from long interviews, with no observations of the mothers' (or doctors') behavior and no indications of how the mothers' thoughts and actions changed over time. Watching this situation progress is critical, for it is the plausible presence of feedback loops that help make sense of the situation.

In spite of the informality of this modeling exercise, the model does tie together much of the important descriptive data presented in the article in plausible ways. The model suggests *how* the children's symptoms, the mothers' behavior and feelings, the level of mothers' anxiety, and the interaction with the doctor could affect one another. The feedback dynamics in the model may help to explain how and why mothers may vary in their beliefs that their children are at risk of long-term damage and/or death. It may also help explain the varying levels of anxiety observable in the mothers—and their disbelief and sarcasm, in some cases, to what the doctor is saying—Together with the knowledge and rapport with parents that general practitioners may have built up over time, an understanding of these potential dynamics may guide doctors in how to respond to mothers who have different configurations

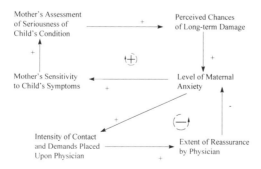

FIG. 5.9. Coughing and countervailing feedback loops.

of their own presenting symptoms. Feedback may also help explain the intensity of some mothers' requests for reassurance and specific forms of treatment that is requested. The doctors may gain guidance on appropriate forms of treatment and gestures of reassurance.

These observations only scratch the surface of options that understanding doctors might choose. They may ask mothers to carefully record just how disturbed their children's sleep cycles are and compare their notes from night to night. They may talk empathetically with mothers about the actual risks of damage and death to their children symptoms the children have. They may talk to mothers who appear to be unduly anxious about how to moderate their own anxiety and why it is important to do so. They may develop office procedures and forms of interaction that provide a context conducive to open and trusting interaction with anxious patients. They may ponder the meaning of the close association between requests for antibiotics and for reassurance. They may investigate what else it is that mothers do before they end up calling them and what patterns might exist among these actions. And they may make use of a simple model such as this one to create opportunities to talk with their colleagues and their staff about what is happening between their patients and themselves.

SUMMARY

Feedback is a pervasive and often confusing aspect of social life. Rather than being intimidated by feedback, however, this chapter should have convinced you that the systematic analysis of feedback loops is helpful in making sense of situations. The Japanese competitiveness example shows how examining feedback loops is a more general extension of elaboration. The hospital lab overtime example shows how distinguishing between shorter- and longer-term effects allows us to be more rigorous in our analysis of unanticipated consequences. Consideration of self-fulfilling prophecies shows how powerful social processes may be understood more clearly by appreciating the role of feedback loops in their generation. Finally, the mother/doctor interaction example shows how descriptive material may be taken to a more analytic level by considering the potential role of feedback in the situation—even without carefully gathered longitudinal, quantitative data.

Making better sense by using modeling as a set of tools is what this book is about. If elaboration as discussed in chapter 4 may be thought of as providing you with a shovel, the systematic consideration of feedback that we have been discussing in chapter 5 should be thought of as a sharp pick. The next chapter adds to this set of tools by considering the leverage associated with becoming sensitive to the contexts within which action takes place. Before leaving this chapter, however, let me urge you to expose yourself to the rich and broad literature on feedback and system dynamics. This chapter should have increased your ability and confidence to dig under the surface of social phenomena, but it barely scratches the surface of the field of system dynamics.

EXERCISES

1. Distinguish between prejudice and discrimination. Is there a problem keeping these two concepts conceptually distinct? How are they related to one another? Are there advantages to adding additional concepts to the model in order to specify the causal mechanisms that might be involved?

2. With respect to prejudice and discrimination, how might the description of these concepts vary from one situation to another? What does this imply about the need to frame the problem being analyzed?

3. Consider the relationship between prejudice and discrimination as a self-fulfilling prophecy. What needs to be added to the model, at a minimum? What else might fruitfully be added to the model?

4. Self-fulfilling prophecies find fertile ground when roles are interdependent, there are training and education differences, and authority differences between the parties. Such situations are ripe for polarization of emotion, negative comments, and conflictual communication. Utilization review departments (responsible for responding internally to patterns of denial-of-payment from government and insurance companies) and their relationships with the physicians who run different departments is a case in point. How can such a situation be modeled?

5. Next time you are caught in a traffic jam, ponder the problem of highway congestion. Start off with the amount of congestion, the number of highways, and the size of the highway budget. What sort of a feedback loop seems to be operative here? Then elaborate with the inclusion of such variables as the number of cars, the amount of driving, and the level of driving safety and comfort. How do these additions change your understanding of the dynamics involved?

SUGGESTED READINGS

A convenient starting point for the system dynamics literature is Richardson and Pugh (1981). At some early point, the pioneering and now reprinted work of Forrester (1990, 1991) should be addressed. The

Systems Dynamics Review reviews current developments in the field. On the Internet, a bibliography of system dynamics literature is available at http://www.psiminst.com/systemsliterature/. A simplified introduction to modeling feedback is available in a newsletter called *The Systems Thinker*; it also contains several practical examples of systems thinking in almost every issue.

Senge's work (1990) reviews several archetypes commonly found in organized, purposive social activities (i.e., organizations). The hospital lab overtime example may be adequately described by using the "fix that failed" archetype.

The counterpart to system dynamics analyses of feedback and its implications in more quantitative work is structural equation modeling. The collection of introductory essays in Hoyle (1995) are both readable and thorough. Brief introductions are available in Francis (1988) and Farrell (1994). More advanced topics are covered in annuals such as Sociological Methodology.

Merton's (1967) early statement on self-fulfilling prophecies is a convenient starting point for exploration of this powerful phenomenon. A series of papers developing and critiquing the application of self-fulfilling prophecies in classroom environments is available in Eder (1981). Farkas et al.'s (1991) work provides an interesting quantitative analysis that lends itself to interpretation in terms of self-fulfilling prophecies with respect to demographic characteristics. This article also digs a bit under the surface to get at the substance of the teacher's beliefs.

6

Conditional and Moderating Relationships: Elaborating the Contexts of Action

Some years ago, Ruth Benedict, a prominent anthropologist, was quoted as saying that if fish could talk, the last thing they would name is water. One implication of this is that we may be least able to talk about those things that are most familiar and taken for granted. This fish story has been used for years to get the point across that what we take for granted may be what we most need to examine and question if we are going to move beyond common sense and the dictates of our computer packages (Abbott, 1988).

In chapter 5, I explored several aspects of feedback in social life within the constraints of an additive model. Feedback effects are puzzling because sometimes they lead to less change than we expect (where they set competing or dialectical dynamics in motion) and sometimes to greater change than we expect (where they set complementary or exacerbating dynamics in motion). Social life does more than feed back on itself, however: It is also *lumpy*.

The lumpiness of social life refers to the observation that things occur in clumps and clusters. More formally, many researchers and theorists believe that the context within which action occurs is essential for understanding social life. Similarly, others argue that relationships between variables and concepts may depend on other conditional, moderator, or conjunctural variables (Ragin, 1989), or that variables and concepts mutually define one another (Salomon, 1991). A problem for us as researchers is that the lumps, clumps, and clusters are sometimes difficult for those studying and those living through various situations of interest to see. To follow the fish story: Context is as difficult for us to see and appreciate as water is to a fish. Consequently, the conditions under which relationships between variables change in magnitude, polarity, direction, or form may be as difficult to see and talk about as water is for fish.

This chapter is about the analysis of lumpiness in social life. Just as with feedback, however, rather than treating lumpiness as an unfortunate complexity that must be dispensed with before we get on to our real

business, the goal here is to give you a conceptual appreciation of the
leverage available with contextual analysis. This leverage for in being
sensitive to context complements the analysis of feedback and elaboration, more generally. The examination of contexts, then, is another tool
that can be added to your repertoire of tools for digging under the surface
of social phenomena.

NECESSITY, SUFFICIENCY, AND SCENARIOS

The larger set of variables and constants that characterize a situation
or context has been called a *causal field* (Einhorn & Hogarth, 1986;
Mackie, 1965; Marini & Singer, 1988), although after Benedict's fish
story and Abbott's (1988) metaphor, *causal pool* might be a more appropriate term. As conditions or conjuncts stand out from this causal field,
they become part of a richer, more complex *scenario* that characterizes
the relationship between two concepts or variables. Consider an apparently simple, non-human example: a fire. Flammable materials, oxygen,
and lack of a sprinkler system are part of one scenario involving a wiring
short that can lead to a fire.

Mackie (1965) used the term INUS to refer to situations in which a
probable cause is an insufficient but necessary component of a complex
scenario that is itself unnecessary but sufficient to predict an effect. To
follow our fire story, in which we are trying to understand the impact of
the wiring short on the fire's starting, the following distinctions obtain:

Insufficient—by itself, a wiring short will not cause a fire;

Necessary—the wiring short is, however, necessary for the occurrence
of this particular scenario;

Unnecessary—the scenario is not the only one that could lead to a fire
(matches, cigarettes, lightning, and other things may cause fires);

Sufficient—but the scenario is sufficient for a fire to take place.

It is useful to break INUS conditions into two parts: the IN and the
US. The insufficient but necessary pair draws our attention to the
essential nature of context. This helps us understand the conditions
under which some things may cause others. There are some things that
are so powerful or so central a part of the action that they may have
consistent effects no matter what the context; others may be conditioned
by time and place. Chevigny (1995), for example, compares the operation
of the police in several cultures in the North and South America:

... to see which practices are so widespread as to seem endemic to police
work, and which are peculiar to a place and a time. (p. 249)

If there were something so common to policing that no matter when or where it occurred, it resulted in violence against the citizens of a country, then a reasonable claim *might* be made that these things were sufficient unto themselves to generate violence. I emphasize the fragile character of such claims because almost all analyses with which I am familiar frame their studies in such a way as to put boundaries around it. Chevigny (1995), for example, chose to compare policing in six urban areas in North and South America where there was at least minimal democracy. Urban areas in Brazil, Jamaica, Argentina, and the United States differ dramatically from one another *if* there are some existential conditions of policing that have the same implications and effects in all of these places, the claim of sufficiency may be stronger. The IN in INUS conditions should sensitize us to the tug of war that is going on in making claims about what constitutes a sufficient explanation: Is it something by itself or is it something *in context*?

The US in INUS claims, on the other hand, should sensitize us to a different set of questions: Is there more than one scenario that makes sense in understanding the phenomena in which we are interested? For Chevigny (1995), it may be that there are different combinations of time periods and cultures that are conducive to high levels of police violence. The expression, "There's more than one way to skin a cat," gets at the main point in this exercise as well. It may be that there are multiple scenarios—multiple combinations of causes-in-context—that have the same impact.

Marini and Singer (1988) used the INUS approach to good advantage to bring order to a variety of partially overlapping studies and observations of the effectiveness of drug rehabilitation programs. They were able to isolate potentially relevant clusters of variables. They linked these clusters of variables with alternative causal mechanisms. Further, in testing alternative scenarios against available data, they were able to lay out an applied research agenda for the kinds of additional data that needed to be gathered in order to develop even more precise and coherent understandings of how, and under what conditions, particular treatment scenarios might have been effective.

Britt (1993) discussed scenarios as one of a number of metaphors for examining process, with particular reference for making sense of the process of leaving welfare. Finishing a training program may be an insufficient but necessary component of a larger scenario. Other components of this scenario might be having experience as a technician in a job market that has a demand for experienced technicians, and a program component that served as a transitional support mechanism. Other scenarios might involve education—rather than training—and still others might involve having a car, access to child care resources in one's family network, and good social skills. Each of these scenarios might be unnecessary but sufficient for the process of leaving welfare to be sustained because any of the scenarios by itself might be sufficient.

The discussion of INUS conditions is more than an academic exercise. Arguments regarding causation cannot be reduced to discussions of how one single variable covaries with another single variable—or by extension to two variables that covary, are contiguous, and have an appropriate temporal order. Neither the realities with which practitioners deal nor the artificial realities that theorists build as vehicles for discussion can be fairly reduced to 2-variable discussions. INUS conditions serve to remind us that situations, context, culture, personality, and all the other factors that form the causal fields out of which scenarios are constructed must be considered. They remind us, in short, that there is more than one way to filet a fish: Just as there are many scenarios for fires to start, there are usually multiple scenarios that may be responsible for the development and timing of social phenomena . . . and all of these complexities may be difficult to see.

CONDITIONS, TRIVIA, ARTIFACTS, AND SUBSTANCE

Being sensitive to the influence of context and conditions helps us by getting us closer to our data and by making us squarely confront the potential oversimplification of assuming that combinations of independent variables have only additive effects on dependent variables (Abbott, 1988; Jaccard et al., 1990). Specifying conditions may: help us uncover the triviality or artifactual nature of a particular process; give us insight into the potentially dangerous uses to which our studies may be put; or, most importantly, give us another much-needed tool for getting under the surface of the phenomena we are seeking to understand, and closer to the contexts within which action occurs.

If a drug rehabilitation program has an effect only when individuals are married and have stable job histories, the impact of the program may be suspected of being trivial or an artifact of a carefully selected client population. It is as if only those who have the best chance of leading a drug-free life have been allowed in the program to begin with. For a program to be considered powerful and nontrivial, it must work with those who need more than a pat on the back in order to change their lives. When the impact of capital punishment as a general deterrent is shown to occur only under a very narrow set of circumstances (such as the choice of years chosen for analysis and assumptions about error terms that are questionable at best [Bowers & Pierce, 1975]), such conditionality might be open to allegations of being dangerous because of the policies that such results might be used to justify. There are, of course, a host of ethical questions also associated with the use of capital punishment. In this case, that means—among other things—taking a look at how sensitive the effects of capital punishment are to contextual conditions. If some conditions lead to the conclusion that putting someone to death saves eight people from being murdered and other conditions suggest that putting someone to death increases the chances that nine other people will be murdered, then we should be alerted to the fact that dangerous oversimplifications are taking place while the ethical questions are being addressed.

The tug of war evident in these examples revolves in part around a question of when causes may be considered important. Are causes important only when they are sufficient unto themselves, or are causes important when we understand the context in which they operate and the scenarios that result? In one respect this is like the riddle, "Where does a 500-pound gorilla sleep?" The easy answer is, "Anywhere he wants to." It may not, however, be the best answer. It is incumbent on the practitioner or researcher working in such situations to justify that the knowledge of scenarios helps clarify what is a complex set of dynamics rather than simply is an artifact that should be passed off as being trivial or attacked for being dangerous.

Researchers, theorists, and practitioners are becoming interested in context, scenarios, and conditions as our understanding of the limitations and real fragility of our additivity assumptions are no longer being swept under the rug (Abbott, 1992; Hage & Meeker, 1988; Isaac & Griffin, 1989; Jaccard et al., 1990; Ragin, 1987, for example). Recall from the discussion of INUS conditions that the conditions under which presumed causal effects occur greatly enrich our understanding of when, where, and how specific causal mechanisms may be operative. Uncovering triviality and artifactuality is one thing; the real action in the analysis of conditions is getting us closer to the when, where, and how of specific causal mechanisms.

THE IMPORTANCE OF CONTEXT:
SOME EXAMPLES

I believe that it is important to understand context and frame arguments properly in order to make sense out of situations. Having done so, even if we end up claiming that something is so powerful that it operates in a wide variety of contexts and situations in the same way, we are on firmer ground because we have checked the other possibilities. To appreciate that posture—rather than taking it for granted—a few examples are offered for review in which understanding context does help us make more sense out of situations we are trying to understand.

A good start is with a relatively simple example in which the addition of a contextual variable helps clarify the nature of what, why, and how some causal dynamics are working themselves out. Henry, Chertock, Keys, and Jogerski (1991) have studied the conditions that create the risk of emotional triangles (a sense of being caught in the middle of conflicts) for clergy and the resulting impact of these triangles on the clergy's symptoms of stress (Fig. 6.1). A history of pastor/parish conflict and more dense and overlapping memberships in the governing body (people related by blood, friendship, and/or marriage) increased the chances of clergy being placed in the middle of such conflicts. Where pastors did not have strong ties with their own families and were therefore more likely to be more dependent on their parishes for their own social ties, the impact of these conflicts were especially telling. Where pastors had strong ties with their own families, these relationships buffered the clergy from being strongly affected by being caught in the middle of parish conflicts.

To consider more closely the value of adding contact with family of origin to the analysis of stress-related symptoms among the clergy, consider the model in two partially overlapping, 3-variable sections that share emotional triangles as a variable. In the first section, there is a simple 3-variable model, with two exogenous variables (history of parish/pastor conflict and density of governing body) stimulating the development of emotional triangles. The model suggests that either of the exogenous variables may stimulate emotional triangles independent of the other. Clergy may get entangled in such problematic relationships either where there has been a history of conflict between parish and pastor, or where a lot of the people on the governing body are related to one another or have other strong emotional ties. Either of these may create emotional triangles by making it difficult for the pastor not to form emotional bonds with parishioners on opposites sides of issues. The combined effects on emotional-triangle complications faced by pastors, then, is assumed to be additive.

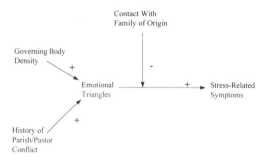

FIG. 6.1. The buffering effects of family ties.

Emotional triangles can be emotionally draining, physically enervating, or to use a now-overworked term, stressful, as the pastors are whipsawed by incompatible entanglements in which they are thrust. The second section of the model—emotional triangles, contact with family of origin, and stress-related symptoms—suggests that the impact of these entanglements on pastors is moderated by or contingent on the extent to which pastors have frequent (and presumably close) contacts with their families. Abstractly, this means that the impact of each independent variable cannot be assessed without considering the other at the same time: Their effects are not additive; they are interactive. More substantively, this summarizes Henry et al.'s (1991) conclusion that in a context of close contact with one's family of origin, the potentially damaging impact of emotional triangles is neutralized, dampened, or buffered—or whatever other aspirin-culture metaphor one could use to get the point across that the power of emotional triangles to effect symptoms of stress is diminished when they occur in conjunction with an external source of social support. Conversely, where emotional triangles occur and pastors do not have such external sources of social support, they are unprotected against the ravages emotional triangles may wreak, and therefore are more likely to experience stress-related symptoms.

So far, the discussion of the model in Fig. 6.1 simply restates what I said in the initial summary of the model. Remembering one of the lessons of sticks and spaces, however, it is just as important to examine what the model suggests does *not* exist. Pace represents the tentative conclusion that some concepts and relationships are relatively unimportant and, for that reason, have been left out of the model. In the present example, a direct, additive effect of family contacts on symptoms of stress *is not considered important enough* to be represented in the model. In considering the reason for this, the contingent meanings represented by the model should be driven home. Pastors, like the rest of us, have probably reached a level of contact with their families that is as comfortable as possible for all concerned and has become a taken-for-granted feature of daily lives. It is only when the potentially stressful emotional triangles are present that contact with one's family of origin stands out and assumes greater meaning than normal. No longer taken for granted, such contact becomes an island of emotional sanity in a sea of emotional triangles.

Without specifying Family of Origin Contacts as context, the contingent power and drama it brings to the model is lost. A competing model, for example, might argue that family contacts exert a strong and continuing influence on stress-related symptoms no matter what else is going on in the situation (see the related discussion of competing models in Dohrenwend & Dohrenwend, 1981). It might suggest, in other words, a direct, additive effect. Contingent effects must always be evaluated against their simpler additive brethren.

Some would argue that there can be no understanding at all without a highly elaborated, rich description of the context within which action takes place (Denzin, 1989; Mishler, 1979). Others would argue that such rich descriptive detail is especially important where we have few cases to study and very complex phenomena to try and understand (Ragin, 1987). My own sense is that scenarios become especially important where contexts differ appreciably from one another, and the meaning of events and actions differs depending on context.

The power, of simple events and changed context, to alter the meaning of everything that happens in a situation must be appreciated, however. Two examples might assist in highlighting this phenomenon beyond what we have discussed in the Henry et al. (1991) example. Meeker and Hage (1991), discussing some of the complexities of theory construction, cited the following:

> An example of the kind of conditional causal link in which a small variation in initial condition can make a large difference in outcome is found in explanations of collective behavior phenomena (McPhail & Wohlstein, 1983). In the development of a riot, for example, a small incident can set off a series of causal processes that lead to a large disturbance . . . On the other hand, the same setting without the incident may proceed without disturbance. The observer who understands the causal links that are involved in the development of crowd behavior may perceive that there is a riot 'waiting to happen' but not be able to predict which time it will occur. (p. 18)

The small incident comes to serve as a symbol of all the perceived oppression, racism, discrimination, demeaning treatment, exclusion, and frustration for many individuals living in an area of the city. The cry against that one person's treatment becomes the anguished and angry cry of many instead of one. It appears as the straw that breaks the camel's back, but its power lies in bringing to the surface old wounds, redefining current situations, and energizing responses.

As a second example of the startling impact that altered meanings as shaped by context might have, consider the impact of divorce and death. The experience of divorce is much less stressful for those who feel their marriages were painful than for those who were relatively happy (Wheaton, 1990). The contingent meaning of trauma should stand out, although sociologists would probably want to argue that the definition of the situation has changed in dramatic fashion. Having a spouse die is also defined in life-event scales as a very stressful event, but imagine how the stress of the death may change depending on the age (young versus old), pain and illness experienced by the spouse (well versus ill and in a great deal of pain), and how expected the death is. Wheaton (1990) is not alone in questioning the meaning of life event scales (for which going through a divorce is taken to be a very stressful life event);

it has been a lively debate for more than 20 years. But these simple expressions of the contingent meaning of divorce and death lay bare some of the oversimplifying assumptions we can make about the nature of stress and its impact on our lives.

All of the examples of contextual effects that I have discussed so far may leave the impression that the elements of context mutually define one another to such an extent that trying to describe, interpret, and explain action outside of the context is a difficult task. Emphasizing context, again, must be evaluated against the competition provided by a simpler additive model. A good test of how nested and mutually defining contextual elements are is to examine how time is treated.

In chapter 3, I considered time solely as a property of relationships that needed to be assessed. Here the focus is much broader. Conventional analyses often assume " . . . 'time' to be a linear organizing device for a sequence of events or an incremental counter 'marking time' in equal units as in a clock or calendar time" (Isaac & Griffin, 1989; p. 875). This assumption is becoming increasingly fragile as it is attacked by both quantitative (e.g., Griffin & Isaac, 1992; Isaac, Carlson, & Mathis, 1994; Isaac & Griffin, 1989) and qualitative (Maines, 1994) researchers. Making the conceptions of time problematic runs the risk of giving the impression that all analysis is potentially chaotic. But in making assumptions about time that are more realistic, chaos is transmuted into leverage for getting under the surface of phenomena.

Quantitatively oriented historical sociologists such as Isaac, Griffin, and their colleagues have done much to bring a more substantive, sociohistorical interpretation of time into focus. What they have called ahistorical time, reflected in clock time or the smooth, linear breaks seen across the bottom of many graphs, manifests itself in two important ways. Methodologically, it allows decisions regarding appropriate temporal periods to be driven by the need for larger samples of temporal units. More substantively, it assumes a seamless continuity to history (Isaac & Griffin, 1989), homogenizing or averaging away differences between then and there and here and now. This domesticates the wild beast of time, but often makes less practical and theoretical sense than it should. Thus, in criticizing some longitudinal studies purporting to explain fluctuations in union membership, the authors argue—in a passage worth requoting—that such parameter estimates are:

> . . . constructed to apply to the entire sets of 150 and 60 years, respectively, through, that is, war and peace, depression and prosperity, the passage of the Wagner Act and its partial dismemberment by the Taft-Hartley Amendment, legal and employ [sic] repression of unions and legislative and employer tolerance or even encouragement, waves of immigration and alien quotas, and times of labor insurgency and quiescence. (Isaac & Griffin, 1989, p. 876)

Domestication of time gives the impression of simple-to-understand relationships between, for example, growth in union membership and changes in strike frequency, when the actual relationships between these may vary considerably depending on clusters of values of the variables alluded to in this quote. Following Ragin's (1987) caveat, however, these are not mere clusters of values, they are the warp and weft of the fabric on which is woven the history of fluctuations in union activity as well as the richer, dialectical activities for which union membership is a proxy. If we were to construct scenarios for the relationship between union membership and strike activity, different scenarios for different eras would be both more realistic and theoretically informative. Time periods might be used to frame the analysis, but these time periods would only be short-hand representations of the very different contexts established by clusters of values on the variables described by Isaac and Griffin (1989).

The alternative to ahistorical time is a conception of sociohistorical time that tries to respect the theoretical importance of periods of time standing as proxies for clusters of values. These values frame different historical contexts that have both practical and theoretical implications for the relationships taking place in these contexts. For example, Isaac and Griffin (1989) argued that the marked changes in the unionization/strike frequency relationship during different periods corresponded to periods of time during which the process of class conflict was dramatically different. Periods during which capitalists had virtually free reign over labor differ substantially from those during which unions are gaining and/or have gained substantial legitimacy. To expect the relationship between fluctuations in unionization and strike activity to be the same during two such periods is to oversimplify the actual relationships and count as insignificant the contextual differences that both theory and practice suggest are relevant to really understanding what is going on.

Modeling may help focus attention on such important aspects of an analysis, especially where many complexities are involved. It seems the struggle to manage the complexity of data regarding descriptive, interpretive, and explanatory claims is larger in most respects for qualitative than for quantitative research. Quantitative research may have very large and complex data sets that merge data from census, archival, questionnaire, and qualitative sources. But this pales in comparison to 20,000 pages of field notes! Miles and Huberman (1994; Huberman & Miles, 1994) suggested several data-management strategies including modeling. Another innovative yet rigorous approach is suggested by Hammersley (1991). He suggested listing the major claims being made relative to a particular situation in outline form, summarizing and indenting the data on which each claim is based and where appropriate, commenting on the credibility of the supporting data.

There is much to say for such outlined, weighted summaries of claims and supporting data. They condense complex arguments into a small space and make explicit exactly what is being assumed and the nature of the data on which the assumptions are based. I believe that there are distinct advantages to carrying the logic a step further to include modeling the claims.

Hammersley (1991) demonstrated his condensing and summarizing strategy using a project by Parker et al. (1981) that compared the punitiveness of justice meted out in two British juvenile courts serving similar urban, working-class jurisdictions. Parker et al.'s (1981) argument is not very complex as arguments go, but it does involve a form of complexity that is difficult to appreciate and grasp: a comparison across contexts involving a contingent relationship. Especially where such complexities are involved, modeling may make the explicit summarizing of assumptions in regard to the nature of important concepts and their interrelationships (in modeling terms, forms of specification) easier and clearer.

Here is Hammersley's (1991) summary of the major claims made by Parker et al. (1981), stripped of the vital presentation of weighted evidence:

1) In Countyside Court [as opposed to City Court] there was 'objectification' of offenders and punitive justice;

2) One possible reason for the punitive treatment was the sharp difference in the social-class backgrounds of magistrates and defendants;

3) The difference in social-class backgrounds is not, in itself, a sufficient explanation since this is also found at City Court. Particularly important at Countyside were deviations from the safeguards of due process and restricted sentencing discretion which allowed magistrates there to act on the basis of class-based, conservative and inaccurate assumptions. (p. 36)

Hammersley's (1991) full verbal summary and his condensation of Parker et al.'s (1981) project should be read for more background. But for purposes of setting up my argument, this short summary is sufficient.

Figure 6.2A (the upper half of Fig. 6.2) is an initial representation of the observation that juveniles in Countyside Court are more likely to be objectified and their cases disposed of more punitively than in City Court. Digging under the surface, it seems that one relevant factor is the social class separation between middle-class magistrates and lower-working-class juveniles. The catch is that the same social class differences exist in City Court.

Context-dependent arguments permit the influence of factors that appear to be constant by bringing to the surface how they interact with

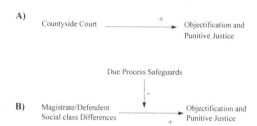

FIG. 6.2. Juvenile justice in two British juvenile courts.

other factors (which vary from one setting to the other) to form a context that has meaning and implications for the participants. In the Parker et al. (1981) case, what varies between the courts is the strength of due process safeguards. Without these, the magistrate/defendant social-class differences are free to operate, producing objectification and punitiveness. Where due process safeguards are in place, the magistrate/defendant social class differences are held in check, producing a more even-handed justice.

Figure 6.2B captures this complexity and subtlety in visual form. And it does so in a manner that has implications for the analysis of other contexts. Armed with this somewhat richer and deeper understanding, a researcher might feel more comfortable predicting the nature of juvenile justice in a given court *if* she knew the magistrate/defendant social class differences and strength of the due process safeguards that characterize the court in question.

COMBINATIONS, SCENARIOS, AND MULTI-CONJUNCTURAL CAUSATION

Modeling Hammersley's (1991) rendition of Parker et al.'s (1981) argument regarding differential punitiveness in two British Courts is instructive for a variety of reasons. In particular, it highlights the mutual definition of elements and the utility of modeling the specification assumptions that characterized the analysis. More concretely, the pressure exerted by social class differences between magistrates and defendants can neither be appreciated nor its implications understood without also trying to grasp the significance of due process safeguards. It is the *combination* of constant social-class differences and variable due process safeguards that leads to the differential outcomes.

Think of the particular combination of magistrate/defendant social class differences and strong due process safeguards as a *scenario*, a combination of concepts, variables, or conditions that are necessary and sufficient for a particular outcome to occur. To the extent that other scenarios lead to the same outcome, we have an even more complex picture emerging. For example, where juvenile courts deal primarily with a middle-class population of defendants, nonpunitive outcomes may be expected whether or not there are strong due process safeguards. If both of these types of situations are put together, they present a picture that has the potential for multiple, alternate scenarios, what Ragin (1987) referred to as *multiple-conjunctural causation*.

Ragin's (1987, 1989, 1993) qualitative comparative analysis (QCA) provides a methodology for analyzing configurations of dichotomized variables and concepts. As an approach to analysis, it seeks a synthetic, middle road between variable-oriented and case-oriented approaches. The following quote is complicated, but it reflects the discussion in chapter 1 of the difficulties and promise of bridging the gap between qualitative and quantitative work:

> A truly synthetic approach would incorporate the respective strengths of the explanatory and interpretive modes while allowing each to speak, as it were, with its own analytic voice. A synthetic method must of necessity find and enlarge the middle ground between rote proceduralism and formulaic scientism on the one hand, and virtually ungrounded speculation or simple description on the other. This methodological synthesis should compel explicit causal reasoning, have the potential for explanatory generality, and allow for replication so that different analysts working with the same material could either produce the same results or be able to identify the source of differences. These criteria are obviously taken from the analytically formal, or explanation, side of the dichotomy. From the interpretive side, a synthetic method should incorporate the use of context, specificity and contingency to discern and signify cultural and historical meaning. This synthesis is both the premise and the promise of formal qualitative analysis. (Griffin & Ragin, 1994, pp. 7–8)

It is not possible to summarize QCA here. The reader is referred to several recommendations at the end of this chapter. Central to the approach, however, is that the configuration of present and absent variables and concepts—what Ragin (1987) termed *causal conditions*—may yield different outcomes. Cases with similar configurations are assumed to be similar for analytic purposes. I prefer the term scenario for these configurations because of its more widespread usage. We may talk, for example, about the different scenarios that could lead to a team's making the playoffs.

QCA forces the researcher to be sensitive to the context within which action occurs. Rather than treating context as some vague abstraction, however, QCA assumes that variables and concepts mutually define one another so that as configurations of concepts take shape, the interpretive meaning and theoretical significance of the resulting configuration or scenario is altered. Each configuration of present and absent concepts represents an explicit, mutually-defined context (cf., Salomon, 1991 about classrooms). One advantage to this approach is that when the end result suggests an additive (i.e., context-free) relationship between the presence of a concept and an outcome, it has been checked against all possible combinations of the other concepts deemed important enough to be in the analysis.

With the added flexibility and power of QCA, it would be possible to extend the Parker et al. (1981) analysis of court systems to a larger number of courts while preserving the need for intimate knowledge of each case. QCA has been used to reanalyze such things as Gamson's data on strategies of social protest (Ragin, 1989), the analysis of employment discrimination (Ragin & Bradshaw, 1991), study how courts manage AIDS disputes (Musheno, Gregware, & Drass, 1991), analyze management styles in textile plants (Coverdill, Finlay, & Martin, 1994), and the conditions leading to social movement success (Amenta, Carruthers, & Zylan, 1992).

The logic of QCA is useful in piecing together tentative context-sensitive theoretical expectations on the basis of current field work and past analyses (cf., Amenta & Poulson, 1994). This feature makes QCA a very useful technique for examining a host of applied problems, such as the conditions under which a particular policy might be effective (or might lead to initially unexpected results). Some of my own research on preschool programs is a case in point.

HIPPY is an education-oriented, home-based, preschool program that works through parents of 4- and 5-year-olds to assist them in getting their children ready for school and themselves ready to be their children's first and most important teacher. It appears that a dilemma surfaces for the program in communities where there are large numbers of multiproblem, poorly educated families who have service needs broader and deeper than the program is designed to provide. Multiproblem, poorly educated families in impoverished neighborhoods are a *context* to which the program must adopt if is to be successful at involving parents.

Without some effective mechanism for adapting to this context and meeting the needs of such families, the expected outcome is poor parental involvement (low attendance at group meetings, prematurely dropping out of the program, perfunctory completion of lessons, and difficulties in negotiating home visits). This is directly parallel to the pressure that magistrate/defendant social class differences put on court systems reanalyzed by Hammersley (1991), except here we are looking at parent responses rather than program responses. Figure 6.3 represents this expectation as a negatively valenced arrow leading from family educational and non-educational risk to parental involvement. This also means that parents in more highly educated, less stressed families will be more likely to be actively involved in the program—no matter what else it does.

Looked at differently, families with high risk in educational and noneducational terms will be actively involved in the program *only* under certain conditions: *if* there is a strong program presence in the homes (assistance in getting to group meetings, patience and effort by staff in negotiating home visits, conscientious role playing with parents, and support for parental involvement) *and* there is family support for other problems confronting the family (drugs, illness, child management, etc.). This alternate scenario is represented as a second, positively valenced arrow from family risk to parental involvement with two contingencies imposed, one involving the penetration of the program in the home and the second involving family support. Together, these represent two scenarios by which parents become involved in the program. This is a multi-conjunctural understanding of the development of parental involvement, summarized in model form.[1]

A NOTE ON RESPECIFICATION AND MODELING

QCA analyses are subject to the same kinds of respecification that other analyses are subject to. Because QCA is deterministic (as opposed to

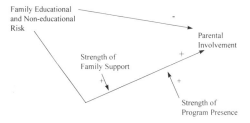

FIG. 6.3. Diagramming a hypothetical example of alternative HIPPY program/context scenarios that may be effective in generating parental involvement.

[1]Technically, the meaning of the arrows is somewhat different with qualitative comparative analysis, or for qualitative analysis more generally, since qualitative analyses tend to be deterministic. Hence, with these forms of analysis, probabilities (and therefore, error terms specifying unaccounted for variance) are not used. In QCA, things are either present or absent.

probabilistic), there is little room for scenarios leading to outcomes most of the time. When results associated with scenarios are ambiguous or conflicting, the analysis turns back on itself. Categories are rethought in terms of the indicators that are used to give it meaning and the relative placement of cases until better sense can be made out of the patterns in the data. The parallel with analytic induction is striking (Hicks, 1994). In analytic induction, relationships and the nature of the concepts brought to bear on the analysis are continually rethought until things make sense and all instances of an outcome can be explained. A major problem with analytic induction is that if there is more than one scenario that makes sense, the analysis hits a wall. With QCA, multiple scenarios can be handled with ease. In the terms I have been using, the models—made up of clusters of scenarios—are continually respecified in terms of which concepts are considered important, what the nature of each concept is, and how the concepts are related to one another.

To tie this to a concrete example from the preschool project, the nature of parental involvement, family support, program penetration and family risk are all complex concepts with several indicators. Change the indicators and the nature of the concept is changed. For example, attendance at group meetings could be dropped as an indicator of program involvement, changing the nature of what is in common with the other indicators. Other concepts might be added to make the analysis even more complex. For example, neighborhood risk could be differentiated from family risk. All of these changes would potentially alter the results. QCA's procedures do not guarantee that solutions will make sense from any of the perspectives we have discussed (Amenta & Poulson, 1994). All it does is keep the researcher(s) close to the data and force respecification to take place. In the final analysis, each of the concepts must make sense descriptively, interpretively, and theoretically. These are the dimensions of making sense that we have talked about previously. The same high standard applies to the implications of the analysis as a whole: Do these multiple scenarios adequately describe how specific outcomes are produced? Are these multiple scenarios grounded in the experience of those living through the various situations represented? Is it possible to make theoretical sense out of the scenarios?

Diagramming these scenarios helps keep them straight and facilitates various dialogues (Fig. 6.4). The positive impact of modeling scenarios should be stronger as the scenarios become more complicated. QCA summarizes its results as an equation, with each term of the equation representing a different scenario, a different combination of conditions that is associated with the outcome in question. With several terms, these equations are as difficult to keep straight as their quantitative counterparts, perhaps more so because many of the scenarios are complex in and of themselves. Modeling the scenarios makes it easier to visualize them and, consequently, talk about them. These dialogues may take place either among colleagues or with (in our case) program staff and families.

Certainly there are situations in which only considering all of the variables and concepts in a model as if they moderated one another makes the most sense. Social life seems far lumpier and more full of complex scenarios than we have heretofore been willing to admit. At the same time, the real world is less pure than that in at least two major respects: Often variables and concepts have both additive and interactive relationships with one another and, conditional variables themselves may have relationships to one another. In practice, researchers avoid having models that are too complicated by focusing on the middle range, analogous to Merton's (1967) discussion of middle-range theories. This theme is taken up again in chapter 8.

SUMMARY

In summary, what should we draw from this discussion of moderating effects? Moderating or contingent effects are much more than simply a "collection of values" (Ragin, 1987). What is represented may be different situations or times, or it may represent combinations of time, situation, and actors. The lumpiness and elusiveness of social life may thus come into better focus by trying to more precisely specify and elaborate the situations within which action takes place. Thus, elaborating the contexts of action helps us in the same way as we examine the pathways through which variables are linked to one another in an additive model. It helps us dig under the surface of our observations to search for the dynamics that are producing what we are observing.

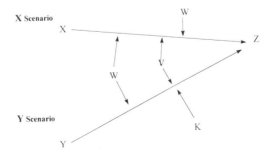

FIG. 6.4. Representing scenarios graphically.

EXERCISES

1. Increased personal, social, and economic resources have been shown to be associated with increased adaptability in a variety of contexts (Eckenrode, 1991). But, often there are inconsistent results across studies, inconsistencies that may be traceable to the fact that variations in resources may make a much larger contribution to adaptability when the context is challenging than when it is not. School transitions are an interesting example of this problem for both parents and children. What might some alternative scenarios be in which school transitions do not have a negative impact on students' adaptability to a new school environment?

2. Pearlin (1983) conceptualized the impact of life events in terms of the extent to which they create or exacerbate difficulties in the enactment of ongoing social roles. Moderating influences on how difficult role enactment is to deal with might include perceptions, social support levels, resilience of coping resources, and so on. Develop some alternate scenarios for the successfulness of role enactment based on some of these moderating influences.

3. Take another look at Fig. 6.2B. All conclusions summarized in models are tentative and are therefore open to being questioned and respecified. The dependent variable in this model combines a couple of different indicators. If they were separated, what implications would there be for the model? Under what conditions should the decision be made to leave them as indicators of the same underlying concept?

4. Still looking at Fig. 6.2B, the credibility of the claim that the model is a factually accurate representation of the differences between the two courts rests in part on the claim that due process safeguards vary between the two courts and that it is these safeguards that critically alter the formation of the contexts of these two courts. These claims are made more credible by documenting as best one can that there really are due process safeguard differences between the two courts *and* that there are no other factors varying between the two courts that could plausibly account for the differing contexts. How does one build such a case?

5. Look at Fig. 6.2B one last time. What sort of picture of these two courts emerges if one attends only to the things that vary between the two courts? How is the interpretive, descriptive and explanatory picture that emerges differ from that represented in Hammersley's (1991) summary.

6. Revisiting Cook's (1993) discussion of speediness of recovery as indicated by length of hospital stay (Figs. 6.E1 and 6.E2), what has all of this got to do with context or the concerns for predictive understanding?

7.   Comparative Analysis
                              by
                    Elizabeth Woolfolk (1995)
                 (Undergraduate Methods, Fall 1995)

I'm a comparative researcher on the move.
I study differences and similarities to get in the groove.
I've got to get familiar with each case I study
To keep the outcomes and results from being muddy.
One of my goals is to explore diversity –
And that's no problem here at the University.
I unravel different causal conditions
Connected to different outcomes and positions.
I like to interpret cultural or historical relevance
'Cause my research approach reveals so much with elegance.
Advancing theory is also a goal;
Each combination of conditions plays its role.
Say for example for lowering crime:
Don't take for granted the cause is the same all the time.
Murder is a crime we can look at for now,
When someone gets murdered, the question is "How?"
What combinations of reasons cause a person to kill?
Fear or anger and a weapon will.
I have to determine alternatives that suffice,
So I'll be able to give some advice.

In this poem by Ms. Woolfolk, what is the main scenario she uses to explain homicide? What other scenarios based on combinations of conditions might there be at the individual level?

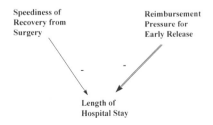

FIG. 6.F1. Panel one.

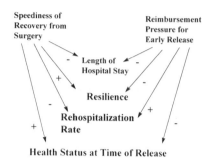

FIG. 6.E2.   Panel two.

SUGGESTED READINGS

There are powerful statements of the importance of context in a variety of disciplines. Technically, good places to start for quantitative analysis are Bryk and Raudenbush's (1987) article on the methodology of cross-level research, a somewhat narrow, condensed and simplified version of their book-length treatment (1992), Jaccard et al.'s (1990) readable *Interaction Effects in Multiple Regression* and Iverson's (1991) *Contextual Effects*. More substantively, Aber's (1994) paper trying to untangle family and community-level effects on child development, Sampson's (1992; Sampson & Laub, 1994) discussion of family management and child development, and Mishler (1979) on the importance of context are useful.

More qualitative treatments such as Burawoy's (1991b) treatment of extended case analysis, Miles and Huberman's (1994) discussion of cross-case analysis, and Ragin's (1987, 1989, 1993) groundbreaking work on qualitative comparative analysis are good places to start. Additional readings applying and/or discussing the challenges and benefits of using QCA in conjunction with other techniques are Amenta and Poulson (1994) and Coverdill et al. (1994). Hammersley's (1991) discussion and analysis of the Parker et al. (1981) court-disposition case is very useful for showing how qualitative data may be organized to increase the credibility of claims regarding relationships.

There are interesting links among thinking about data in detail, looking at alternative facets of a phenomenon to cross-check one's initial conclusions, reframing an argument, respecifying, contextualizing observations, and examining interaction effects. A good example of how these ideas come together in quantitative research is Achen's (1991) discussion of a media-impact study.

The impact of context on parenting and family relationships more generally has been investigated in a number of disciplines. Ecological psychologists, for example, consider both the moderating and mediating roles of context in parenting. Luster and Okagaki (1993) distinguished among multiple influences on parental behavior and give some excellent examples of parenting in context. With respect to moderating influences, for example, they briefly described Elder, Nguygen, & Caspi's (1985) work on how fathers' experience of a sudden drop in income during the Great Depression selectively influenced their parenting styles.

7

Criteria for Evaluating Models

A picture of a friend is useless if it covers a football field and exhibits every pore. (Achen, 1991, p. 13)

Is it possible to know when a model is a good one? This question may be answered in two ways. It may be argued that the goodness of models depends on what you want the model to do, so that there may be different criteria for models with different objectives. Getting the big picture, an insightful picture, a memorable picture of a friend probably does not mean having it blown up to the size of a football field. The detail of the pores may get in the way of the kind of effect you are looking for. In past chapters, I have talked about four types of understanding (description, interpretation, explanation, and prediction) and associated forms of validity drawn from the critical-realist work of Cook & Campbell (1979) and Maxwell (1992). One way of evaluating models, then, is in terms of how well they facilitate the iterative dialogue that leads to greater understanding of our ability to make sense and generate meaning in one or more of these four areas. Does the model increase our capacity to describe what is going on and how it takes place? Does it increase our ability to understand how different actors living through the situation being analyzed think about it? Does it increase our capacity to understand how various theories apply to the situation being analyzed, what they lead us to expect, what surprises we encountered in the field, and what else is going on that particular theories miss? And finally, does it increase our ability to predict what is going to happen in the future or in different situations?

Second, it may be argued that there are standards by which goodness may be judged. Within a critical realist framework, all such judgments are approximate. The primary mechanism for justifying claims is the specification and/or elimination of alternative interpretations, no matter what type of understanding is being considered (Cook & Campbell, 1979; Hammersley, 1991; Maxwell, 1992).

This chapter explores these questions. We look at the ways in which they interpenetrate, and the extent to which there are tradeoffs. Does, for example, focusing on the predictive aspects of models potentially undermine their use in interpretation or explanation? We will also

132

briefly examine the ways in which qualitative and quantitative researchers construct answers to these questions.

GOODNESS IS IN THE EYE OF THE BEHOLDER

Dozens of questions could be asked about models in the effort to judge how good a job they do in helping us understand different aspects of a situation. I organize these into four basic types corresponding to description, interpretation, explanation and prediction. Descriptive questions focus on the factual accuracy of the model, presumably with as little contamination by theory and interpretation as possible. Interpretive questions focus on getting inside the worlds of the individuals living through a tangle of events. Explanatory questions emphasize the specification of causal mechanisms. Predictive questions emphasize only what is supposed to happen in the future or in other situations, not necessarily *why* certain events might be more likely than others or *how* they are interpreted by the people in the situations being studied.

Discriminating among these four kinds of questions, however, conceals a much larger number of more specific questions that those interested in modeling may ask about the models they are developing and using with their colleagues and clients. Box 7.1 condenses a series of questions that Randers (1980) developed in reviewing practice in the field of system dynamics. He believed that the kinds of questions asked are driven by the objectives of the model:

> . . . a modeling procedure will differ according to the objective it is intended to satisfy. Any model has several characteristics; the model objective determines which of these will be emphasized. (p. xviii)

Randers (1980) imposed nine categories on the questions he gleaned from the literature. These nine categories are not always easily subsumed under one of the forms of understanding with which I have been working in this text. How we evaluate models is strongly influenced by the objectives served by the model, as Randers pointed out. But the kinds of questions we ask, how we ask them, and what we mean by them are conditioned as well by our perspectives and tools as well as by the model's objectives. System dynamics emphasizes the structure of the feedback loops present in a model. It sees evolving relationships as the key to understanding how things change over time. Consequently, in the system dynamics literature, there are fewer model-evaluation questions dealing with concepts, and more dealing with relationships. The essential work of operationalizing is something that is to be done prior to the formal evaluation of the model.

Box 7.1
Adapting Rander's (1980) Evaluation Criteria

Insight Generating Capacity and Fertility

• Does the model increase our understanding of the situation being investigated?

• Does it improve the mental models of model builders and clients?

• Does it produce surprising effects that are obvious after the fact?

• Does the model generate new ideas, new ways of looking at the problem or new policies that might have been overlooked?

Descriptive Realism

• Do the model components represent the situation in a way that corresponds closely to how persons experienced with the system perceive it?

• Does each component have a perceivable or conceivable real-world equivalent?

Mode Reproduction Ability

• Can the model reproduce important modes of dynamic behavior observable in the situation, under the same conditions which reproduce such modes in the situation being analyzed?

Transparency

• Is the model easily understandable even by a non-professional audience?

Relevance

• Does the model address problems considered important by experienced persons in the situation being analyzed?

Ease of Enrichment

• Can the model be adapted to represent systems related but not identical to the situation originally represented?

Formal Correspondence With Data

• Does the model incorporated credible real-world observations?

• Can the model reproduce under historical conditions a reasonable fit to historically observed data?

Point Predictive Ability

• Can the model predict events with a minimum of error?

Note. Condensed with some modifications from Randers (1980, p. xviii–xix). Reprinted with permission.

The same words mean different things in different perspectives. Consider Randers' (1980) descriptive realism questions, for example. Models were descriptively real for Randers (1980) when they corresponded to how experienced participants viewed the dynamics of a situation and the extent to which the elements in the model matched some real world equivalents. Such questions fall more easily within interpretive understanding in the framework I have been using. By and large, however, it is possible to use these questions as stepping stones in reconstructing the meaning of these various forms of understanding as they relate to the evaluation of models. If nothing else, such questions are a powerful reminder that there are multiple ways of making sense, and that the questions we ask alter the shape of the model evaluation process.

Descriptive Questions

Descriptive questions focus on the specification processes that have been described in earlier chapters from a critical-realist perspective. What concepts are considered important—and by implication, which ones are unimportant (Remember the spaces!)? What is the descriptive essence of the concepts considered important—and by implication, what is considered to be irrelevant or different from these concepts? Where, when, and how are these concepts related to one another—and by implication, where, when, and how are they not related to one another? For models as a whole, how factually accurate do they seem to be in capturing what is going on in the situation and how it takes place? Whether the specific questions have to do with concepts, relationships or models as a whole, the logic of increasing the credibility of the claims involved is the same. All estimates about the nature of concepts, relationships, and the dynamics of the phenomena being modeled are taken to be approximations. The credibility of claims regarding the truth of concepts, relationships, and models is increased to the extent that alternative descriptive claims may be eliminated.

Concepts. For concepts, a part of factual accuracy should be concerned with—as Randers (1980) suggested—perceivable and conceivable real-world components. There should also be a sense that these components correspond to credible real-world data. In looking at suicide data across jurisdictions, for example, are the patterns attributable to actual variations in suicide rates, or are they attributable to differences in the classification procedures used by various jurisdictions to distinguish among accidental deaths, homicides, and suicides (Douglas, 1967)? All organizational data reflect something about practical organizational concerns and realities as well as what is presumably being measured. In the suicide-data example, the *reported* suicide rate in Pittsburgh, PA in 1975—just to pick a year and place—may underrepresent Pittsburgh's *actual* suicide rate in 1975. Some of the actual suicides may have been reported as homicides or, perhaps more likely, accidental deaths.

If the misclassifications that take place are random—so that sometimes deaths in each category are misclassified as something else—then there is not much of a problem, at least as far as describing suicide rates. However, if there is a systematic bias to how deaths are classified, there are competing interpretations for what the reported suicide rate actually means. It may be that there is a systematic classification of suicides as accidental deaths, for example. In the language of specification, what we are calling the suicide rate may be a misspecification. We cannot have much confidence in it because we do not know what it means.

Consequently, claims regarding what is being measured by an organization cannot be accepted at face value. We need to know something more about procedures, potential biases, sampling, definitions, access, competencies of those gathering and reporting the data, and so on. Whereas these items of information may have some inherent value, their real value here is that they offer explicit, concrete information for specifying and eliminating alternative interpretations of the observed patterns in the data. Organizations are not alone in the extent to which there may be other interpretations of the data that are gathered. Individuals may fudge their responses to questions for similar reasons. We may be misspecifying, for example, when we classify some individuals as civic-minded. It may be that they are not really civic-minded, but they are answering questions as if they were, either because they think that is what we want to hear or because they want to create the impression that they are civic-minded. Just as with suicide rates, then, there may be alternative, competing interpretations regarding what our concepts mean. To paraphrase an old saw, "The credibility is in the details."

For both individual data and that gathered by organizations and communities and reported as rates, it is useful to think of the actual observations as a composite of two components: a true observation and errors. True observations may never really be attainable, but it is convenient to imagine that they exist. Researchers try to get to them by eliminating, as best we can, the alternative descriptions. I need a caveat at this point as well. This discussion of concepts involves description only. We are assuming that there is so much consensus on what is being observed that alternative theoretical meanings and alternative interpretations by different people living through a situation do not exist. Because alternative explanations and interpretations exist in many cases, the idea that true scores can only be approximated is even more compelling.

Qualitative researchers are inclined to go through repeated checks of how appropriate indicators are, how weighty or credible they are, which ones are so similar as to be considered interchangeable, whether or not they hang together, and whether the range of phenomena that could occur in the situation is being adequately represented (Hammersley, 1991, 1992; Maxwell, 1992; Miles & Huberman, 1994). These are iterative procedures, performed again and again, over time, with slight but deliberate variations until the same answers keep coming back. Finding the same answers, however, is credible only if plausible alternatives have been surfaced and eliminated.

Quantitative researchers are more likely to pretest their data-gathering instruments and rely on statistical manipulation to uncover patterns among the indicators from which scales might be constructed (Carmines & Zeller, 1980). These scales may then be judged by how internally consistent they are for certain populations in certain situations at certain times. Models in which appropriate use of previously generated scales and indices has been made will have a stronger claim to descriptive validity than those in which such care has not been exercised. Central to this process is clustering together indicators that converge on one another, and separating and discriminating the indicators that do not descriptively belong together.

Procedures and practices vary, but for us to judge that models are doing a good descriptive job about concepts, there should be a sense that the data in models have been gathered in a way that either emulates or surpasses best practice in the field (e.g., Silverman et al., 1990). Emulating best practice increases the credibility of claims about the descriptive validity of concepts. Increasingly, there is interest in complementing best practice from qualitative and quantitative approaches (Daly, 1993; Morse, 1991; Reichardt & Rallis, 1994; Rossman & Wilson, 1985; 1991). Combining best practice from both fields may or may not yield converging descriptions of concepts, but at the very least, a much richer, detailed potentially complementary description of how indicators may hang together and converge, or require some separation to make better descriptive sense.

In the language of specification, if we are going to judge that a model is doing a good job of conceptual description, there should be evidence of conceptual respecification: some evidence that alternative ways of grounding the concepts in use have been examined. Respecification is inherently an iterative process. It implies the devotion of time and effort to describing just how, when, and where indicators may be clustered together and, by implication, where they do not hang together. "The Devil is in the details" is a useful saw . . . just make sure that you use the saw to cut up alternative descriptions of what concepts are.

Relationships and Models.   Randers' (1980) list of questions for judging relationships and models is drawn from the system dynamics literature and practice. It is a list that is biased toward the analysis of relationships, treating conceptual respecification matters as a preliminary to the actual examination of a model. Accounting for what has happened in the past (part of formal correspondence) and being able to reproduce large shifts in how concepts are related to one another and when they are important (model reproduction ability) are key questions in a system dynamics approach. They also have some interesting analogs in both quantitative and qualitative research.

In quantitative research, the credibility of descriptive claims about the nature of relationships rests on the same fundamental commitment to the elimination of alternative descriptions that obtains concepts. For experimental and quasi-experimental work, the importance of this approach was developed by Campbell and Stanley (1963) and subsequently elaborated by Cook and Campbell (1979). In these kinds of designs, increasing the credibility of the descriptive claim that there is a relationship of some form and strength between a manipulated variable and an outcome is defined as an internal validity problem. The major vehicle for establishing the credibility of the observed relationship is eliminating alternate descriptive interpretations. For nonexperimental quantitative work, the same logic implies. We try to eliminate alternative ways that the observed relationship could have been generated by eliminating potential spuriousness and other variables that might be intruding in more complex ways. The procedures differ, but the objective is the same: Increase the credibility of the described relationship by eliminating alternative descriptive interpretations.

When multiple variables are considered in a nonexperimental context, questions of descriptive adequacy in quantitative research tend to examine the fit between patterns and expectations for existing data, with more sophisticated assessments even being able to assess the fit for measurement and substantive models simultaneously, should that be desirable (Hoyle, 1995b; Hu & Bentler, 1995, for example). We may think of *fit* as a series of the same specification problems we have considered before. Are the descriptively important concepts and variables in the model? When links are presumed to exist, are they represented? Where links are not presumed to exist from patterns in the data, are they left out? Are appropriate assumptions being made about the concepts and linkages that are left out of the model (Achen, 1991)?

Suppose we asked this series of questions and were able to give a tentative "Okay" to each question, so that a credible claim regarding fit could be made. Would we be in a position to assert that we had found the true model? I know of no discussions of this matter that do not answer this question with a resounding "No!" Consider how Berry (1993), in a recent discussion of assumptions in multiple regression, described what is meant by a true model and what an appropriate posture for quantitative researchers might be:

> In the regression literature, a true model is usually conceived as one that explains all variation in the dependent variable in the population of interest. Alternatively, it can be viewed as the model that completely describes the process determining the value of the dependent variable for any case in the population; thus the equation reflecting the true model would include *all* variables that have an effect on the dependent variable, and accurately reflect the nature of all of these effects. It would be *incredibly naive* [my emphasis] to believe that in a concrete social science application the true model would be known . . . perhaps it is more plausible to presume that this model exists, yet it is unknown to the researcher . . . For virtually every social science dependent variable I can imagine, I doubt there is a true model. Even if there is I am convinced that I will never be able to identify it. (pp. 6–7, 8)

Berry's (1993) position is critical realist: The best we can do in descriptive terms is to approximate a true model. Berry goes far beyond believing that approximation is necessitated because of imprecise measurement and other idiosyncratic factors, however. Were those the only problems, surely his feelings about his being able to identify such a model would be more positive.[1]

The main culprits that Berry (1993) blames for having multiple, potentially true models are *different levels of aggregation* and *different causal distances*. For example, there are some educational phenomena like grade attainment that may be studied at the individual level or aggregated so as to look at them across blocks of schools or school districts. Each model might have its own theoretical explanation and be internally coherent, but the models may be very different. At the individual level, researchers and teachers might be interested in the implications of how involved a child's parent is in school-related activities, how often the child comes to school, or how undernourished a child seems to be. The development of a model gives them a window for viewing and organizing their experience on these matters. At a higher level of aggregation (such as comparing schools with one another), there may be some overlap in interest, but the view from the window is very different. Parent involvement and parent-involvement strategies may be of interest. Poverty rates in the area that the school serves and the adequacy of school lunch programs may be of interest. Dropout rates and dropout prevention programs may be of interest, as are other factors (Wilson & Allen, 1995). There is nothing more or less true about each of these approaches. They may even be combined (Aber, 1994). Berry's point is that they may both claim to be true models dealing with school achievement phenomena.

Similarly, models using different conceptions of causal distance may be used to study the attainment of grades in junior high school. Some models may focus on the role of friends' behaviors and attitudes, current plans for the future, course of study, time spent with parents around educational matters, cultural capital (Farkas et al., 1990), and course mastery as a "close quarters" (Berry, 1993, p. 7) modeling effort. A different model might focus on things from afar, such as early IQ scores, preschool experiences, parental education, and so on. Just as with different levels of aggregation, it is conceivable that models constructed at different causal distances could be both informative and descriptively adequate. Further, in both cases, it is possible that cross-level (as with Bryk & Raudenbush, 1992) or cross-distance (as with Farkas et al., 1990) could be constructed as long as very strong associations among sets of concepts did not make the combination problematic.[2]

---

[1]"Pun intended" (Lofland, 1995, p. 64).

[2]Quantitative researchers would treat this as a multicollinearity problem. Qualitative researchers would perhaps find that they could reach a point of saturation using either set of categories and concepts.

Arguing that there may be many different true or equivalent (Mac-Callum, 1995) models that could descriptively fit a data set is not an idea that just cropped up in the analysis of regression assumptions. For social scientists, it goes back at least to Popper (1959). It seems, however, that there are two important points regarding the evaluation of models with respect to goodness on descriptive criteria *after* one is convinced that the level of aggregation and causal distance are appropriate for the analysis of the situation. One is that models have to be *disconfirmable* (Mulaik & James, 1995), or, potentially eliminated. One has to be able to tell when models are descriptively inadequate. The second point is that even though the one Truth with a big T cannot be found, suggesting that it is there (perhaps as a little t truth) and should be looked for is a reasonable working assumption.

Such a posture for quantitative researchers is parallel to the posture of several leading qualitative researchers working in the general area of ethnography (Altheide & Johnson, 1994; Hammersley, 1992; Lofland, 1995; Maxwell, 1992; Miles & Huberman, 1994). Believing in a capital-T Truth that may simply be recorded in detail and accepted at face value is considered naive. As Lofland (1995, p. 48) puts it, however, these "realists" believe that there is a ". . . (small t) truth to which we can have some reasonable degree of access." Claims made by qualitative researchers regarding such matters usually rest on the coherence and detail of the data gathering, analysis, and reporting practices of the researcher involved (Lofland, 1995; Miles & Huberman, 1994).

Common to both quantitative and qualitative work is the need for "consistency between analysis and facts" (Lofland, 1995, p. 48). Truth may be approximate, but where researchers are able to show that alternative descriptions of the data do not hold, they may establish a firmer claim. Just as qualitative and quantitative work may *complement* one another by highlighting different aspects of a problem, so different models may complement one another by highlighting different aspects of a different problem. This gets us a bit ahead of ourselves and into the realm of theory, but it is interesting that Berry (1993) offers a similar resolution: "In this view, there is no such thing as true models, there are only theories" (p. 7). A less stringent criterion here would be seeking as much specificity and explicitness as possible: If relationships among variables and concepts are not specified, the authors are begging the question of how good the model is by allowing it to be resolved solely in terms of variance explained or the amount of detail presented.

Discussions of fit merge into Randers' (1980) second interesting question regarding the capacity of a model to reproduce important modes of behavior. In blunt terms, when big things happen or big shifts occur, is the model sensitive to them?

Quantitative analogs are available in a variety of forms. At a basic level, this question asks whether the big things are in the model. If there are gorilla concepts lurking out there, are they represented? At a more advanced level, if feedback is central to understanding the patterns in the data, are feedback relationships properly analyzed? At a more subtle level, however, such a question may refer to the sort of argument put forward by Isaac and Griffin (1989, for example) in a number of papers on the subject of the importance of historical periods that shape the nature of relationships among variables and concepts in important ways. When such changes in context are present, does the model have a way of representing them? Even more generally, if there are important things going on at different levels of analysis, is the model able to discriminate what these are (Bryk & Raudenbush, 1992)? If these sensitivities do not exist, a goodness claim in descriptive terms for quantitatively derived models would not be credible.

Qualitative researchers, as discussed in previous chapters, have a very different approach to establishing a legitimate claim to descriptive validity. Establishing the factual accuracy of an overall account (Maxwell, 1992) is comparable to examining the overall fit of the model with the multiple forms of data that it summarizes. At a minimum, there must be a sense that the model does not represent a naively realistic (Hammersley, 1992) view of what is happening in the situation being modeled. Beyond that, an intangible objective of getting it right (Kirk & Miller, 1986) seems close to the concept of fit. Lifting the veil to get a look at the essence of a situation does no good if one focuses only on the pores in the face. Massive detail without some credible order-developing strategies simply generates overload, not greater descriptive understanding. Hammersley (1991) could have presented a massive amount of detail concerning the operation of the individual juvenile courts—everything from transcriptions of court proceedings to numerous observations on these proceedings. Instead, he chose to focus on the most important claims being made and the evidence that could be amassed to support each of these claims.

Wolcutt (1994) flipped getting it right on its head. He wondered whether a more appropriate goal may not be at least not getting it all wrong. I find a strong parallel between that turn of phrase and arguments that ask about the big things. Being sensitive to context and agency are not subtle requirements in qualitative research; they are almost taken for granted. And with enough detail, any local situation may be made sense of descriptively in the same way that having lots of variables and concepts in regression equations can help explain more variance. In neither case, however, is there any guarantee that the most important things are being examined or that the influence of context is placed in perspective (Becker, 1990; Burawoy, 1991b). Without some evidence in support of a claim to having picked up on the big things that are going on, a claim of descriptive validity is baseless. To return to Hammersley's (1991) discussion of Parker, Casburn, and Turnbull's

(1981) court study, one of the big things going on is the differential presence of due process safeguards between the two courts. These safeguards changed how status differences between judges and families of the juvenile defendants played out in the two situations. Without the systematic clarification of how this element shaped the context of the two courts, the comparison fails to make good descriptive sense.

When assessing descriptive adequacy within context, it is important to ask how properly framed the context is. This is a matter of being skeptical about the descriptive validity of one's measurement and substantive models in the context being studied. Unless one may be assured that the concepts are grounded the same way in all aspects, and unless evidence is brought to bear that the relationships are the same in all aspects studied, claims to descriptive validity must be questioned. This is not a new argument, although the terms may have changed a bit over the years. Isaac and Griffin (1989), for example, cited Moore's (1958) early work on political power by saying:

> . . . a particular historical event can do more than confirm or disconfirm a hypothesis. It can change the situation so that one hypothesis or another *becomes* correct. (p. 888)

Providing evidence that such events are not altering either the descriptive validity of the concepts being examined or the nature of their relationships bolsters claims to descriptive validity.

In sum, descriptive validity questions draw our attention to claims regarding what and how events take place and situations unfold. Credible answers to these questions involve bringing evidence to bear regarding both what *is* and *is not* going on in a situation. In the language of specification, descriptively valid models make it easier for us to establish what concepts are important and unimportant, what indicators of these concepts hang together or are interchangeable and which ones are not, and what relationships are important and which ones are not. Similar questions may be asked about the extent to which the models we are constructing reflect the lived-in worlds of people and institutions as opposed to the research-oriented worlds of the model builder.

Interpretive Questions

Interpretive questions focus on the extent to which our models implicate the experience (Altheide & Johnson, 1994) of those living through a situation. The implication of experience is an involved undertaking that may be broken up into questions similar to those we asked about descriptively valid claims. Do the concepts used in the analysis make sense in the terms used by people living through the situation? Is the nature of the observed relationships interpretable in terms used by the people living through the situation? At a more complex level, are the mental models used by participants compatible with the model constructed by the researcher? Meaning is generated not so much by how things hang together empirically as by how people define the situation and think that these things hang together.

With descriptive validity, a common thematic response to such questions involved increasing credibility by eliminating alternative descriptions to concepts, relationships, and models to more closely approximate the true (note the lower case) model. Establishing the credibility of interpretive claims is more complicated because there are potentially as many versions of what is going on in a situation as there are participants. Specification of alternatives is still very important, but rather than elimination of alternatives being the only relevant strategy, we see that respecting the differences among alternatives is a viable strategy as well.

Concepts. Randers' (1980) descriptive realism questions are a good place to start because they provide a new twist to the nature of interpretation. This is an emic concern: Do the concepts in the model make sense in the terms used by those experienced with the situation? Rossman and Wilson (1991), for example, give the following example of how building more interpretive sense with multiple forms of data increased the quality of their understanding of how a state testing program improved the curricula in 12 schools:

> . . . One problem associated with quantitative research is that researchers cannot be sure that the meanings they attach to words on a survey and to the resulting statistical summaries are similar to those held by respondents; the data have become de-contextualized.
>
> To compensate for this potential problem, [our] design stipulated a third phase when we returned to the original twelve sites and sought educators reactions to the survey results. Essentially, we summarized key survey findings and then asked for their interpretations. The qualitative responses provided detail and enhancement to the numbers from the survey. For example, we found that the majority of the survey respondents indicated that the curriculum had improved as a result of the state testing program. Yet when we probed this in the follow-up interviews, we found that most of the interpretations of "improvement" focused on tightening of the curriculum with adjectives like "structured," "more focused," "coordinated," "more systematic." Thus the qualitative results offered an elaboration not available if just the quantitative results were analyzed in isolation. (pp. 321–322)

In this example, perceptions of improvement derived from the state testing program are probed. The goal is to elaborate the meaning of improvement in the eyes of the teachers who are experiencing the changed policy. This enriched understanding ". . . lends strength to an argument and *provides alternate perspectives*" (Rossman & Wilson, 1985, p. 637). Metaphorically, the authors characterized this strength-building exercise as illuminating the different facets of a gem.

The gem metaphor as Rossman and Wilson (1985) used the term is a dramatic way of capturing the convergence of indicators that forms part of the process involved in evaluating any of the forms of validity that we have discussed. Rossman and Wilson also suggested that exploring participant interpretations may lead to *divergent* (rather than *convergent*) outcomes. Extending the discussion of the last quote in a hypothetical direction, suppose that the probes of teachers about the meaning of improvement yielded differing interpretations of improvement gains. Imagine that some of the teachers thought of improvement in terms of structure, focus, and coordination, while other teachers thought of improvement in terms of excitement, innovation, and creativity (Fig. 7.1). These are divergent interpretations of improvement. Had this actually been the result of Rossman and Wilson's (1985) probing, the two meanings of improvement would have been confounded. Consequently, the concept of improvement would have been confused, and the analysis of relationships involving improvement might have been nonsensical.

Suppose, for example, that it had been found that teachers with longer years of service were more likely to feel that the state testing program had created a lot of improvement. Given the divergent but confounded interpretations of improvement, the possibility of understanding this relationship would be almost nonexistent. Armed with the hypothetical information regarding the different clusters of meaning, improvement could be respecified as having two dimensions: one in which meanings converged around structure and another in which meanings converged around creativity.

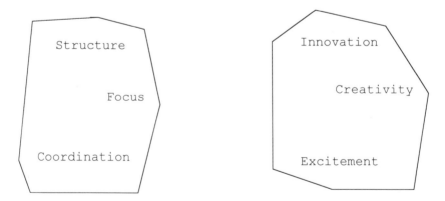

FIG 7.1. Hypothetical extension of Rossman and Wilson's (1985) curriculum improvement example into two clusters of meaning.

Respecifying the concept using this interpretive information would do more than simply make the concept more understandable. As we have talked about before, forms of specification interpenetrate one another. Consequently, there would be an increased chance of making sense of the relationship of improvement to other concepts and variables, such as years of teacher service. It might be, for example, that younger teachers appreciate improvements in innovation and creativity and older teachers appreciate the increased structure and coordination.

The liberties I have taken with the example drawn from Rossman and Wilson's (1985) analysis are intended to highlight an important point about the evaluation of concepts in models from a vantage point of interpretive validity. Probing for the meanings associated with emerging concepts is an essential part of the research process. Without some evidence that such efforts have been made, it would be hard to give a good grade (to follow the teaching analogy) to the resulting model in terms of interpretive validity—at least as far as concepts are concerned. The results of probing and gathering additional observations may either converge or diverge. In either case, a more plausible and useful model should be the result.

Relationships and Models.   A different facet of interpretive questions for Randers (1980) focuses on relevance, the extent to which the model addresses problems deemed by experienced participants as being important. More generally, if investigations are driven by policy questions, such an interpretive question makes a good deal of sense. On the other hand, there may be many occasions when it is exactly those things that are either taken for granted or considered trivial or bizarre, or even nonevents that are important to examine. Consequently, it is not an easy matter to make a hard and fast decision as to what constitutes goodness in such situations.

Rossman and Wilson's (1985, 1991) point about the need to build in greater interpretive validity to conclusions is well-taken here. Lest it be concluded, however, that these are simply academic exercises of no relevance to those living through the situation, note that the authors asked important questions regarding the effectiveness of policy interventions in the schools where the informants teach and administer classes. Such matters of relevance are not confined to educational concerns, however. Consider the following summary discussion of how results of a study had an impact on a general practitioner:

> The response of the general practitioner to the results was the recognition that he and his patients were operating on different levels of knowledge concerning their problem. As one who regarded himself as a champion of these patients and the legitimacy of their illness, this came as something of a shock. (Denz-Penhey & Murdoch, 1993, p. 17, cited in Miller & Crabtree, 1994, p. 349)

Relevance is at the heart of this discussion. Implicit in the discussion but worth noting is that there appears to be no condescension of researcher to doctor and patients in this analysis. There are several risks involved in breaking situations into concepts and analyzing them. Aside from de-contextualizing the meaning of the concepts, it also implies detaching oneself from what is being studied. A certain amount of detachment is useful analytically (Lofland, 1995), but trying to assure relevance is a step away from becoming overly analytic and detached. The downside risk is associated with the implication that what is being studied is somehow less powerful and less compelling than the social scientist's discussion. The risk appears greater in quantitative research than in qualitative. Burawoy (1991b), for example, argued that participant observation breaks down barriers between researcher and researched:

> It shatters the glass box from which sociologists observe the world and puts them temporarily at the mercy of their subjects. Instead of watching respondents through two-way mirrors, reconstructing them from traces they leave in archives, analyzing their responses to telephone interviews, or reducing them to demographic data points, the ethnographer confronts participants in their corporeal reality, in their concrete existence, in their time and space. (p. 291)

For us to judge that a model is doing a good job interpretively, some sense of confronting participants in their corporeal reality should be present: Context should never be pushed under the rug, but a certain analytic detachment must also be present (Lofland, 1995). Are participants forcing convergence among events where there might plausibly be divergent interpretations? Is there selective attention to events (and interpretations of events) that fit pre-established ways of thinking about what is going on? Is there even more deliberate falsification of positions in order to conceal discrediting or uncomfortable information (Douglas, 1976)? Implicating experience, as Altheide and Johnson (1994) put it, requires both confronting the corporeal reality of participants and not being seduced by it.

A third facet of interpretive validity is addressed by Randers (1980) as part of insight. System dynamicists use the term *mental model* to refer to how participants understand the dynamics of a situation; in other words, what they consider important and how they view these things as being causally related to one another. This stretches the typical questions about interpretation as qualitative researchers view it. Mental models are concerned with the dynamics of cause and effect through the eyes and thought processes of the participants. Much qualitative analysis is primarily concerned with how participants carve up a situation into concepts. Just as Maxwell (1992) reminded us that there are two parts to theories—concepts and relationships—so there are also two parts to interpretation and emic concerns: How people carve up a situation into concepts and how and why they believe these concepts are related to one another. Models essentially force researchers to consider both sides of this issue. Goodness here would refer to the extent to which both concepts and relationships are embedded in the experience of those living through a situation. Adapting an injunction from Groves and Lynch (1990):

> [B]egin with concrete, socially situated experiences. Only after analyzing these experiences does the inductive methodologist attempt to build more abstract theoretical models of social life. (p. 358)

This was the advice a colleague and I followed in the preschool study in developing a child-as-student role development scale for the HIPPY program. Only after figuring out how parents and paraprofessionals thought about what was going on in the lesson sessions did we try to translate that into some tentative questionnaire items. Even then, there was a rechecking process with the paraprofessionals as to the wording of the questions to make sure that they not only were transparent and easily understood, but also that they captured how the parents and paraprofessionals were themselves thinking about what was going on in sessions.

It is interesting what questions Randers (1980) did *not* feel were relevant to descriptive realism, transparency or insight. Conflicting accounts and interpretations were not considered in Randers' list of questions. The process of meeting frequently with all clients involved in a particular analysis is supposed to iron out differences in mental models. This may often occur, and I suppose that one way of assessing goodness in such situations would be to ask for some documentation showing how initially divergent mental models have converged—much along the lines of Hammersley's (1991) argument that claims that are not self-evident need to be buttressed by data that are themselves weighted by their credibility.

As with relevance, however, there are distinct alternative interpretations of what goodness might be and how it might be achieved as far as insight. It may be exactly the conflict among mental models in a situation that is of greatest interest to the researcher. These differing models may be traceable to, for example, ideological differences (conservatives versus liberals over funding of the Humanities), positional differences (such as engineers and marketing personnel in an auto company), class differences (wealthy versus working class views of the social security system), racial differences (Blacks versus Whites on affirmative action), or gender differences (males versus females on parental responsibilities).

Underneath the areas in which these differences may occur lies a more important distinction. These differences may have a dialectical relationship with one another, with each reacting to, taking energy from, or forming an identity in opposition to the other. Divergent perspectives regarding dynamics need to be respected. If the dialectical relationship is itself of interest or of crucial importance in understanding something else—such as varying levels of polarization between groups in a community—then including the divergent perspectives in the same model may be the best route. If the divergent perspectives are tied to context so that they fundamentally alter how concepts are related to one another, it might be more useful to develop two separate models. More complicated situations may require some combination of these strategies, but one thing to be avoided is simply averaging out the differences and assuming that the variation that occurs does not have important implications.

In sum, we should address questions of model goodness in interpretive validity terms in a similar manner to that established with descriptive validity questions. Concepts should be examined to assess the extent to which they reflect the worlds of participants, and may therefore be justifiably called emic. Relationships and models as a whole should be similarly examined, and good models from this vantage point should have evidence of this grounding process.

Convergence and divergence take on new layers of meaning with interpretive concerns, however. There may be strong differences in how people or groups in different positions of power and authority, different backgrounds, or different cultures organize in their minds what is important in a situation and what the dynamics are. The same sort of divergence may also be expected in theoretical or explanatory approaches to validity, the topic of the next section.

Explanatory Questions

Explanatory questions focus on the extent to which a model and its specifications are embedded in one or more theoretical perspectives. *Embeddedness* is a nice term and appears to be a powerful way of describing the fit between a model and the theoretical perspectives to which it is related, but it conceals the fact that there is a two-way exchange going on here in theoretical terms. The kinds of questions we ask, however, will be similar to those already encountered in descriptive and interpretive validity concerns. Are the concepts used in a model compatible with relevant existing and emerging theory? Are the concepts considered central to a theory in the model? Are the additive and interactive relationships expected by a theory present? What does the theory predict should occur that does not—so that these expectations were initially in the model and subsequently left out? What is happening in the situation (and reflected in the model) that is unexpected or surprising from a particular theory's point of view? This section reviews these kinds of questions, again using as a stimulus the work of Randers (1980) summarized in Box 7.1.

This cyclic process has been described as a true two-way dialogue by authors such as Burawoy (1991a) and Maines (1993), although they are not concerned with models per se, only with a continuing reformulation in which theories and research efforts mutually inform and revise one another. Miles and Huberman (1994) incorporated models as one strategy for making sense in their multiple attempts to convey the iterativeness and tentativeness of the research and theory-development process. Randers' (1980) list of questions seemed to favor the flow of ideas and information from data, as they were organized and understood by a model. This is the ground-up, inductive side of the cycle advocated by grounded theorists (Glaser & Strauss, 1967; Strauss, 1987; Strauss & Corbin, 1990). The other side would be represented by theoretical perspectives suggesting that concepts organized the welter of observations, what relationships might be crucial, and what the nature of facts is (Burawoy, 1991a).

The iterative, cyclic dialogue has as its purview the same three specification problems that we have encountered before. The first is the transaction between indicators and concepts that results in having indicators converge on one another and discriminates concepts from one another. Meaning and understanding emerges here from the dialogue between what we are observing in the field and finding in our analyses, and what the theory tells us should exist. The second focus is on those concepts that are considered important. Unlike the case of descriptive validity, where such decisions are driven by observed patterns, or the case of interpretive validity, where such decisions are driven by the perceptions of participants, with explanatory validity, such decisions are driven by theoretical concerns. Theories might tell us exactly what concepts are important and what we should be looking for as indicators that such things are present in the situation being analyzed. Finally, a theory may offer some concrete expectations regarding how concepts are related to one another. A theory of social support as buffer, for example, might tell us what social support is, conceptually and operationally. Further, it might suggest that the level of social support one enjoys does not have a strong impact on one's well-being except during periods of high stress. This is a very specific hypothesis that conveys both what should and should not be observed in a particular situation in a particular period of time.

Whether one starts with theory or the problem to be analyzed, there are ample opportunities for using models to assist in the theory-reconstruction process. When theories clash with the realities we are studying, ambiguities and contradictions present themselves (Burawoy, 1991a; Ragin, 1987) and demand a reanalysis. The nature of concepts may be reassessed. Those variables and concepts considered to be important may shift. The relationships among concepts may change. The context within which the work is being done may be reframed. Models may serve as a vehicle for organizing this iterative process, allowing it to be pushed forward into new territory either for the theoretical perspective or the interpretation of the situation being analyzed—or both. For a model to be credible in this regard, there must be evidence that the model summarizes a developed treatment (Lofland, 1995), that it has gone through a reconstruction or respecification process (Burawoy, 1991a), or that it has gone through a few iterations. Similar concerns are expressed by quantitative researchers. Byrne (1994), for example, argued that structural equation models that cross-validate their modified models over independent samples are more credible than those that do not.

Insight is perhaps the most important criterion for Randers (1980) because ". . . the ultimate objective [of the modeling process] is increased understanding" (p. xix). Seeing things that were not seen before, either because they were taken for granted, not understood as a pattern, or simply too complex to be penetrated by the theoretical perspectives and experience of those engaged in the process extends and reformulates the theoretical perspectives involved. When such efforts produce "surprising effects that are obvious after the fact (of modeling) (Randers, 1980, p. xix)," useable theoretical knowledge has been gained (see also Burawoy, 1991a; Lofland, 1995).

Although not formally stated by Randers (1980), one interpretation of this incorporation of "surprising effects that are obvious after the fact (Randers, 1980, p. xix)" is that plausible causal mechanisms by which variables and concepts affect one another are being developed and understood within a theoretical perspective. The *hows* and *whys* make greater theoretical sense than they did before the surprise was encountered. We think of this metaphorically as a light bulb going on, as a breakthrough, a lifting of the veil, as taking us beyond common sense, or as an A-ha! phenomenon. However we think of it, seeing something that was not obvious before and being able to tentatively account for it theoretically is a characteristic that good models have. Models that do not tell us anything new, or do not get us beyond common sense may be considered sufficiently mundane and hardly worth the effort (cf. Burawoy, 1991a).

Just as with interpretive validity, however, there are apparent problems with complexity and diversity. With interpretive validity, I argued that one must respect the different voices of participants . . . and try to understand why their voices were different. With explanatory validity, the sources of diversity are the multiple theoretical perspectives that may inform our understanding of particular situations. The resolution should be the same: respecting the alternative theoretical formulations as best one can rather than ironing out their differences.

In some cases, it may be possible to develop partial models that specify the implications of particular theoretical positions, and then to follow that with the development of a synthetic model based on the results of the analysis. Jenkins and Kposowa's (1990) analysis of the sources of military coups in Africa is a good example of this strategy (Fig. 7.2). They first specified the implications of four different theoretical positions ranging from ethnic antagonism theories to dependency the-

• *Political Development Theory*

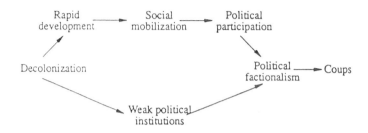

• *Military Centrality Theory*

• *Ethnic Antagonism Theories*

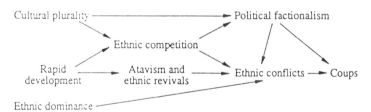

• *Dependency Theory*

FIG. 7.2. Jenkins and Kposowa's (1990) competing partial models of the sources of military coups in Africa (figure one in their presentation). Reprinted with permission.

ory. They then developed a synthetic model in which the overlapping implications of the partial models were exposed to a test.

Partial models may also be of considerable use in summarizing a complex literature where there seem to be multiple, competing theoretical and practical positions. Dohrenwend and Dohrenwend (1981) used this approach to good advantage in their early discussion of six alternative models of the relationships between life stress and health status (Fig. 7.3). Each of these partial models is given a convenient label that serves to reinforce the fact that there are several different ways to think about how life stress and health are related to one another across time.

There are limits to the strategy of developing partial models and then exposing them to test. For one thing, it may not be possible to decide on a common set of indicators for the concepts involved. I used the social-support-as-buffer hypothesis to illustrate the extent to which particular theories could generate expectations that could then be put to a test. Suppose, however, that an alternative to the buffer hypothesis was an additive model predicting that stress undermined health and support increased it. The capacity to fairly pit these hypotheses against one another is contingent on being able to agree on a common set of operations for the analysis. If the two hypotheses defined social support very differently (for presumably sound theoretical reasons), using a single measure of social support would underrepresent one or both of

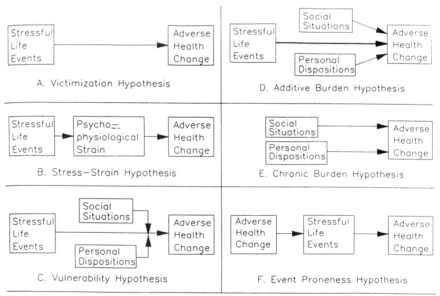

FIG. 7.3. Dohrenwend and Dohrenwend's (1981) presentation of six alternative models for the relationships between life stress and health.
Reprinted with permission.

the theoretical positions. In such cases, it might be more reasonable to simply have two models.

A very difficult problem to surmount is the fact that, often, alternative models will specify feedback or contingent relationships either as competing models or part of a synthetic model. Such complexities require the infusion of a great deal of information, longitudinal analyses, and/or the combination of analyses in ways that bring the complexities to life. That problem notwithstanding, however, whether one is engaged in qualitative (Burawoy et al., 1991), comparative (Amenta & Poulson, 1994), or quantitative (Jenkins & Kposowa, 1990) research, the development of competing models may make it easier to be surprised (and learn something) about what is going on in a particular situation.

In sum, goodness in terms of explanatory validity rests in part on how infused our choice of concepts is, our conceptual and operational definitions, and our expectations about how and why concepts should be related to one another by particular theories. This is the deductive side of what is really an iterative, cyclic process. On the deductive side, good models should be conceptually dense in the sense that they have a lot of the concepts in them that are considered central to the theory. They should also have concepts that make sense in terms of at least one theoretical position. If more than one theory is being used to inform the model, the links to each should be clear and fairly represented. Finally, the expectations of the theories as to combinations and relationships should be explicit.

The other side of explanatory-validity goodness is the extent to which the model helps us learn something new, surprising, or useful about the situation and theories that are used to inform the model. What have we learned about the nature of concepts in context? What have we learned about the relevance or irrelevance of particular concepts in context? What have we learned about relationships among concepts in context that should be expected in the future? This is the inductive side of the respecification process, and it corresponds to concerns of the reconstruction of theory (Burawoy, 1991a). What we learn from models is bounded by time and space. These are the issues confronted in discussions of predictive validity.

Predictive Questions

On their face, predictive questions regarding models seem straightforward. As Randers (1980) put it, "Can the model produce a precise prediction of a future event or of the future magnitude of important elements in the system" (p. ix)? In this form, prediction is stripped of all but descriptive meaning, but whereas descriptive questions engage us with the present and the past—as in, "Can this model adequately describe these historical data?"- predictive validity questions make us look to the future and/or to other situations. The narrow interest of prediction is in being able to forecast the future or the extent to which what we have learned from our analysis may be extended to the understanding of other situations, times, and places. Such a narrow position has two major problems: lack of usefulness and poor generalizeability.

In the first place, prediction stripped of other forms of understanding has little usefulness. It is highly context-dependent in the sense that it must depend on what is virtually a closed system. Nothing changes except that which is in the model at the present time. Further, such an approach cannot provide reasons for how or why things occur, when they are likely to occur or what the events will mean to those who are living through them. It may be possible to predict fairly accurately what the suicide rate will be in Pittsburgh in a year's time simply by using Pittsburgh's current suicide rate and unemployment rate. We might even be able to reduce the margin of error by including some information on the trends or trajectories in these variables. At its most absurd level, this is like predicting how old you are going to be on your next birthday from information regarding how old you are now. We can predict; we can explain variance. But everything interesting from a theoretical, interpretive, and even descriptive point of view is collapsed into itself when to predict something in the future we rely heavily on the level of that phenomenon in the past and present.

Such a stripped-down version of prediction is something of a straw man. But in combination with either understanding or explanation, it becomes a more legitimate position. Consider how it is discussed by Huberman and Crandell (1982) for example:

> Like other data sets, qualitatively derived findings are valid if they successfully explain, interpret and—in the best of all possible worlds—predict the empirical phenomena under study. (p. 69)

Within an interpretive framework of understanding, prediction would entail knowing the logic of how individuals think about events and situations so that how people would react to an event could be anticipated. Explanation involves a different tension. The touchstone is not so heavily influenced by the worlds of the individuals involved—although that certainly helps—as it is by the theoretical perspectives that are guiding the analysis. Expectations for the future involve justifying predictions on the basis of theoretical implications. When interpretation and explanation proceed in tandem with prediction so that the forms of understanding interpenetrate one another, the result can be much more useful—at least for the context being studied.

In the hands of researchers like Huberman and Crandall (1982), prediction can become an effective vehicle for furthering overall understanding and usefulness of research projects (see also Miles & Huberman, 1994). They generated a long list of specific expectations for the sites in their school-improvement project at the end of their data collection and sent them to informants one year later for comment and further discussion. Aside from the direct benefits of such a dialogue between researchers and practitioners, such a procedure can be enlightening in other respects. In commenting on their use of prediction as a tool, for example, Huberman and Crandall (1982) stated:

> [Predicting what will occur at a given site] is, to our knowledge, a newcomer to qualitative research, and proved most fruitful and encouraging. Most feedback on the findings was confirmatory . . . most of our predictions were on the nose . . . [and] when predictions were off the mark, it was largely due to unanticipated events—mostly unpleasant ones—at the site in the intervening year. (p. 70–71)

A key phrase in this discussion by Huberman and Crandell (1982) is "unanticipated events." A quick reaction to that might be that the expectations for sites that the authors had (or more generally, their model for generating expectations) was mis-specified in the sense that I have talked about unanticipated events in chapter 4. That does a disservice to the authors, by whose account most of their predictions were on the mark, indicating that their understanding of what was happening was descriptively adequate, was incorporated the world views of the important actors at the sites, and was theoretically informed.

The second problem associated with a stripped-down version of prediction is a poor generalization to other situations. What may have been missing in some instances from Huberman and Crandell's (1982) site-specific predictions was a sense of how features of the site that were constant over the year interacted with changes. This is a problem of generalizeability: Prediction must refer to more than just chronological time extensions. To be useful, it must incorporate what Cook and Campbell (1979) and Maxwell (1992), for example, have called external validity or generalizeability:

> Generalizeability refers to the extent to which one can extend the account of a particular situation or population to other persons, times or settings than those directly studied . . . Generalizability [in qualitative research] is normally based on the assumption that this theory may be useful in making sense of similar persons or situations, rather than on an explicit sampling process and the drawing of conclusions about a specified population through statistical inference. (Maxwell, 1992, p. 293)

The second part of this is overdrawn. Cook (1993) argued that sampling provides only a very soft and incomplete basis for generalization, and that the best way to facilitate generalization would be on the basis of theory—another instance of a plea for the interpenetration of these forms of understanding. Unfortunately, theories in the social sciences are usually so underdetermined that it is hard to get much help from them. Hence, there is not as much of a gulf between the qualitative and quantitative positions here as Maxwell (1992) and Yin (1984) suggest.

There are two complementary ways of thinking about the problem of generalization. First is to ask what the contextual limits (other persons, times or settings than those directly studied) are to the model that has been developed in only one context. More directly, does what we have learned in one context help us make sense out of what is occurring in another? Alternatively, one could approach this problem as Becker (1990) did, by asking why the same processes may create different outcomes in different contexts. These are two sides of the same coin—and the coin of the realm here is not a stripped-down version of prediction, but prediction in conjunction with (and in the service of) greater theoretical and interpretive understanding.

When one puts these aspects of generalizeability together, as Ragin (1987, 1989, 1993) has coherently done, the result is a comparative analysis that ties matters of prediction directly to efforts to interpret and explain what is happening in different contexts, and how and why it is happening. In this light, the evaluation of predictive questions becomes more complex. It is not simply a matter of being able to predict with a modest degree of error how much of something there will be at a particular point in time, or what particular events might be expected—although those by themselves are massive achievements that deserve high marks on predictive criteria. What also must be considered is the extent to which matters of context interact with one's models in making sense out of a set of situations. Here we should be interested not only in things that were theoretically expected that did occur, but also in things that were not expected but occurred (Ragin, 1987). Precision may not be the hallmark of this latter approach—a feeling shared by system dynamics theorists (Randers, 1980)—but greater understanding on all fronts definitely is.

Cross-context prediction as the systematic consideration of other contexts is not uniformly welcomed by researchers. Abbott (1988) reminded us that there are method-driven tradeoffs that make it difficult to consider exceptions to the general linear model. Interaction effects have begun to receive more respect and treatment (Aiken & West, 1991; Jaccard et al., 1990). Hierarchical linear modeling techniques are beginning to diffuse through the social sciences (Bryk & Raudenbush, 1992). In spite of these trends, there are probably still many quantitative researchers who feel that the search for universal laws (i.e., prediction unfettered by context) is incompatible with piling on lots of contingencies, or that considering such complications is a painful constraint to be eliminated so that the *real* work of analysis may begin.

Many qualitative researchers will not be interested in the evaluation of such cross-context prediction either. As Burawoy (1991b) pointed out, ethnomethodologists may deny the relevance of such constraints, arguing that the search for invariant properties may take place in any setting. Similarly, those working out of an interpretive case method framework may treat the individual setting as representing the larger society of which it is a part, so that bull fights, cockfights, weddings, and other presumably significant events may be analyzed with the understanding that key elements of the larger society are being analyzed in the process. For many other qualitative researchers, however, for whom establishing the importance and significance of relationships means painstakingly studying them in different contexts (Glaser & Strauss, 1967; Miles & Huberman, 1994), or using context as a substantive wedge to better understand a situation (as in Burawoy's [1991b] extended case method), context is not a bothersome constraint or something whose relevance is to be denied. Rather, the consideration of context is central to the theory building and reconstruction process (See chapter 8). These approaches are, I believe, right on the money . . . in a predictive sense, of course.

Judging the goodness of models with respect to prediction, then, is not so easy a task as it might first seem. Evaluating predictions of what is going to happen in the future is at first glance simply a matter of calculating the amount of error involved. But predictive questions turn out to be richer, more rounded, and more complex once it is realized that we cannot take an ahistorical position on time. The future then shares much in common with other contexts, so that it really becomes difficult to appreciate prediction without considering its overlap with other forms of understanding. I turn to this discussion in the next section.

TENSIONS AND TRADEOFFS AMONG CRITERIA

I have already briefly discussed Huberman and Crandell's (1982) statement of the value of multiple, interpenetrating forms of understanding. Their argument is substantive: Research that combines description, interpretation, explanation, and prediction will be more trustworthy and credible than research that does not. I believe the same statement may be made for models, but there are also reasons to suspect that this is a difficult goal to reach. To begin with, there are some confounding factors whose presence must be reiterated. Second, there are hidden sources of resistance to allowing predictive elements, especially those having to do with context, to interpenetrate with other forms of understanding. Finally, there is tension among these forms of understanding that represents legitimate dilemmas for researchers. Let's consider these in turn.

Interpenetration as Confounding. Some interpenetration of forms of understanding are attributable to the theory-ladenness and interpretive content of facts (Hammersley, 1992; Maxwell, 1992; Miles & Huberman, 1994; Reichardt & Rallis, 1994; Wolcott, 1994). Theoretical perspectives bias what we look for, what we see, and how we interpret what we see. The values and experiences of the researcher color what is attended to, how it is examined, and what is reported. Thinking of these biases as sources of potential spuriousness is appropriate. When things make sense theoretically, for example, one should always ask whether the sense that is being made is spuriously attributable to the theoretical perspective's influence on what facts are amassed and how they are interpreted. Good analyses, whether models are used or not to facilitate the grasping of the argument, are those in which there is a realization that these sources of spuriousness exist. Models constructed from organizationally compiled data without a critical evaluation of alternate theoretical meanings imposed by the agency and/or by the members as they routinely use these categories are suspect. Where evidence of such a critical examination is presented, we may more comfortably judge models to be better.

Interpenetration and Contextual Oversimplification. When it is the researcher who is bringing theoretical perspectives and values to the situation, we tend to think along the lines of a methodological problem. When the explicit or implicit theoretical perspectives and values are part of the context within which something is being analyzed, their substantive impact becomes more pronounced. Out of convenience, context is usually thought of as having tangible properties. For example, we think of neighborhoods, organizations, and communities. The defining, critical elements of context, however, are more intangible and focus on meaning. It may show up as organizations, neighborhoods, and communities change, but it is perhaps easier to grasp with historical periods. Commenting on historical discontinuities in their analyses of union growth and the influence of the National Association of Manufacturers, for example, Griffin & Isaac (1992) suggested that such patterns reflect:

> ... real social change of the 'deepest' sort. Briefly our interpretation is that the historical contexts and social structures governing labor-capital conflict and labor's position in the polity were transformed at least twice and probably three times during the 40 years or so of our analysis. These contextual transformations, in turn, resulted in what we see as time-dependent, historically contingent relationships between [the growth and decline of unions and the National Association of Manufacturer's] 'counterorganization'. . . (p. 25)

When we strip analyses of the context within which they occur, we run the risk of losing the frame of reference that allows descriptive, theoretical, and interpretive sense to be made of a situation. Needless to say, models that properly frame the context of their analyses are more credible than those that do not. As Mishler (1979) put it, context should not be treated as an enemy; it should be treated as a resource for furthering our understanding. I will come back to this problem again in the next chapter because such arguments touch directly on questions regarding the relative simplicity of models, but there are also aspects of this problem that are central to questions of interpenetration. To these I now turn.

Contexts do not just happen, nor are they fixed; they evolve. Further, the relationship between context and the social entities (individuals, groups, etc.) that are represented in a context is complicated by the negotiations, transactions (Sameroff, Seifer, & Zax, 1982), or dialectical processes (Groves & Lynch, 1990; Sameroff, 1975) that implicate the lived experience of participants. Lived experience, in other words, is not passive. Although it may be the case that "social structure takes its toll whether or not its effects are registered in people's minds" (Kornhauser, 1978, p. 117), it cannot be automatically assumed that the relationships are unidirectional. If we were to assume that classroom climates affect children and teachers, but children and teachers do not have an impact on classroom climate, and introduce classroom climate into an analysis without any critical analysis of this assumption of unidirectional influence, we would be making this sort of potentially unwise simplification.

Neither should it be uncritically assumed that the impact of the climate is the same for all children and teachers. Some children and teachers may be much more susceptible or resistant to the impact of the classroom climate than others. This is becoming a familiar assumption in quantitative research as researchers have tried to use census and other archival data in their questionnaire analyses to obtain leverage for removing interpretively and theoretically valid explanations of their results (Aber et al., in press, for example). More credible modeling efforts will at least be sensitive to the issue and, in some cases, may even be able to bring other evidence to bear on the reasonableness of such an assumption.

Interpenetration and Noncontextual Tradeoffs.   There are other substantively interesting dilemmas and tradeoffs present between forms of understanding that less directly implicate context. Geertz (1983), for example, sketched the dilemma which researchers face in choosing the relative balance of etic and emic concepts:

> Confinement to experience-near concepts leaves an ethnographer awash in immediacies as well as entangled in vernacular. Confinement to experience-distant ones leaves him stranded in abstractions and smothered in jargon. The real question . . . is what kinds of roles the two concepts play

in anthropological analysis. To be more exact: How, in each case, should they be deployed so as to produce an interpretation of the way people live which is neither imprisoned within their mental horizons, an ethnography of witchcraft as written by a witch, nor systematically deaf to the distinctive tonalities of witchcraft as written by a geometer [a specialist in geometry]. (p. 57)

This dilemma has been talked about as the danger of going native (Kirk & Miller, 1986), or as the need to implicate the experience of participants without taking what they say at face value (e.g., Altheide & Johnson, 1994). Of more relevance here, however, is the sense of tradeoff implied by being "awash in immediacies as well as entangled in vernacular" or "stranded in abstractions and smothered in jargon." The construction and deployment of concepts is represented here as a balancing act between maximizing interpretive understanding and maximizing theoretical understanding. Good analyses—and for our purposes, good models—are those that have confronted these options and successfully engaged in this balancing act.

The tension among description, interpretation, explanation and prediction have been played out in several other venues as well. Among quantitative researchers, there are periodic arguments regarding whether it is more important to maximize the amount of variance explained (R^2)—a somewhat ill-conceived prediction argument (King, 1986)—or understand the dynamics by that the variance which is explained becomes so, a position closer to explanation. In point of fact, King (1986) argued that "[t]he best regression model usually has an R^2 that is lower than could be obtained otherwise" (p. 677). As a charicature of the search, King (1986) went on to say:

> If the goal is to get a big R^2 . . . include independent variables that are very similar to the dependent variable; your R^2 will be 1.0. Lagged values of y usually do quite well. In fact, the more [such variables] you add, the bigger your R^2 will get. Another choice is to add variables or selectively add or delete observations in order to increase the variance of the independent variables . . . These strategies will increase your R^2, *but they will add nothing to your analysis, nothing to your understanding [of the phenomena in which you are interested], and nothing useful in explaining your results to others.* (p. 677)

Models constructed in such a way as to maximize explained variance without regard to the discreteness among variables that are needed to develop explanatory understanding cannot be viewed as being as good as those in which there are some sensitivities with respect to such issues.

A similar distinction shows up in the systems dynamics literature. In the set of criteria Randers (1980) developed for evaluating system dynamics models, he found underlying differences between the shape of cross-criteria ratings generated for predictive purposes and for purposes of understanding. He traced these differences to the driving forces of what the models are used by clients for rather than to theoretical perspectives or research traditions from which the model builders come. The tension is there, nonetheless, and it is useful to be sensitized to it. For those interested in prediction, concern is greater over a model's relevance to problems at hand, the formal correspondence of the model with the data available, and the model's ability to predict specific outcomes. For those interested in understanding the transparency, mode reproduction ability, descriptive realism, and insight, generating capacity is more important. Sidestepping for the moment the lack of shared meaning that some of these terms have, one lesson should be clear: What one finds interesting or good about a model is going to vary depending on whether one is interested in description, explanation, interpretation, or prediction—or some combination of all four.

Building off Randers' (1980) discussion one last time, there is a very interesting bias built into the system dynamics approach as he conceived it:

> In system dynamics, much weight is usually placed on the upper entries in the list, whereas the lower ones are seen as less critical. This is rational when the ultimate objective is increased understanding, both of the past and of the likely consequences of future actions. The system dynamics approach is finely tuned to this objective and is therefore less useful if the goal is short-term, high-precision forecasting. (p. xix)

The upper entries Randers is referring to *combine* explanatory and interpretive forms of understanding. Good models of any kind may focus on this combination while downplaying the extent to which predictive accuracy is maximized.

Yet it is also the case that these three forms of understanding may be combined. Schreckengost (1980) described the relative effectiveness of system dynamics over econometric modeling in situations where there are important variables for which only soft estimates are available. As exercises, the Central Intelligence Agency pitted their soft- and hard-modeling groups against one another to develop estimates. In one such exercise, the task was to estimate the number of tanks that the Chinese would be amassing along the Sino-Soviet border. The econometric group was able to predict the number of tanks with about 25% error. The soft-modeling group was able to reduce this to 2% error by including night soil (the use of human excrement as fertilizer) in the model—something that needed to be left out of the econometric model because of its sensitivity to measurement error. The more night soil used to fertilize the crops, the less oil had to be diverted from gas and oil products to fertilizer, leaving more oil available for the mobilization of tanks. Such an approach reveals much more about the mobilization of the Chinese than just tanks! And although this may be the clearest example I can think of regarding Hirsch et al.'s (1987) distinction between elegant and clean econometric models versus dirty and more realistic sociological models, the essential point is that system dynamics may yield much better predictions than econometrics or more general quantitative approaches under certain conditions. More generally, not allowing ease of measurement to drive what ends up in our models is much preferred over using only what we think we are able to measure precisely. Predictive, explanatory, interpretive, and descriptive validity should all be better served.

PROCESS OVER PRECISION

If it were a simple matter to assess the credibility or goodness of descriptive, interpretive, explanatory, and predictive claims, it would be possible to assign numbers to these various ratings and develop profiles for models that summarized their ratings of different criteria. Comparing the shapes of ratings of a number of identified criteria is a tempting simplification. If the criteria are artfully selected, the shapes could highlight strong differences in approaches to modeling among those for whom understanding, explanation, or prediction are disproportionately important. It is, however, another instance of developing an overly precise approach in an area that masks many problems of softness and uncertainty.

Developing sensitivities to the various ways of thinking about good models is more important than developing some sort of precise estimate as to just how good a model is. If fit criteria are examined as if they were the only path to a good model, model evaluations can quickly become mechanical and routine. The process of thinking hard about the problems of specification, not as a mechanical exercise, but more as a way of achieving greater balance in one's approach to modeling is, consequently, a better path.

A good model, then, is not necessarily a definitive model. A definitive model may even be trivial or boring. More to the point, however, a good model is one that facilitates dialogue and systematically incorporates surprises. The process, then, is more important than the model. What holds for system dynamics, then, also holds for the paper and pencil models which we have been discussing. As Forrester (1985) put it:

> ... models are always in a continuous state of evolution. Each question, each reaction, each new input of information, and each difficulty in explaining the model leads to modification, clarification, and extension. (p. 133)

The next chapter focuses on one particular aspect of modeling choices and continuing reevaluation: the relative degree of simplification or elaboration of variables and concepts contained in the model. It is intended as a complement to this discussion of the alternate ways of thinking about goodness.

SUGGESTED READINGS

There are some useful discussions in the quantitative literature regarding the meaning of fit and some of the abuses associated with it. King's (1986) discussion of the Coefficient of Determination (R^2) and Luskin's (1991) rediscussion are essential reading to complement Achen (1991) and Berry's (1993) discussions of regression assumptions and interpretations. Both MaCallum (1995) and Hu and Bentler (1995), in the collection of essays on structural equation modeling put together by Hoyle (1995), are readable discussions of alternative ways of thinking about the nature of fit of data to models.

In the qualitative literature, the whole issue of fit revolves around discussions of realism. Lofland's (1995) article on analytic ethnography is a good, short review of the issues. Other discussions of these issues include Altheide and Johnson (1994), Hammersley (1991; 1992), Maxwell (1992) and Miles and Huberman (1994). All of these sources agree either that there is some version of the truth of a situation that may be identified in an approximate way, or that assuming that there is such a truth is a useful heuristic. For alternative perspectives in a qualitative vein, the *Handbook of Qualitative Sociology* offers a number of references (Denzin & Lincoln, 1994).

With regard to the different forms of understanding that models may help develop from a critical realist perspective, Maxwell (1992) offers a ground breaking discussion with respect to qualitative fieldwork. An interesting exercise is going back to Cook and Campbell (1979) to examine how they approach these issues within the constraints and needs of quasi-experimental designs.

Miles and Huberman (1994) present a cogent, concrete program for the making, testing, and feeding back to participants of site-specific predictions. It should be required reading for those doing qualitative *or* quantitative work who want to put their feet in the fire of the implications of their models for site evolution and development.

Meehan's (1986) continuing work on the meaning and use of organizational records is useful for assessing alternative interpretations of the descriptive and explanatory adequacy of such records as data. It continues a tradition of skepticism traceable to Garfinkel and Bittner's (1967) good organizational reasons for bad organizational records, together with Douglas's (1967) *Social Meanings of Suicide* and Cicourel's (1968) *The Social Organization of Juvenile Justice*.

The use of qualitative and quantitative data in tandem in various parts of the research process as a way of strengthening descriptive, interpretive, explanatory, and predictive claims has become more wide-spread in recent years. Rossman and Wilson's (1985; 1991) work in education is illustrative, especially when combined with Miles and Huberman (1994) and Hammersley (1991). Sieber's (1973) early work on combining surveys and fieldwork is very important. More extended recent treatments are available in Reichardt and Rallis (1992). Integration is not as important as the provision of alternate perspectives (where qualitative and quantitative complement one another by using the strength of their different voices) for thinking about and interpreting what is going on in each of the iterative dialogues. Groves and Lynch's (1990) work in criminology is a general case in point.

Finally, perhaps the most well-known treatments involving the elimination of alternative interpretations to establish the credibility of relationships is Campbell and Stanley (1963) and Cook and Campbell (1979). The implications of their work go far beyond experimental designs. Maxwell's (1992) comparison with field studies in a qualitative vein should be read in tandem with this.

EXERCISES

1. Take one of the main concepts of interest in your area. How dependent is it on one or a few indicators? Is it gathered in such a way that the operating theories and practices of the data gatherers might have systematic biases built into it? How can you increase the theoretical validity of this concept by eliminating alternative interpretations of what it means?

2. For this same concept, how well does it reflect the language of those living or who lived through the situation being analyzed? Are there alternative emic interpretations that may be attributable to positional, status, and so forth, differences? How can these be specified? Should a single interpretation be sought?

3. For this same concept, how context-dependent does it seem to be? Make a quick list of the places, times, and people for whom the concept makes sense. Now make a list of the places, times, and people where the concept would lead to erroneous conclusions. How can the chances of these kinds of errors be reduced?

4. Repeat exercises 1 through 3 for one of the main relationships of interest in the area in which you are immersing yourself.

5. Repeat exercises 1 through 3 for the model as a whole.

6. Considering the area of your interest as a long-term area, are the ways in which the prospect of using both qualitative and quantitative approaches might be useful in specifying and/or eliminating alternative interpretations, thereby increasing certain validity claims?

7. Cook's (1993) example of the confounded meaning of length of hospital stay (Figs. 7.E1 and 7.E2) is an excellent vehicle for examining issues having to do with the evaluation of models along several dimensions. What does this example tell us about the relative goodness of these models in descriptive, interpretive, explanatory, and predictive terms? With the second panel, what are we learning besides the unconfounding of the meaning of length of hospital stays?

8. Pick up three or four issues of a journal in your primary field in which there might be quantitative analyses of competing theoretical positions. Do you find any tendency for a self-fulfilling prophecy in these discussions? Specifically, are some of the theoretical positions poorly conceptualized, poorly measured, underdeveloped in their expected relationships, and then blamed because they do not explain as much variance as other positions? The lesson, of course, is that if you are going to choose a competing-model approach, you should give the contending theories a fair chance of explaining the phenomena being analyzed.

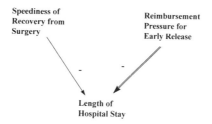

FIG. 7.E1. Panel one.

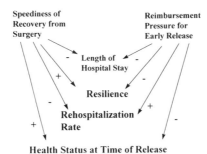

FIG. 7.E2 Panel two.

8

Strategies for Moving From Elaborated to Working Models

> I suppose [the model] captures a lot of what's going on, but it's so complex I have no idea what the hell it all means! (Comment by a student when confronted by a 14-variable model)

The model elaboration processes that I described in the chapters on elaboration, feedback, and context are driven by the need to capture more of the complexity that characterizes the realities of the situations we are investigating. Quantitative theorists and researchers talk about gaining a greater fit between their models and these underlying realities (Blalock, 1964; Hoyle, 1995a, for example). Qualitative researchers may talk in terms of realizing more developed treatments (Lofland, 1995) or developing greater conceptual density (Strauss, 1987). Both qualitative and quantitative researchers may refer to the elaboration process as one in which there is movement toward greater realism, more sensitivity to context, and closer contact with what is happening in a particular situation (Hirsch et al., 1987; Miles & Huberman, 1994).

Those who favor the incorporation of both qualitative and quantitative data in their models view the elaboration process as an opportunity to incorporate both structural and subjective perspectives in their analyses. Groves and Lynch (1990), for example, in decrying the structuralism/subjectivism dichotomy in criminology, argue that:

> . . . just as we object to a bald or naked structuralism which mechanically links structural characteristics with behavioral regularities, we believe that it is equally undesirable to opt for detached and abstracted versions of subjectivism that rely exclusively on the actor's attributions of meaning and intent . . . [we believe that criminology should] deepen its understanding of the structural background as well as the subjective foreground of crime. (p. 357)

With elaboration and modification, more generally termed *respecification*, models may become sufficiently complex so that it becomes difficult to understand their implications. As complexity increases, researchers begin considering how to manage the developing complexity.

166

Consequently, as the research process moves through a few iterations, researchers are trying to balance elaborating and simplifying their models. Strategies for engaging in this balancing act are the topic of this chapter.

The processes of elaboration and simplification are not linear. Models increase and decrease in complexity as their objectives change. More developed and complete models will be referred to as *elaborated models* even though all models represent simplifications of both reality and theoretical perspectives. Simplified models that may be useful as vehicles for communication and guides for action will be called *working models*. It is important to remember, however, that elaborated and working models are relative points in a process of continuing respecification.

This chapter develops guidelines for moving from more elaborated to working models by making decisions in three overlapping areas: simplifying tests for reducing complexity to manageable proportions, sufficiency tests to reduce the risk of oversimplifying, and action tests to ensure that informed action by those participating is not jeopardized. I also develop some presentational suggestions for expanding the capacity of models to convey complex ideas in a small space, à la Tufte (1983, 1990). A prior issue, however, is the varying nature of simplification, which means very different things to different research traditions.

THE MULTIPLE MEANINGS OF SIMPLICITY

The pervasiveness of the balancing act alluded to in the last two paragraphs has been associated with a variety of interpretations of the process and the meanings of simplicity. Simplicity may convey elegance (Hirsch et al., 1987), core or basic concepts and processes (Arminger & Bohrnstedt, 1987; Berry, 1993; Lieberson, 1985; Ragin, 1987), formal grounded theory (Strauss, 1987), identifiability (Hoyle, 1995a; MacCallum, 1995), or communicability (Miles & Huberman, 1994). These denotations and connotations overlap, but they do reveal some of the continuing tensions associated with the management of complexity.

Elegance and parsimony are properties of theories and models that have a barely sufficient number of concepts in them to adequately explain the phenomenon of interest. What constitutes a barely sufficient number of concepts and how these concepts should be chosen are, however, open to debate. Hirsch et al., (1987) discussed parsimony and elegance as it relates to contemporary economics:

> . . . contemporary economics exemplifies a highly abstract, deductive approach to social science. Its style is characterized by the development of models based on deliberately, vigorously and rigidly *simplified* [my emphasis] assumptions. (p. 318)

Such a position is comparable within the other social sciences to those who believe that the essence of situations requires getting to a reduced set of concepts that somehow make context irrelevant. Witness the following discussion of Lieberson's (1985) *Making It Count*:

> Lieberson's distinction between basic and superficial causes is certainly important, and it must be addressed if sociology is to be taken seriously. The vast majority of the research papers in sociological journals focus heavily on superficial causes, i.e., *on causes tied closely to time and context* [my emphasis]. Very few link these to more basic causes, to causes that represent more *fundamental* social processes operating in all social contexts. (Arminger & Bohrnstedt, 1987, p. 370)

Superficiality is explicitly tied to the consideration of context and time in such a formulation. Context and time are enemies (Mishler, 1979) rather than sources of understanding, with the hope that looking for more basic processes will increase a discipline's claim to being a serious social science.

The effort to strip down quantitative analyses to a fundamental core does have some merit. King (1986) argued that "[t]he best regression model usually has an R^2 that is lower than could be obtained otherwise" (p. 677). The closest approximation to a true model will have the best adjusted R^2 across samples, but as Luskin (1991) pointed out, it "is apt to be outdone in any particular sample by models catering shamelessly enough to that sample" (p. 1041). One interpretation of this is that from a substantive point of view, King and Luskin made a statistically oriented plea for focusing on the big things. But there is also a darker side of this argument that I come back to.

Such views are not peculiar to quantitative approaches. Burawoy (1991b) pointed out, for example, that both ethnomethodology and interpretive case studies seek something more universal in their analyses, denying the relevance of situational and contextual factors that characterize the particular situations that they are investigating. That there should be something more fundamental or higher level about theorizing and model building is also reflected in grounded theory's distinction between substantive and formal theory:

> . . . while most sociologists seem not to be personally interested in developing these higher-level [formal] theories, being content either to develop substantive theories about particular topical areas . . . nevertheless the writing of formal theories is, from the grounded theory perspective, viewed as being ultimately of the greatest importance. (Strauss, 1987, p. 241)

Substantive theory is first developed within contexts. Following that, a more formalized version is developed across contexts in an attempt to get at a higher level, more formal theory.

What is being dispensed with in these formulations—whether qualitative or quantitative in origin—are contextual parameters that may provide meaning for the overall analysis. Context does not have to be an interactive or combinatorial conception, although we usually think of it in that way (e.g., Burawoy, 1991b; Isaac & Griffin, 1989; Ragin, 1987). Within an additive framework, context is more implicit, more fluid, taking shape from the sum of the variables and concepts that are in the model. Where combinations of variables and concepts are presumed to be more important, an appreciation of context may be easier.

An interest in context puts pressure on social scientists to increase the number of variables and concepts in their models for reasons divorced from explained variance. The goal is trying to get it right, *not* explaining the most variance. Their models will be messier (Hirsch, et al., 1987), but they will be more realistic and interpretable, and they will less likely to be reduced to a few assumptions about human nature.

The same may not be true for those who take a combination approach, for such an approach relies on using conditions, context, historical periods, and so on as *leverage* in trying to tentatively make sense of comparative observations. Burawoy's (1991b) extended case method and Ragin's (1987) qualitative comparative analysis share this commitment. Parsimony and elegance cannot come at the cost of stripping observations from context *without putting the assumption to a test that particular features of context make no difference.*

One aspect of the dark side of achieving elegance in one's models, then, is stripping from them any sense of the context that shapes the meaning of everything that is taking place. Elegance may be achieved at a very costly price. But there is also a second aspect to the dark side of context-stripping as part of the simplification process. Contexts shape the meaning of what occurs in them, but they are also shaped in a variety of ways by what takes place in the context. Singer (1993) gives the following example from medical anthropology regarding the spread of malaria:

> The Anopheles mosquito that serves as a vector for the parasite that causes malaria was greatly influenced by human environmental reshaping for purposes of food cultivation, a development that reflected and expressed significant changes in the human social relationships and polity associated with production of a surplus and food storage. Cultivation created sunlit pools of stagnant water favored by Anopheles mosquitoes for breeding while storage of a food surplus allowed the concentration of a large number of human victims in settled villages. During this process, there is little doubt that the mosquito changed to facilitate more effective exploitation of human created environments for breeding and humans as a major source of the blood needed for reproduction. (p. 943)

The transactional nature of context/social entity relations should be taken into account whether it is as simple and local as high school and college students choosing their friends and the organizations they join, (e.g., Britt & Campbell, 1977a, 1977b), or as complicated as the transactions that organizations have with their environments (Hirsch et al., 1987), or as far-reaching as the unanticipated consequences reflected in the relationship between social organization and malaria or AIDS (Singer, 1993).

DEVELOPING SOME SIMPLIFICATION GUIDELINES

Table 8.1 lays out tests in three decision areas: simplification tests, sufficiency tests, and action tests. Simplification tests look for sources of redundant information in elaborated models. Some of the redundancy may come simply from variables that are so closely tied to one another empirically that eliminating one of them loses no useful information. More subtle are redundancies that are more theoretical in origin. Variables that measure the same underlying construct offer such possibilities, as do variables that are analytically separate but that mutually influence one another and variables that are parts of a simple causal chain. In each of these cases, the explanatory power of the model may be maintained while simplifying the overall complexity of the model.

There are risks associated with moving toward greater simplification, however. A companion set of sufficiency tests helps reduce the risk of losing touch either with the underlying theoretical perspective(s) that inform the model or the causal dynamics that are being represented. There must be sufficient variables in the model that are interpretable in terms of the underlying perspective to prevent slippage into an actuarial exercise where only prediction matters. Because the most robust dynamics in models are often represented by feedback loops and an appreciation of feedback is often associated with the generation of insight, it is also important to have important feedback loops that characterize a situation in a working model. The need for theoretical interpretability must be balanced against a need for including variables in the working model that are associated with important shifts in the situation being modeled. And the variables in these working models must leave reliable and valid traces so that observations of situational changes can be made.

For those interested in developing interventions, an additional set of constraints should be imposed. Action takes place in context. The same action in different contexts may mean entirely different things to the

TABLE 8.1
Simplification, Sufficiency, and Action Tests

Simplification Tests

1. Conceptual Redundancy: Can variables be eliminated that are related to the same underlying construct?

2. Empirical Redundancy: Can variables be eliminated that are highly intercorrelated?

3. Path Redundancy: Can variables be eliminated that would make compelling hypothetical constructs?

4. Blocking: Can variables be eliminated that are part of a feedback loop?

Sufficiency Tests

1. Perspective Ties: Are there a sufficient number of variables in the working model to permit coherent representation of the underlying perspective(s)?

2. Reality Ties: Are there a sufficient number of important variables in the working model to be able to predict what will be happening in the system under consideration?

3. Assessment Feasibility: Can values of the trace variables in the working model be quantitatively or qualitatively estimated?

4. Loop Representation: Are all major feedback loops represented in the model either directly or indirectly?

Action Tests

1. Variable Mutability: Do the variables in the working model focus on elements of reality that are mutable?

2. Context Representation: Are there variables in the working model that reflect the context within which action is taking place?

3. Program Ties: Are there variables in the working model that capture the time, effort, and resources devoted to different aspects of an intervention?

people in the situation. Consequently, oversimplifying models by eliminating important contextual variables may preclude effective intervention: As in the example we discuss shortly, it is context that is being
altered, not individual behavior. Similarly, if the variables in a model do
not lend themselves to change, the model may predict well but be of little
use in guiding policy. And if the model does not also capture the time,
effort, and resources devoted to different aspects of an intervention, it
will be difficult to establish links between what is being done and what
is happening in terms of process and outcomes.

Getting to the heart of this process is difficult without working
through an example. As a basis for discussion, I have taken an article
on wife battering by Anderson and Rouse (1988) and developed a series
of models based loosely on their discussion. Wife battering is a useful
problem area to model because the literature is very rich and there are
a number of approaches to intervention independent of the theoretical
perspectives out of which one is working. Wife battering is also a useful
example because it shows dramatically that no model can ever be fully
specified: *No* model ever captures all of the theoretical, interpretive, and
descriptive richness—let alone the pain—present in discussions of wife
battering. What we hope for in modeling, whether we are coming from
a qualitative or quantitative orientation, is to develop insight into the
driving forces that shape the context within which battering occurs and
that have explicit predictions regarding what, why, and how various
interventions might work.

The Anderson and Rouse (1988) piece is useful to consider in this
manner for three reasons. First, it is insistent on the role of theory in
making sense of interventions. Modeling is a useful supplement to this
process of applying theory to practical situations because it forces us
to be explicit about the assumptions we are making as to what concepts
are important, what they mean, and how they are related. Second, the
discussion is sufficiently complex that it exposes many of the dilemmas
confronted by researchers as they try to become more explicit about
what is important to consider, and what might be downplayed. In this
case, for example, feedback and context are important both in terms of
making sense of the interventions Anderson and Rouse considered but
also in terms of bringing to life the politics of intervention in a post-industrial society undergoing many changes in male/female relationships.

The authors draw from two sociological perspectives, symbolic interaction and critical theory. Different theoretical perspectives sensitize us
to different aspects of wife battering, and these sensitivities guide our
choices about how to explain what is happening and what to do about
it. Had they drawn from other theoretical perspectives, their discussion—and my initial specification of it—would be different. So, for
example, there is little in their approach that could be labeled as

psychological (aside from self-esteem, which crosses several disciplinary boundaries) or that focuses on the early-childhood experiences of battered spouses or their husbands. And there is little in their approach that concentrates medically on the physical and emotional trauma suffered by the wife across time.

More interpretively, had the primary focus been the husband instead of the wife, the model would have been specified differently. Because I am only loosely basing the models on their discussion—trying to capture the spirit rather than the letter of their argument—there could also be several alternative specifications drawn from their discussion. It should be noted, however, that even if I were doing a close and detailed reading of their presentation and the perspectives on which they base their discussion, there would be a large number of alternate interpretations (Berry, 1994).

Getting to the point of putting a tentative model down on paper is a multistep process that corresponds to the specification decisions we have discussed concerning the nature of concepts, which concepts are important, and what the relationships are among them. Although not a linear process, it is convenient to think in terms of three steps that correspond to the specification problems we have been discussing in several chapters: What concepts do we claim are important, what do we claim the concepts mean, and what relationships do we claim exist among them.

The first step is simply listing the concepts from the different theoretical perspectives that the authors claim are important (Hammersley, 1991).[1] As we have discussed before, listing concepts is more complicated than it might seem because it represents the authors' interpretations of what is important and relevant in symbolic interaction and critical theory *and by implication*, what is not important. Concepts that are tentatively not considered important do not show up on the list.

To get back to the example, Anderson and Rouse (1988) suggest several concepts drawn from symbolic interaction and critical theory as being relevant to wife battering. From symbolic interaction, they emphasize the importance of situational definitions and the influence of others on the sense of self. From critical theory, they emphasize the influence of power differentials between actors. An initial list of these concepts is:

---

[1]Had this been an exercise in evaluating whether symbolic interaction or critical theory gives a better descriptive, interpretive, and predictive understanding of wife battering, it would have been useful to develop partial models based on discrete from one another across perspectives. Anderson and Rouse's (1988) interests, however, are in trying to bring these two perspectives together in an eclectic fashion to increase both their understanding and the success of the interventions they design.

frequency and severity of wife battering
repressive domination
social resource asymmetry
social isolation of wife
social support
economic isolation of wife
self-esteem of wife
coping strategies
assertiveness of wife's communication
clarity of wife's definition of the situation
dependence of wife on husband for self-validation
dependence of wife on husband for situational definition
number, complexity and competency of wife's roles

A companion step corresponds to the second form of specification that we have talked about: evaluating and re-evaluating the indicators of, and ways of thinking about, concepts that the authors claim are important for each concept. For example, frequency and severity of wife battering is a label I inferred from references to wife beating, constant criticism, abuse, physical assault, and verbal abuse. For the authors, the pairing of physical assault and verbal abuse is especially prominent in their discussion of symbolic interaction. Self-esteem is a label I attached to references regarding sense of self, good definitions of themselves, self-concept, loss of self-worth, and emotional numbness.

Definition of the situation is an especially complex and potentially confusing concept for the symbolic interaction perspective. For Anderson and Rouse (1988), confusion about the meaning of violence in the relationship, internal contradictions in the situation, and confusion over where the causes of battering lie and what is contributing to the battering situation are the ways they ground definition of the situation. Just as with questions regarding what concepts are important, dialogue regarding what each concept means and how it differs from the others would lead to changes in how these concepts are grounded.

There is nothing pure about the distinction between elaborated and working models; the latter is just simpler and takes more for granted. Even elaborated models are simplified and have been shaped by what the researcher tentatively has decided to include and exclude. In order to keep the number of concepts manageable in the present case, for example, I have combined some of the concepts Anderson and Rouse (1988) refer to both within and across perspectives. I collapsed social and economic isolation on grounds that isolation as a dominance strategy seems such an important part of their argument that it outweighed differences in the source of the isolation. I also included social support in this concept. Collapsing social resource asymmetry and repressive domination into isolation further simplified the analysis without losing the importance of power differentials in the situation. I applied the same argument to dependence: In their discussion, dependence on the husband stands out as the most important element for both self-validation and definition of the situation. Because dependency on the husband for validation is shared for these two concepts, collapsing them seemed appropriate.

I altered definition of the situation not by collapsing it with another concept, but by specifying the dimension along which it varied. The clarity of the definition of the situation from the interests of the wife (as defined in part by the counselor) seems especially important to Anderson and Rouse's discussion, so I chose that as the defining dimension.

Additionally, coping strategies seems very important to include in the model, so as to give a sense of the give-and-take between husband and wife and to reflect how feedback effects might play a role in the situation. Coping strategies by itself, however, contains no references to the dimensions along which they may vary. Merging coping strategies with assertiveness of wife's communication, however, results in a more general concept of assertiveness that would cover both verbal and nonverbal forms of coping with the situation on the wife's part.

With short-hand labels in parentheses, the remaining set of concepts is:

frequency and severity of wife battering (battering)
social and economic isolation of wife (wife's isolation)
self-esteem of wife (wife's self-esteem)
clarity of wife's definition of the situation (situational clarity)
dependence of wife on husband for self-validation and situational
    definition (validation dependence)
number, complexity, and competency of wife's roles (wife's role multi-
    plexity)
wife's ╌╌ertiveness

Any list is tentative. Any list should be challenged descriptively, interpretively, theoretically, and predictively. For this example, it is a place to start.

The third step in the process is the specification of relationships among concepts and the graphing of these specification decisions. In some areas, Anderson and Rouse are very clear about how they believe these concepts are related to one another. In the following brief passage, for example, they are explicit not only about the polarity and direction of the influence of battering on self-esteem, they also directly confront the usually implicit assumption of whether the relationship is contingent on the initial level of self-esteem that the wife brings to the relationship:

What does abuse do to a woman's sense of self? Even for women who enter what will be come a battering relationship with good definitions of themselves, the experience of repeated abuse can negatively alter self-concept. For other women involved in battering relationships, an already low sense of self worth is reinforced by the batterer's behavior. (Anderson & Rouse, 1988, p. 138)

Although it is somewhat unclear what mechanisms are linking the extent to which battering erodes self-esteem, the authors give an example drawn from their own intervention/research experience regarding the link:

I felt like I had done everything I could. But he got me feeling so inadequate I was wondering, 'God, am I so inadequate that I don't even know I'm doing it right?'" (p. 139)

In trying to get a fix on what this quote meant in terms of the concepts Anderson and Rouse considered important, I came to see it as expressing the multipath nature of the influence of battering on self-esteem. A part of the mechanics of battering that Anderson and Rouse talked about seems traceable to being physically brutalized and not being able to stop it. In Fig. 8.1, this is represented as the direct effect of battering on self-esteem. Additionally, however, there are some indirect effects of battering that reinforce the direct effect. Battering increases the social and physical isolation of the wife. Whereas isolation by itself may not have direct implications for self-esteem, three other concepts are implicated by Anderson and Rouse's discussion: dependency, situational clarity, and multiplexity. As the wife becomes more cut off from social and economic support, she not only becomes more dependent on the husband for validation of her self (dependency), she also becomes more uncertain of what the situation means (situational clarity) and becomes removed from alternative roles that might give her a different basis for believing in herself.[2] These indirect effects are summarized in Fig. 8.1.

The authors also referred specifically to the impact of the wife's coping on the escalation of battering by the husband. So, for example, they argue that males may be subject to some violence by wives, but that the wife's violence is usually "self-defensive and men are more likely to escalate the level of violence, and women are more likely to be hurt" (Anderson & Rouse, 1988, pp. 134–135). In another passage, they go on to argue:

---

[2]Note that in the model, I have explicitly left the relationship between isolation and situational clarity as an indirect effect. By doing so, I am assuming that as the wife becomes more isolated, her dependence on her husband for validation and situational clarity becomes greater, and as a result of that, her own definition of the situation becomes less realistic and clear.

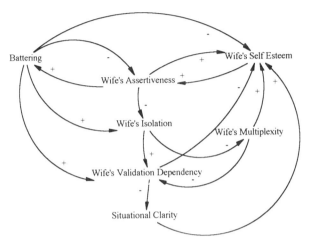

FIG. 8.1. Elaborated model of Anderson and Rouse (1988).

. . . change in the [wife's] behavior may be experienced as highly threatening by the [husband]. Despite popular beliefs regarding provocation, the victim does not "cause" the batterer's behavior . . . but his inability to deal with changes in the relationship may lead, even if only temporarily, to more, rather than less violent behavior. (p. 142)

This passage and the quote are especially revealing with respect to both the influence of feedback and the dilemmas created by talking about endogenous change.

These references reflect the presumed existence of feedback relationships that have implications for how much battering the husband engages in and how assertive the wife is. The short-term loop involving only battering and assertiveness (Fig. 8.1) has dampening implications for the relationship between how much the husband batters and how assertive the wife is. But this loop is a potential powder keg because it *seems* to lay the blame for causing battering on the wife. She tries to assert herself in one way or another, and the husband (interpreting her assertiveness as a hostile and threatening act) physically and verbally assaults her to bring her to her senses. The danger of blaming the victim for what is happening is palpable.

The longer-term feedback loops activated as the implications of change in levels of battering or assertiveness ripple through the rest of the important concepts have the same implication. As one scenario, imagine that the wife was simply to become more assertive *and nothing about the context changed*. The implications may be traced along the paths linking the concepts in Fig. 8.1 to one another. It would be expected that more would ensue than physical and verbal assaults. Attempts would be made by the husband to further isolate the wife from any economic and social resources and to make his wife more dependent on him for any sense of identity, value, and competency.

Leave battering out of this model for a moment. Note that no matter where you make changes in the remaining system, the changes lead to escalation because all of the feedback loops among these concepts are positive. The negative polarities observed among these five variables are attributable to the fact that two of the concepts are defined negatively: wife's validation dependency and wife's isolation. Because they all feed back on assertiveness, and because assertiveness generates more battering, changing any might have the contrary effect of making the wife even more of a victim than she already is! This threat is more clear with the model than it would be without a close reading of Anderson and Rouse (1988).

The elaborated model represented in Fig. 8.1, then, should be seen as reflecting the dynamics that allow this situation to continue. Further, by highlighting the powerful feedback loops present in the situation, it points to two dilemmas in such analyses. First is the dilemma of partial interventions: Helping the wife to temporarily be more assertive may have the unintended consequence of making her situation worse. Second is the dilemma of focusing on endogenous sources of change represented by the feedback loops. They cannot be avoided because they assist greatly in making sense of the situation, but pointing them out runs the risk of having the victimized wife blamed for what is happening to her.

Are such situations hopeless? No, but as Anderson and Rouse pointed out, they may take time to change. To appreciate why and how effective change is possible, let us consider again the nature of battering as a part of a larger dominance strategy enacted by the husband. Aside from the physical and emotional trauma caused in the short term, the power of battering lies in its ability to shape the *context* within which the husband and wife interact. By isolating the wife and making her dependent on the husband for self-validation and her definition of the situation, the husband is able to unilaterally control the context of their interaction. His dominance defines the situation and its social and economic boundaries, and it is he who dictates the cruel benchmark by which his wife must judge herself. Hence, it becomes virtually impossible for the wife to alter the situation on her own. Anderson and Rouse suggested that the answer to effective change in this situation is in altering the context, although they did not use the same term.

How does the context need to be changed? Two general things must be accomplished *in combination*: The positive feedback loops among the concepts other than battering must be stimulated to allow them to mutually reinforce one another in a positive direction, leading to greater self-esteem and assertiveness rather than to fluctuating but low levels of both; and the battering must be constrained either by getting the wife out of the situation or, for cases in which the husband's behavior seems amenable to change, making nonbattering a condition for treatment (Anderson & Rouse, 1988). Context, as a combination of mutually defining elements, then, has more than the analytic component we discussed in chapter 6. It has compelling applied implications as well.

What I have termed an elaborated model could be tested, respecified, refined, and further elaborated amongst researchers and practitioners. Models such as this should be considered a starting point for these discussions and tests. Different models would surely evolve out of them. To be of use to individuals trying to intervene in situations so as to reduce the incidence and prevalence of wife battering, however, models must be conceptually simpler. They must reflect what practitioners and participants are individually and collectively doing, and give them ways of thinking about outcomes that are both theoretically and practically coherent. Last, models must sensitize them to the contexts in which the abusive relationship is embedded.

This is a tall order, but one that can be met at least in part by following the suggested guidelines for model simplification. Suppose, for example, that the model in Fig. 8.1 was further simplified by leaving out the extent to which the wife is involved in multiple roles (multiplexity), the extent to which the wife is dependent on the husband for validation of herself and her definition of the situation (wife's validation dependency), and the extent to which she has a realistic, clear picture of what is happening to her (situational clarity). These concepts all mediate between how isolated the wife is (wife's isolation) and the level of her self-esteem (wife's self-esteem). They help us understand how and why isolation has an effect on self-esteem, but understanding that, perhaps they can be left out of the model.

What does the resulting simplified model tell us (Fig. 8.2)? It suggests first that there are three important feedback loops whose implications

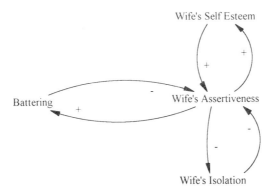

FIG. 8.2. Simplified model drawn from Anderson and Rouse (1988).

must be understood. Two of these are positive feedback loops involving how assertive the wife is (assertiveness), how economically and socially isolated the wife is (wife's isolation), and how positively the wife is able to think about herself (wife's self-esteem). The third is a negative feedback loop that operates between how assertive the wife is in her attitude and behavior (assertiveness) and how frequently and severely the husband resorts to battering as a strategy of control (battering). Secondly, it strongly suggests that to effectively intervene in such situations, the positive feedback loops must be stimulated and the nature of the negative feedback loop must be changed *in combination*. Doing one without doing the other will not work.

These are contextual changes. Prevention researchers use the analogy of a scaffold for such comprehensive interventions. The scaffold is put in place to accomplish a specific combination of effects, then removed as the system becomes self-sustaining. Consider the potentially useful working model used by a programs staff. The staff has developed a comprehensive intervention to reduce the frequency of physical and verbal wife abuse among at-risk couples (Fig. 8.3). The model focuses on battering, wife's self-esteem, wife's isolation and wife's assertiveness—a subset of the concepts in the elaborated model—plus therapeutic context.

From a substantive point of view, the therapeutic context would have several interdependent components. One component would focus on increasing the wife's self-esteem. A second component would focus on assertiveness training for the wife. A third component would concentrate on reducing the wife's economic and social isolation—and by so doing, increase the roles in which the wife felt comfortable and competent, giving her an independent sense of who she is and providing her with a clearer and more realistic definition of the situation in which she had

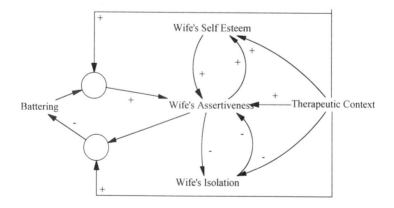

FIG. 8.3. Working model drawn from Anderson and Rouse (1988).

been trapped—including the fact that she is not to blame for continued battering.

These components all focus on stimulating the positive feedback loops in the second model. They must be combined with components that alter the structure of the feedback loop between how seriously the husband batters (battering) and how assertive the wife is (wife's assertiveness). Although the former interventions are designed to alter the levels of self-esteem, assertiveness, and isolation, this latter set of components must accomplish a different task. It must alter the *relationships* that exist between battering and assertiveness. Recall from chapter 6 that contextual effects may operate both additively and interactively. This example illustrates both forms of contextual effects.

Without the therapeutic context, the husband's battering controlled the wife's behavior and established the context for interactions with each other. The ability of battering to undermine the wife's assertiveness must be undermined, either by getting the wife out of the relationship or by establishing that the continuation of the therapeutic relationship was contingent on no battering. Secondly, if there is to be a relationship between the husband and the wife, the wife's assertiveness must control the context of their relationship, not be a victim of it.

In sum, then, the working model preserves the power and drama of the elaborated model while permitting a representation of how the therapeutic-context intervention must work. It represents a way of bringing to bear, in an explicit form, the situational dynamics and programmatic imperatives that are important for understanding battering and what to do about it.

These are all substantive implications of this particular modeling exercise. Let us now turn to a consideration of this exercise in terms of the kinds of criteria for altering the specification of models that we have been using in this example: the simplification, sufficiency and action tests represented in Table 8.1.

Conceptual Redundancy

Conceptual redundancy claims permit the simplification of models where it appears justifiable to collapse together concepts whose theoretical meanings are close to one another or else leave one of the concepts out. The confidence with which we can convince ourselves and others that this conceptual respecification approximates the essence of what you are after is the touchstone by which you should judge the goodness of the decision to simplify the model in this way.

Sometimes one concept may be a lower-level or less complex representation of another. The Anderson and Rouse (1988) illustration contained several examples of this kind of simplification. For example, I collapsed social isolation and social support together on grounds that they both dealt with access to social resources.

Such respecification decisions about concepts are relatively straightforward and a bit uninteresting. More challenging and potentially useful are those situations in which the concepts are not quite the same, but by synthesizing them, it is easier to make sense of the situation conceptually. In Anderson and Rouse (1988), for example, how the wife copes (coping strategies) and how assertively she communicates her positions (assertiveness of wife's communication) are similar in that they deal with reactions of the wife to the situation in which she finds herself. Both concepts have weaknesses, however. With coping strategies, it is unclear what is the underlying dimension that is varying. With assertiveness of wife's communication, the problem is that it deals only with the wife's communication, not her more general behavior. By combining them into a more general concept labeled assertiveness, however, the two together are more revealing than they are separately. More generally, the tension that exists among concepts that are close to one another in one sense or another may be a useful lever for moving the analysis along and simplifying the model at the same time.

Empirical Redundancy

Empirical redundancy may be thought of in a couple of different but related ways. In the first, it may be that concepts share a large number of indicators. In the Anderson and Rouse illustration, for example, I applied the label battering to a collection of observations including wife beating, constant criticism, and abuse. Others could just as easily call similar sets of observations abuse. A question for discussion, then, would be whether or not these two concepts have the same descriptive meaning by virtue of having the same indicators. If the descriptive meaning appears to be the same, collapsing the two concepts or choosing just one as a proxy for both of them simplifies the model.

In other cases, the actual indicators may be different, but a credible case may be made that the indicators are interchangeable. This is a descriptive problem as well. Quantitatively, split-half reliability tests rely on the fact that different versions of the same scale may correlate highly. To the degree that they do, alternative versions of the test may be used. The logic can work in the other direction as well: If observations, questionnaire items, or other forms of data appear to be interchangeable, attaching a common label may be appropriate.

Certain more advanced statistical programs like LISREL or EQS on the quantitative side and HyperResearch or NU*DIST on the qualitative side facilitate making simplification decisions empirically. But such a level of sophistication is not necessary for empirical criteria in order to make simplification a reasonable strategy. The existing literature relating elements of the elaborated model may provide clues for ways of simplifying models by using such empirical criteria. Were there actual studies that documented qualitatively or quantitatively that socially isolated wives were also very likely to be economically isolated, then collapsing the two together may be more confidently done.

Path Redundancy

The search for redundant paths is a form of explanatory simplification. The touchstone here is whether or not by leaving mediating variables out of the working model the causal mechanisms become less clear. As a general rule, if the paths by which one concept affects another are mutually reinforcing *and* are well-understood, leaving them out of the elaborated model in order to achieve some simplicity may be appropriate.

In the Anderson and Rouse (1988) case, comparing Figs. 8.1 and 8.2 shows that three variables were left out of the more simplified model: how dependent the wife is on the husband for self and situational validation (wife's validation dependency), how clear and realistic the wife's understanding of the situation is (situational clarity), and in how many different roles with which the wife is involved (multiplexity). These concepts primarily explained how and why the wife's isolation had an impact on her self-esteem. Notice that in the elaborated model, there is no direct link between wife's isolation and wife's self-esteem. This indicates that the impact of wife's isolation is being mediated by other concepts. These paths do mutually reinforce one another, and they appear to be well-understood by the authors as being central to their explanation. Hence, leaving them out to achieve some simplicity seems warranted.

Blocking

Blocking is a procedure Blalock (1971) suggested for taking variables that are reciprocally related to one another and using one as a proxy to represent the influence of both. This can be a useful simplification if the variables are related in similar fashion to the model's other variables. If they are not, the risk of oversimplification is greater. This assumes, as well, that you are not interested in the precise relationship between the two variables because one is being left out to make the working model simpler.

There do not appear to be any occasions in which blocking would be justifiable in the Anderson and Rouse illustration. The feedback loops are too important both conceptually and practically to permit the use of this sort of technique. Where loops are somewhat peripheral both descriptively and theoretically, it may be more useful.

Perspective Ties

Being applied and problem-driven creates pressure to be almost atheoretical about what works. Not having sufficient ties to the underlying perspectives that should be informing one's work, however, reduces the chances of understanding the richness of what is being observed. In the present case, the more simplified working model has ties to the fully specified model through the variables that have been given the status of hypothetical constructs. This is not an empty exercise, as Anderson and Rouse (1988) pointed out. The kinds of changes that can be expected are how to achieve these through various intervention techniques, how to understand how comprehensive interventions have the potential for mutually reinforcing one another in a consistent, integrated approach. All of these are much more feasible when the perspectives out of which one is working are explicitly brought to bear through a modeling exercise.

The working model also has ties with critical theory through the inclusion of battering and wife's isolation, both of which reflect the influence of dominance. Symbolic interaction theory is represented in the working model through wife's self-esteem and the hypothetical constructs that mediate the impact of the wife's isolation on how assertive she is.

Reality Ties

Perspectives shape how we look at situations and what we define as being important concepts. What is actually going on in the situation is a partial construction of the participants. If there are patterns of action taking place, however, that appear to be important to the participants and to an understanding of the risk of wife battering, it behooves those who intervene to try to incorporate these patterns in their models—whether these patterns do or do not fit the theoretical perspective out of which one is working. We can look at the four nonprogram variables in the working model and see whether they have any face valid interpretive importance. A better check is to examine work done from other perspectives or combinations of perspectives to see whether there are any analogs for the kinds of things being represented in the model. In the present case, many interventions look at coping (or some analog), self-esteem (or some control or efficacy-oriented analog), and support of one kind or another. This is not an armchair exercise; it is, rather, a call for immersing oneself in the situation to evaluate what is happening.

Assessment Feasibility

All of the concepts in the working model can be assessed by using a variety of qualitative and quantitative techniques. The feasibility of measuring variables should *never* be allowed to drive the choice of variables and concepts. Assessment is useful in providing feedback to the program staff and participants, however, as to how much progress they are making with respect to assisting the wife in asserting herself in her communication, assisting her in the development of both economic and social resources, working with her to increase the assertiveness of her coping tactics being battered, and preventing the reoccurrence of battering both in the short and longer term.

Loop Representation

Both the elaborated model and the working model contain numerous feedback loops. Loops need not be completely represented, but at least one of the assessable variables in a loop should be represented in a model so that the loop's impact shows up in the model's changing levels of variables. But as I talked about in considering blocking, leaving loops out of a model is a high-risk enterprise, both descriptively and theoretically. Loops may be the most insight-generating part of models. They may also be the best clue as to how things are going to change over time.

Program Ties

Each of these variables represents a potential intervention site in a comprehensive program. Tying variables in a working model to what is actually being done grounds the model in tangible efforts and resource-allocation decisions, and facilitates the communication and mutual understanding of individuals engaged in different aspects of the intervention. Articulate and credible sanctions may be brought to bear to directly suppress the frequency of battering. Counselors made up of professionals with special training, and/or women who have gone through the program, may intervene directly to reestablish and sustain the wife's sense of self. These efforts may be supplemented by initiatives to increase the wife's social support and economic ties. And there may be direct role playing or other training with the wife to increase the assertiveness of her coping tactics.

In our hypothetical example, these four program elements adequately represent the major operational aspects of the intervention program. If they did not, the model would have to be altered to incorporate additional elements. In this example, the potentially discrete elements relating to social and economic ties have been combined. Were this not possible, other variables would have to be added to the model.

Context Representation

Developing an appreciation of context has been one of the major themes of this book. Rather than being a complication that must be neutralized before the real work of modeling can proceed, I have joined those taking the position that context must be incorporated into analyses. This is more than a theoretical point about gaining leverage for making interpretive and explanatory sense, although such leverage is appreciable. There are also strong practical implications such as those we encountered in the Anderson and Rouse illustration. To not understand that a combination of factors had to be put in place at the same time in order for some success to be achieved in reducing battering and augmenting the wife's sense of self runs the risk of making the situation worse for the wife rather than better. To not understand that the context within which the interaction between husband and wife takes place needed to change runs the risk of allowing the wife to be blamed for causing the battering in the first place.

Variable Mutability

Many of the current models that predict program effectiveness have a large number of demographic factors in them. Race and sex, are to all extents and purposes, immutable. Income and education levels are more mutable, but they take a fair amount of time—and resources—to alter. Certain personality traits appear to be relatively unchanging. Other variables may have a delayed impact or be difficult to assess in the short term (Zigler & Trickett, 1979). If models do not focus on aspects of situations or individuals that are mutable, then no change (either positive or negative) could be observed. Whatever interventions are being examined are at risk of being considered failures.

In the present illustration, all of the concepts in the working model are amenable to change, although perhaps not all at the same speed or at the same time. Assertiveness training with respect to coping tactics may take place relatively quickly, but follow-up and practice will take some time. It may be possible to alter an individual's self-esteem in the short run, but much of the improvement in self-esteem will be as a result of the feedback loops contained therein. Altering clients' social and economic isolation is a more long-term endeavor. Whether all of these can appreciably change during the course of the intervention requires some assumptions about time and some skill in constructing ways of assessing these variables.

In sum, the balance of complexity and simplicity, abstractness and concreteness, theoretical elegance and practical usefulness alters the nature of the models with which we work. Working in applied and clinical settings pulls us away from more elaborate and abstract models both because of the need to conceptually share what we are doing and the need to act with others. There are no simple guidelines for this enterprise, but the set of tests developed in this chapter should be of some use to those engaged in such efforts. Simplification tests move our models toward greater simplicity, creating working models. But in moving toward greater simplicity, we must also be careful not to simplify in ways that destroy our ability to stay in touch with what we are trying to understand, or the logic of the inventions and interventions with which we are trying to alter the processes systems operate under. Sufficiency and action tests serve as useful reminders in keeping us in touch with these other constraints.

INCREASING MODELS' CAPACITY
TO CONVEY COMPLEXITY

Models are intended to be vehicles for creating and disciplining dialogues among data, theoretical perspectives, the lived-in worlds of participants, and the practical needs of policy analysts. These are higher-level, complex goals for models. The visual display of the model should convey the complexity of the assumptions contained according to principles similar to those espoused by Tufte (1983) for the visual display of quantitative information. Clarity and efficiency of communication are to be valued, and for the presentation of quantitative information, precision is also valued. As we have seen, however, precision may be a false goal for the presentation of relationships where both quantitative and qualitative data are used. Instead, the density, specificity, coherence, and richness of the information that is brought to bear on the elements of the model are to be valued. Still, there are strong parallels. Tufte (1983) summarized excellence in tabular data by saying:

> Graphical excellence [in tabular form] is that which gives the viewer the greatest number of ideas in the shortest time with the least ink in the smallest space. (p. 51)

Transposing these ideas to models, we have:

> Graphical excellence in models is that which gives the viewer the greatest number of ideas in the shortest time with the least ink in the smallest space.

This is a relative statement. All models are simplified, and as researchers try to balance partially competing objectives, they are seeking to capture as parsimoneously and simply as possible the complexity of the situations they are modeling.

At whatever point researchers decide they cannot further simplify their models, they can use a variety of presentational devices to present complex ideas as simply as possible. Such efforts capture the spirit, at least, of Tufte's (1983) expectations for graphical excellence. In this section, I consider techniques for presenting the flow of influence, time, and events; techniques for orienting the reader to the main parts of one's argument; techniques for being explicit about what is and is not being considered; techniques for presenting alternative specifications; and techniques for visually conveying results.

Breaking Up the Flow of Time, Events, and Influence

There are two almost universally accepted presentational conventions for spatially ordering the flow of influence, time and events: Represent influence and time as flowing from left to right, and minimize the number of crossed lines of influence. These two conventions serve to reinforce implicit assumptions about movement and simplicity in our Western culture. In the process, for additive models, they serve to keep alternate paths of influence clear and explicit.

To represent influence flows, more exogenous, distal, antecedent, or earlier-occurring variables and concepts are placed on the left of the page. More endogenous, proximal, consequent, later-occurring variables and concepts are placed nearer the right-hand side of the page. Byrne (1994), for example, used this convention to array a set of nine concepts in a coherent fashion to show burnout among elementary-school teachers (Fig. 8.4). Her model is the end product of a structural equation modeling exercise. As such, it contains information both on the underlying concepts (represented in large ovals) and on the variables (represented in small rectangles) whose commonality defines these underlying concepts, as well as on the error terms associated with each of the concepts. All of this follows the conventions of structural equation modeling. As a summary of the argument, the model could be simplified even more by including only the concepts in the diagram.

The exogenous concepts in Byrne's model are arrayed around the left-hand side of the page and their influence filters through a succession of more proximal (in terms of influence), intervening concepts to the trio of interrelated concepts that plumb the dimensions of burnout. The second presentational convention serves to keep separate and distinct the two main paths of influence that flow, respectively, through emotional exhaustion on the one hand, and self-esteem and external locus of control on the other.

Basic and applied journals in the social sciences have many examples of the use of such conventions. Simons and Whitbeck (1991), for example, used them to reinforce the impact of their argument that running away from home as an adolescent is a precursor to adult homelessness. Miles and Huberman (1994) used these techniques to assist in ordering patterns of relationships across cases in preparation for the construction of cross-case scenarios. Kaniasty and Norris (1993) used them to help

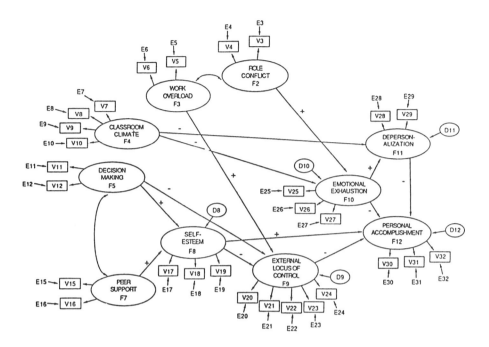

FIG. 8.4. Final model of burnout for calibration sample of elementary school teachers (Byrne, 1994).

clarify a potentially confusing argument about the direct impact of a disaster on subsequent depression and its indirect impact on depression through the erosion of social support. Both Kaniasty and Norris (1993) and Feist, Bodner, Jacobs, Miles, and Tan (1995) supplemented the implicit flow of time by including a notation regarding time (T_1, T_2, etc.) with their associated concepts to reflect the time period during which the observations were made.

The left-right and overlap-minimization tactics increase the capacity of models to convey complex ideas in a straightforward manner. They can, however, become a straitjacket if they are improperly used. If, for example, there are not sound reasons for the ordering of variables and concepts, so that it is more realistic to treat them as being reciprocally related rather than assuming a unidirectional flow of influence, trying to squeeze them into a pre-established form will oversimplify the model. Leaving arrows out of a model simply to clean it up runs a similar risk of oversimplification. When faced with a decision to have a more elegant, oversimplified model or a somewhat messier, more realistic model (Hirsch et al., 1987), the appropriate choice is messiness.

Alternate Specifications

Increasing the credibility of models in a variety of senses rests on the ability to, at least, specify and, at most, eliminate alternative interpretations of what is happening in a situation. This is true for such widely divergent approaches as structural equation modeling (Hoyle, 1995) and qualitative analysis (Maxwell, 1992). Specifying these as partial or plausibly competing models may be very helpful in structuring these credibility-building processes, as we have already seen in chapter 7. I revisit the issue here to emphasize the use of partial models as presentational devices.

Smith et al. (1994) used partial models to lay out three competing models that claimed status as explanations of the impact of top-management-team characteristics on organizational performance. A first model focused solely on the more distal demographic attributes of the management team: factors such as size, tenure, and heterogeneity. A second model focused on the impact of more proximal, process-oriented factors such as social integration and the informality and frequency of communication. A third model treated the demographic factors as exogenous and the process-oriented factors as potential intervening factors. There are, of course, other ways of setting up such an argument. Alternative direct and indirect paths of influence from the demographic factors could be specified ahead of time on the basis of previous research, for example. Smith et al.'s (1994) reading of the literature, suggested that specifying the demographic and process of partial models placed the basic arguments of the existing literature into perspective.

When alternative specifications involve some of the *same concepts*, the use of partial models can be even more useful. Muller and Seligson (1994), for example, used this partial-modeling technique to set up two alternative interpretations of a prior model of the economic and cultural determinants of democracy. Both interpretations involved the same four concepts. The competing models differed in how the concepts were depicted as influencing one another. By visually specifying these as alternative, competing models, the actual analysis becomes more focused on the questions of the relative descriptive and explanatory validity of the competing models.

Similarly, Telles (1995) used the partial or competing-model specification technique to facilitate laying out four alternative interpretations of the impact of industrialization and inequality on segregation in Brazilian metropolitan areas. Dohrenwend and Dohrenwend (1981) used this technique to specify six alternative ways of thinking about the relationship of stress and social support on mental health. Jenkins and Kposowa (1990) separate out competing interpretations of the causes of African *coups d'etat* so as to bring alternative ways of understanding this phenomenon into focus.

There is nothing about the specification of alternate or partial models that limits the technique to quantitative analyses. Miles and Huberman (1994), for example, specified potentially competing models for job mobility from each of 12 cases. These were a preliminary step in collapsing these partial models into four alternate scenarios that were useful in explaining how job mobility takes place in the collection of sites they analyzed. The development of partial or competing models prior to iteratively engaging in comparative (cross-case) qualitative analysis may help put into practice suggestions made by Burawoy (1991a), Miles and Huberman (1994) and Amenta and Poulson (1994). All of these authors suggested tentatively and explicitly summarizing expectations before going into the field. Specifying these as *competing alternatives* in the form of tentative, partial, or competing models provides a greater opportunity for both systematic reflection and discussion.

There is one caveat to bear in mind when using the partial or competing-model-specification technique to set up and/or organize arguments. Most uses of this technique focus on the same set of concepts and the same sets of indicators. Because there are really three specification processes going on simultaneously with researchers trying to understand the nature of concepts, which are important, *and* how they are related to one another, focusing on only one aspect of this respecification process may detract attention from the other two. The meaning of concepts may change across contexts and, here may be alternate ways of understanding the specification of concepts. Different concepts may be important in the same or different contexts, and so on. All of these complex possibilities make the specification of alternate, competing models even more potentially useful than they already have proven to be.

Blocking and Highlighting

In complicated models, giving special emphasis to certain aspects of an overall picture is difficult without the use of some additional props. Specifying partial models is a useful technique. Alternative, complementary techniques are collecting descriptively and conceptually related concepts and variables together in larger blocks and highlighting crucial processes and scenarios *within* the context of the larger, more complex model.

Liem and Liem (1990) used both of these techniques to focus attention on the critically important feedback processes involved in the impact of involuntary unemployment on individual and family functioning (Fig. 8.5). Three variables and concepts related to individual functioning are clustered together. The same is done for six variables and concepts related to family functioning and four variables and concepts related to family characteristics. Overall, 15 variables and concepts are collapsed into five abstract categories. Overlaid on this blocking, Liem and Liem

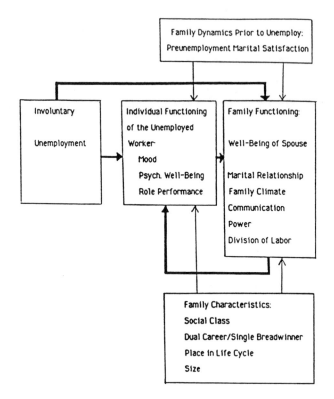

FIG. 8.5. Effects of unemployment (Liem & Liem, 1990, p. 177).
Reprinted with permission.

used heavier lines to relate what they saw as the critical feedback process that makes sense of the impact of involuntary unemployment.

Severe blocking such as that engaged in by Liem and Liem (1990) is very helpful *if* the variables and concepts that are blocked together make compelling descriptive and explanatory sense *and if* the blocking does not oversimplify relationships among variables and concepts outside of the block. In the Liem and Liem analysis, the severe blocking does appear to make such sense. The five variables and concepts collapsed under the family functioning block, for example, appear to fit together as if family functioning were either a higher-order factor defined by these concepts-as-indicators, or whose interrelationships were so tight that collapsing them together does not violate the relationships of these concepts to other concepts outside of the block.

These techniques do not need to be used together. Their use by Liem and Liem (1990) mutually reinforce one another, but there is no reason why highlighting, for example, cannot be used separately. Miles and Huberman (1994) used what amounts to a highlighted arrow to contextualize job-mobility changes within the other changes that are taking place at sites. Without some form of highlighting, the 35-concept model would be so complicated that it would defy use as a communication vehicle. With the highlighted arrows to focus attention on those particular aspects of the overall model, how job mobility changes relate to other things happening at sites stands out in relief, making communication and analysis easier.

SUMMARY

I made a distinction between elaborated and working models in this chapter as convenient representations of models with different levels of complexity. More developed and complex models (elaborated models) capture more of the complexity of theoretical and empirical realities. Working models trade off the capacity to mirror the complexities of situations in favor of greater ease of communication and use. There is no fixed definition of these terms, however, because the process of respecification of models to achieve different ends is continuous.

Three sets of tests are introduced to serve as guides in moving from elaborated to working models. Simplification tests focus on reducing redundancy in elaborated models by respecifying so as to reduce the number of variables and their relationships. Sufficiency tests serve as a brake for the simplification process to keep models from oversimplifying either the empirical or theoretical realities of situations. Action tests serve to focus attention on the practical relevance of the working models for interventions.

The chapter ends with a discussion of increasing the capacity of models to express complex ideas. Strategies for breaking up the flow of influence, time, and events are presented. The use of partial and competing models, highlighting, and blocking are also discussed.

SUGGESTED READINGS

Miles and Huberman's (1994) discussion of cross-case analysis highlights several of the techniques involved in presenting models in a way that maximizes their effectiveness as a means of facilitating and making explicit various dialogues. More generally, their discussion of alternative organizing and presentational devices for qualitative data is without peer. Hoyle (1995a) contains several useful discussions of formal criteria for identifiability, disconfirmability and equivalent models. Tufte's (1983, 1990) work with the display of tabular data is a singular achievement and should not be missed.

EXERCISES

1. In chapter 6, I modeled a pattern of interactions among mothers and their children and mothers and their children's doctors so as to highlight the influence of two feedback loops. Can this model be simplified? How would you respecify a simpler form? What must be preserved? What are the risks of simplifying the model at all?

2. For an area of investigation in which you are interested, how does context figure in? What sorts of contexts might be relevant to understanding descriptively, interpretively, and theoretically what you are interested in?

3. For this area of your interest, take a single phenomenon that you are interested in understanding, and in conjunction both with about five articles on this topic and some of your colleagues, brainstorm a list of concepts and variables that you believe are at least minimally important for understanding this phenomenon.

3a. Which concepts and variables may be collapsed conceptually? Why?

3b. Are there any variables and concepts that are so highly related that one of them may be taken as a proxy for the others?

3c. Are there any variables and concepts that could become hypothetical constructs? On what does this decision depend?

3d. Are there any nonessential feedback loops that can be collapsed?

3e. Are there clear ties between the variables and concepts in the model and the underlying perspectives to which they are tied?

3f. Are there a sufficient number of important variables and concepts in the model to predict what will be happening in the situation being examined?

3g. Are the variables and concepts in the model descriptively valid?

3h. Are all major feedback loops represented in the model?

3i. Are the variables in the model capable of being changed?

3j. Is context adequately represented?

3k. Are there concepts in the model that reflect the time, effort, and resources devoted to different aspects of the intervention?

4. Figures 8.E1 and 8.E2 return one last time to Cook's (1993) discussion of the meaning of hospital stays. If one is interested in comparing the speediness of recovery of patients across hospitals, can the model in Fig. 8.E2 be simplified? Why or why not? Justify your answer in terms of being able to separate alternative meanings of the concepts under investigation.

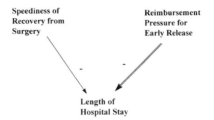

FIG. 8.E1. Panel one.

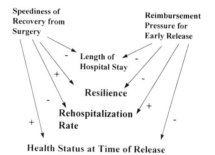

FIG. 8.E2. Panel two.

9

Epilogue

Plausibility is the opiate of the intellectual. (Miles & Huberman, 1994, p. 264)

Residents of changing environments need a tent [—not a palace]. (Hedberg et al., 1976, p. 45)

Wow! Can that ditch digger dig! (Overheard at a construction site)

An epilogue traditionally reviews and summarizes the major themes of a monograph. This chapter does that . . . with a few twists and mixed metaphors. The multiple, iterative, cyclic dialogues involved in conceptual modeling have been the focus of this book. The continuing, processual nature of the enterprise is of greater importance than any single model, and there are limits to what we can do with models. This chapter discusses the major themes of as they relate to these two key features.

If we successfully organize what we know about a situation, we may be able to give viewers—à la Tufte (1983)—a vehicle for quickly and vividly grasping a large number of ideas without using much space or ink. In doing so, however, we may be tempted to get comfortable in its warm plausibility, but as Miles and Huberman (1994, p. 264) reminded us in their nicely turned phrase, getting comfortable can have the unintended consequence of having us miss the point. Rigidity and selective perception follow comfortable plausibility. Remembering logo sets, the point is that if we are going to build models, we should be trying to emulate the flexibility and tentativeness of tents rather than elegant but fixed-in-concrete palaces.

Getting too comfortable with what we have accomplished with a particular model is a risk to be avoided. I have tried to build a sensitivity to this risk into the definition of models: organizing devices for a continuing, explicit dialogue between multiple sources of data and assumptions. I have tried to reinforce this sensitivity by embedding the definition of models in a framework of critical-realist assumptions that permit the use of both qualitative and quantitative data to ground the model's claims.

The tentative claims about the nature and dynamics of situations made by models are formally titled specification decisions. We have considered three interdependent, ongoing *specification decisions*. One set of decisions focuses on the nature of the concepts we are considering: What are they and, by implication, what aren't they? A second set of decisions involves deciding which concepts are important and which are unimportant. A third set of decisions focuses on relationships among concepts: What is the nature of each relationship and which relationships are important?

Guiding these interdependent specification decisions are four forms of understanding, or ways of making sense. We make descriptive sense of concepts by bringing together empirical indicators so that through the cycles of data gathering and analysis, those occurring together may be given conceptual names and differentiated empirically from other concepts that are grounded in different clusters of indicators. To the extent possible, these concepts should be grounded in the experience of individuals, groups, and institutions living in the situations that we are studying. This process helps make interpretive sense of what we are examining. A third process of explanatory sense-making creates a continuing dialogue between what we are observing in a situation and what it means from a variety of theoretical perspectives. And a final process of predictive sense making asks us to consider what changes must be made in these concepts if they are to applicable in other temporal and situational contexts, and how the same concept may have different meanings in different contexts.

Relationships undergo a similar continuing scrutiny and assessment. The direction in which influence flows between concepts and how strong that influence is must be examined and claims substantiated. We must also bring data of various sorts together to validate claims regarding the polarity, linearity, asymmetry, and timing of relationships. Just as with concepts, we should also be pursuing what these relationships mean to the people and groups living in a situation (interpretive sense-making), what they mean in terms of various theories (explanatory sense-making), and how context-dependent their various meanings are (predictive sense-making).

All of these ways of making sense of concepts and relationships have in common the consideration and potential elimination of alternatives in an effort to increase the credibility of claims. There are often good substantive reasons, however, for being able to only approximately make sense of concepts and relationships. Theoretically, for example, there may be a potentially large number of alternate theories into which we could embed a particular model. Interpretively, there may be varied groups or individuals who have different power or experiences that impose different interpretations of what is going on in a situation.

Descriptively, there may be alternative ways of combining indicators and concepts that are equally plausible and credible.

The specifications from one cycle become the grist for these multiplex dialogues during the next cycle. As a result, models tend to become more complex as these respecification cycles take place. Complexity and diversity (or messiness [Hirsch et al., 1987]) are not to be avoided. We turn them into sources of leverage. We have considered three sources of leverage: elaborating by simply adding concepts with different properties to additive models, elaborating by considering the special insight available from considering feedback, and elaborating by considering combinations of concepts as context.

Adding concepts to additive models gives us a sense of what it means to have a fluid, changeable context. In the process, we can begin to dig under the surface of our observations by facing the challenges of spuriousness and mediation. Tracking down spuriousness, considering direct and indirect effects, pursuing unanticipated consequences, and teasing out mutually reinforcing and antagonistic mediating effects are sources of leverage comparable to shovels that social scientists have been using for some time to dig under the surface of our observations.

We move from shovels to ditch diggers with the other two forms of leverage. An appreciation of the role of feedback in social life dramatically alters both how we look at situations and the rigorousness of the questions that we may ask about patterns that may emerge over time. Feedback allows us to ask questions about how situations evolve and how social phenomena feed back on themselves over time. Appreciating context is similarly liberating. It permits a much more rigorous approach to understanding how and why combinations of elements of social situations come together to create scenarios associated with what we observe happening in different situations and times.

Evaluating models that are using these sources of leverage are complicated by the fact that there are multiple, overlapping ways of making sense of situations. We may question how well models do at describing current and past patterns. We may ask how well models do at implicating the experiences of those living through situations. We may ask how well models do at stimulating a dialogue between theoretical perspectives and observations. And we may ask how well models do at predicting what is going to happen in other situations and times.

Respecification of concepts and relationships is not simply a matter of always trying to capture more complexity. We may maintain the same relative level of complication and revise our models to highlight those aspects of the situation that appear most important for us to understand descriptively, interpretively, theoretically, or predictively. We may also simplify our models to make them more useful in establishing dialogues with various audiences. For example, we may wish to sensitize ourselves and others to the powerful role of feedback or the importance of a combination of program elements in creating an effective therapeutic context. Alternatively, we may wish to focus solely on the implications of a particular theoretical perspective. We may even want to concentrate on scenarios that characterize a relatively narrow segment of historical periods and contexts. Working models, as opposed to their more elaborated brethren, are useful in pursuing these objectives.

The modeling process, then, is a continuing one, and the particular models we develop are like tents. With tents rather than castles, the modeling process—as the building, tearing down, rebuilding, and so on—stands out as being more important than the models themselves (Forrester, 1985). It is the modeling process that over time pairs descriptive, interpretive, explanatory, and predictive understanding—or more generally, insight—that makes it easier to understand where things are going and why. It is also true that there are limits to what we can do with models. Appreciating these limits is a way to put the lessons learned in this introduction to conceptual modeling in perspective. Let us look at some things that might be termed limits.

The language used in conceptual modeling often conveys the impression that the impact of one concept on another is linear and constant across the range of observed variation (Richardson, 1986). Even a phrase as apparently neutral as "There is a positive relationship between the amount of migration into a community and the size of the population of that community" may convey more than we want to imply about the nature of the relationship between these two concepts unless we continue to be explicit about exactly what we claim the nature of that relationship is. The cautionary note should be clear. When we believe a relationship between two concepts is contingent on the initial value of the influencing concept, or we believe that asymmetry is present, or we believe that the relationship is curvilinear or changes in some other fashion, we should make sure that these qualifications are clear both in the text and in our models. These are limits, then, in what we can take for granted as we develop and talk about our models.

There is an upper limit on our models imposed by the fact that we have carved the world up into concepts and relationships. Models are simplified compared to the realities of situations. Even when we reabsorb some of this complexity by constructing scenarios composed of combinations of mutually defining concepts, we are still simplifying.

We can push back the limitations of simplification somewhat by incorporating greater numbers of concepts and relationships into our models. The more we do this, the more dependent we become on computer simulations to help us understand the implications of our models. Limits conceived of in this way then become trade-offs. We trade our capacity to wrap our minds around the implications of relatively simplified models in order to capture more of the complexity associated with the realities we are studying. In practice, whenever it is possible to simulate models, we should do so, just as we should be combining methods of gathering and analyzing data whenever there appears to be an advantage in doing so. Yet there are limits to how complicated we can make our models without ceding control to computers.

There are other ways of addressing limits as well. For example, we might ask whether any of our major conclusions are altered by apparently slight changes in the situation or changes in the values of the variables and concepts we start with. Phrased as such, this is a question of description and prediction—or more particularly, robustness (Little, 1995). The same issue may also apply to interpretation and explanation, however. When elements of the situation change, does the interpretation of events and changes shift in the minds of those living through the situation? When elements of the situation change, does the theoretical meaning of what is being observed change?

Questions of robustness blend into questions of context dependency. What may seem from one point of view to be minor changes in context may from another point of view be substantively meaningful changes that alter the meaning of the context either theoretically or through the eyes of the actors living within it. Context is not something to be trampled—either in the name of robustness or in the name of elegance (Hirsch et al., 1987). It is a source of leverage and insight. But do these questions represent limits?

I believe robustness questions do remind us to be concerned about limits. More to the point, they make us rethink how parsimonious and context-free our models are becoming. There is a limit—albeit an intangible one—to how context-free we can make our models without trampling on context. When apparently small things appear to alter our conclusions, let us treat these as signs that we may not yet have achieved an adequate rendering of the situation and that we might be missing the nature of the context within which what we are studying is taking place.

Let me rework the nature of the limits question to get at a different aspect of the problem. A better question might be not whether we are describing all the details, but whether we can describe the central elements of situations. Similarly, we might not ask whether we can interpret all the details, but if we can capture the meaning of the central issues; not whether we can understand theoretically the smallest events, but if we can explain the major changes that are taking place and if we are gaining insight; not whether we can predict with absolute specificity, but if we can predict where the major sources of change and cleavage will be, and what else we must know about the situation. These are limits questions too, and it should be clear that we can redefine the limits of our analyses by caring less about the small details than the larger picture.

A related question about limits derives from the incompatibility between carving the world up into variables and concepts and examining relationships on the one hand, and gathering stories to get at process on the other (Maines, 1992; Maxwell, 1992). Stories capture power and drama (Daly, 1991) and are one approach to process. Models capture pattern and speak to structure. The tension between the two approaches should be viewed as being healthy. Miles and Huberman (1994), for example, argued that

> . . . both approaches need to be combined for careful description and explanation . . . [to create] a deeper story, in effect, that is both process-oriented and variable-oriented. (p. 91)

The combination also speaks to the interpenetration of forms of understanding. Stories may capture power and drama, but . . .

> if a story describes a [social entity] and environment that no longer exist, the story's predictions will fail, and its power to generate behavior will undermine the [social entity's] effectiveness. (Hedberg et al., 1976)

Combined with models that substantively embrace both context and history, such unintended consequences should be less likely. Each approach has strengths and weaknesses. Moving to a deeper level by using the tension between the two approaches to good advantage should create greater insight.

This emphasis on depth brings us to the center of the problem of limits. In its most general form, Orum, Feagin, and Sjoberg (1991) phrased a similar concern as follows:

> The social order has been constructed by human agents, and although social patterns emerge, these patterns can, within broad limits, be revised. (p. 35)

These are substantive limits. We deal with them by arguing that there are patterns that exist independent of how people define the situation (Miles & Huberman, 1994), by acknowledging the interpenetration of forms of understanding (Maxwell, 1992), and by actively incorporating both subjective and objective data and perspectives in our models (Groves & Lynch, 1990).

Such limits might be better thought of as challenges. We should know going in that models are tools and all tools are imperfect. That human agents can reconstruct situations is part of what makes the challenge exciting. But there is an aspect of this limit-as-challenge we should be particularly sensitive to.

We discussed in earlier chapters the number of alternative ways of modeling and the number of different ways that models may be embedded in alternate perspectives. The darker side of this is that the diversity and complexity may lead us to focus on the wrong things. In part, this is a detail/big-change problem. We spent some time developing and respecifying a model of wife battering in the last chapter. Looking at wife battering the way we did, however, is but one aspect of a much larger social problem. Developing a model to better understand the implications of a particular therapeutic context should not be confused with, nor divert attention from, the larger social issues involved (Anderson & Rouse, 1988).

Another part of looking at the wrong thing is less a detail/big-change problem than it is a superficial cause/basic-cause problem (Lieberson, 1985). Because of limitations of technique, time, training, theoretical development, or values, we may trap ourselves into a cycle of respecification that never gets beneath the surface. The answer, as some might have it, is to keep a sense of humor about our work. Fine. But as we are laughing, let us keep ourselves open to new perspectives, ideas, and techniques that may help us embrace the complexities of social life and make better sense of them. Enjoy the tent building and ditch digging.

References

Abbott, A. (1988). Transcending general linear reality. *Sociological Theory, 6*, 169–186.

Abbott, A. (1992). From causes to events: Notes on narrative positivism. *Sociological Methods and Research, 20*, 428–455.

Aber, J. L. (1994). Poverty, violence, and child development: Untangling family and community level effects. In C. Nelson (Ed.), *Threats to optimal development: Integrating biological, psychological and social risk factors*. The Minnesota Symposium in Child Psychology, (pp. 229–272). Hillsdale, NJ: Lawrence Erlbaum Associates.

Aber, J. L., Gephart, M., Brooks-Gunn, J., Connell, J., & Spencer, M. (in press). Development in context: Implications for studying neighborhood effects. In J. Brooks-Gunn, G. Duncan, & J. L. Aber (Eds.), *Neighborhood poverty: Context and consequences for child and adolescence* (ch. 3). New York: Russel Sage.

Achen, C. H. (1991). *Interpreting and using regression*. Newbury Park, CA: Sage.

Aiken, L. S., & West, S. G. (1991). *Multiple regression: Testing and interpreting interactions*. Newbury Park, CA: Sage.

Althauser, R. P., Heberlein, T. A., & Scott, R. A. (1971). A causal assessment of validity: The augmented multitrait-multimethod matrix. In H. M. Blalack (Ed.), *Causal modeling in the social sciences* (pp. 374–398). Chicago: Aldine.

Altheide, D. L., & Johnson, J. M. (1994). Criteria for assessing interpretive validity in qualitative research. In N. K. Denzin & Y. S. Lincoln (Eds.), *Handbook of qualitative research*. Thousand Oaks, CA: Sage.

Altman, I., & Rogoff, B. (1987). World views in psychology: Trait, interactional, organismic and transactional perspectives. In D. Stokolis & I. Altman (Eds.), *Handbook of environmental psychology* (pp. 1–40). New York: Wiley.

Amenta, E., Carruthers, B. G., & Zylan, Y. (1992). A hero for the aged? The Townsend movement, the political mediation model and U.S. old-age policy. *American Journal of Sociology, 98*, 308–339.

Amenta, E., & Poulson, J. D. (1994). Where to begin: A survey of five approaches to selecting independent variables for qualitative comparative analysis. *Sociological Methods and Research, 23*, 22–53.

Anderson, C., & Rouse, L. (1988). Intervention in cases of woman battering: An application of symbolic interactionism and critical theory. *Clinical Sociology Review, 6*, 134–147.

Arminger, G., & Bohrnstedt, G. W. (1987). In C. Clogg (Ed.), *Sociological methodology*. Washington, DC: American Sociological Association.

Asher, H. B. (1976). *Causal modeling*. Newbury Park, CA: Sage.

Babbie, E. R. (1992). *The practice of social research*. Belmont, CA: Wadsworth.

Baron, R. B., & Kenny, D. A. (1986). The moderator-mediator variable distinction in social psychological research: Conceptual, strategic and statistical considerations. *Journal of Personality and Social Psychology, 51,* 1173–1182.

Becker, H. S. (1990). Generalizing from case studies. In E. W. Eisner, & A. Peshkin (Eds.), *Qualitative inquiry in education: The continuing debate* (pp. 233–242). New York: Teachers College Press.

Bernard, H. R. (1988). *Research methods in cultural anthropology.* Newbury Park, CA: Sage.

Bernard, H. R. (1994). *Research methods in cultural anthropology* (2nd ed.). Newbury Park, CA: Sage.

Berry, W. D. (1993). *Understanding regression assumptions.* Newbury Park, CA: Sage.

Blalock, H. M. (1964). *Causal inferences in non-experimental research.* Chapel Hill: University of North Carolina Press

Blalock, H. M. (1966). *Lectures in casual modeling.* Chapel Hill: University of North Carolina Press.

Blalock, H. M. (1969). *Theory construction: From verbal to mathematical formulations.* Englewood Cliffs, NJ: Prentice-Hall.

Blalock, H. M. (1971). *Causal models in the social sciences.* Chicago: Aldine-Atherton.

Bowers, W., & Pierce, G. (1957). The illusion of deterrence in Isaac Ehrlich's research on capital punishment. *Yale Law Journal, 85,* 187–208.

Brannen, J. (1992a). *Mixing methods: Qualitative and quantitative research.* Aldershot, Great Britain: Avebury.

Brannen, J. (1992b). Combining qualitative and quantitative approaches: An overview. In J. Brannen (Ed.), *Mixing methods: Qualitative and quantitative research* (pp. 3–38). Aldershot, Great Britain: Avebury.

Brewer, J., & Hunter, A. (1989). *Multimethod research: A synthesis of styles.* Newbury Park, CA: Sage.

Britt, D. W. (1991). A clinical perspective on organization development. In H. Rebach & J. Bruhn (Eds.), *Handbook of clinical sociology* (pp. 259–278). New York: Pergamon.

Britt, D. W. (1993). Metaphors of process: Scenarios, trajectories, pathways and routes. *Applied Behavioral Science Review, 2,* 115–124.

Britt, D. W., & Campbell, E. Q. (1977a). A longitudinal analysis of alcohol use, environmental conduciveness and deviance. *Journal of Studies on Alcohol, 38,* 1640–1647.

Britt, D. W., & Campbell, E. Q. (1977b). Assessing the linkage of norms, environments and deviance. *Social Forces, 56,* 532–550.

Britt, D. W., & Wilson, L. (1995). Developing and validating parent-as-teacher and child-as-student role development scales in a home-based preschool program. *Journal of Applied Sociology, 12,* 73–86.

Brown, M. C., & Warner, B. D. (1992). Immigrants, urban politics, and policing in 1900. *American Sociological Review, 57,* 293–305.

Bryk, A. S., & Raudenbush, S. W. (1987). Application of hierarchical linear models to assessing change. *Psychological Bulletin, 101,* 147–158.

Bryk, A. S., & Raudenbush, S. W. (1992). *Hierarchical linear models: Applications and data analysis methods.* Newbury Park, CA: Sage.

Bryman, A. (1988). *Quantity and quality in social research.* London: Unwin Hyman.

Burawoy, M. (1991a). Reconstructing social theories. In M. Burawoy, A. Burton, A. A. Ferguson, K. J. Fox, J. Gamson, N. Gartrell, L. Hurst, C. Hurzman, L. Salzinger, J. Schiffman, & S. Ui (Eds.), *Ethnography unbound: Power and resistance in the modern metropolis* (pp. 8–27). Berkeley: University of California Press.

Burawoy, M. (1991b). The extended case method. In M. Burawoy, A. Burton, A. A. Ferguson, K. J. Fox, J. Gamson, N. Gartrell, L. Hurst, C. Hurzman, L. Salzinger, J. Schiffman, & S. Ui (Eds.), *Ethnography unbound* (pp. 271–287). Berkely: University of California Press.

Byrd, H. R., & Rebennack, M. [Professor Longhair Music/Skull Music BMI]. (1992). Cabbage Head [Dr. John]. On *Goin' Back to New Orleans* [Compact disc]. New Orleans: Warner Brothers, Inc.

Byrne, B. M. (1994). *Structural equation modeling with EQS and EQS / Windows.* Thousand Oaks, CA: Sage.

Campbell, D. T., & Fiske, D. W. (1959). Convergant and discriminant validation by the multitrait-multimethod matrix. *Psychological Bulletin, 56,* 81–105.

Campbell, D. T., & Stanley, J. C. (1963). *Experimental and quasi-experimental designs for research.* Chicago: Rand McNally.

Campbell, D. T. (1974). *Quantitative knowing in action research.* Kurt Lewin Award Address, Society for the Psychological Study of Social Issues. Presented at the Annual Meeting of the American Psychological Association, New Orleans.

Campbell, D. T. (1979). "Degrees of Freedom" and the case study. In T. D. Cook & C. S. Reichardt (Eds.), *Qualitative and Quantitative Methods in Evaluation Research* (pp. 49–67). Beverly Hills, CA: Sage.

Carmines, E. G., & Zeller, R. A. (1979). *Reliability and validity assesment.* Newbury Park, CA: Sage.

Chevigny, P. (1995). *Edge of the knife: Police violence in the Americas.* New York: The New Press.

Cicourel, A. (1968). *The social organization of juvenile justice.* New York: Wiley.

Collins, R. (1982). *Sociological insight: An introduction to non-obvious sociology.* New York: Oxford University Press.

Cook, T. D. (1993). A quasi-sampling theory of generalization of casual relationships. *New Directions for Program Evaluation, 57,* 39–82

Cook, T. D., & Campbell, D. T. (1979). *Quasi-experimentation: Design and analysis issues for field settings.* Chicago: Rand McNally.

Cook, T. D., & Reichardt, C. S. (1979). *Qualitative and quantitative methods in evaluation research.* Beverly Hills, CA: Sage.

Cornford, C. S., Morgan, M., & Ridsdale, L. (1993). Why do mothers consult when their children cough? *Family Practice, 10,* 193–196.

Coverdill, J., Finlay, & Martin (1994). *Sociological Methods and Social Research, 23.*

Daly, K. (June, 1991). *Of numbers and narrative.* Paper presented at the Law and Society Annual Meeting, Amsterdam.

Daly, K. (1994). *Gender, crime and punishment.* New Haven: Yale University Press.

Davis, J. A. (1985). *The logic of causal order.* Beverly Hills, CA: Sage.

Delaney, W., & Ames, G. (1993). Integration and exchange in multidisciplinary alcohol research. *Social Science and Medicine, 37,* 5–13.

Denz-Penhey, H., & Murdoch, J. C. (1993). Service delivery for people with chronic-fatigue syndrome: A pilot action research study. *Family Practice, 10,* 14–18.

Denzin, N. K. (1978). *The Research Act: A theoretical introduction to sociological research methods* (2nd ed.). New York: McGraw-Hill.

Denzin, N. K. (1989). *Interpretive interactionism.* Newbury Park, CA: Sage.

Denzin, N. K., & Lincoln, Y. S. (1994). Entering the field of qualitative research. In N. K. Denzin & Y. S. Lincoln (Eds.), *Handbook of Qualitative Research* (pp. 1–17). Thousand Oaks, CA: Sage.

DeWalt, B. R. (1979). *Modernization in a Mexican ejido.* New York: Cambridge University Press.

Dohrenwend, B., & Dohrenwend, B. S. (1981). Socio-environmental factors, stress and psychopathy. *American Journal of Community Psychology, 9,* 123–159.

Douglas, J. (1967). The social meanings of suicide.

Douglas, J. (1976). *Investigative social research.* Beverly Hills, CA: Sage.

Eckenrode, J., & Gore, S. (Eds.) (1990). *Stress between work and family*. New York: Plenum.

Eder, D. (1981). Ability groupings as a self-fulfilling prophecy: A micro analysis of teacher–student interaction. *Sociology of Education, 54*, 151–162.

Einhorn, H. J., & Hogarth, R. M. (1986). Judging probable cause. *Psychological Bulletin, 99*, 3–19.

Elder, G. H., Nguygen, T. V., & Caspi, A. (1985). Linking family hardship to children's lives. *Child Development, 56*, 361–375.

Farkas, G., Sheenan, D., Grobe, R. P., & Shuan, Y. (1990). Cultural resources and school success: Gender, ethnicity and poverty groups within an urban school district. *American Sociological Review, 55*, 127–142.

Farrell, A. D. (1994). Structural equation modeling with longitudinal data: Strategies for examining group differences and reciprocal relationships. *Journal of Consulting and Clinical Psychology, 62*, 477–487.

Feagin, J. R., Orum, A. M., & Sjoberg, G. (1991). *A case for the case study*. Chapel Hill: University of North Carolina Press.

Feist, G. J., Bodner, T. E., Jacobs, J. F., Miles, M., & Tan, V. (1995). Integrating top-down and bottom-up structural models of subjective well-being: A longitudinal investigation. *Journal of Personality and Social Psychology, 68*, 138–150.

Forrester, J. W. (1990). *Principles of systems*. Portland, OR: Productivity Press.

Forrester, J. W. (1991). *Industrial dynamics*. Portland, OR: Productivity Press.

Francis, D. J. (1988). *An introduction to structural equation models*. 623–637.

Freedman, D. A. (1985). Statistics and the scientific method. In W. Mason & S. E. Feinberg (Eds.), *Cohort analysis in social research: Beyond the identification problem* (pp. 343–366). New York: Springer-Verlag.

Freedman, D. A. (1987). As others see us: A case study in path analysis. *Journal of Educational Statistics, 12*, 101–128.

Freedman, D. A. (1991). Statistical models and shoe leather. In P. V. Marsden (Ed.), *Sociological methodology* (pp. 291–313). Washington, DC: American Sociological Association.

Garfinkel, H., & Bittner, E. (1967). Good organizational reasons for "bad" clinic records. In H. Garfinkel (Ed.), *Studies in ethnomethodology* (pp. 186–207). Englewood Cliffs, NJ: Prentice-Hall.

Geertz, C. (1983). *Local knowledge*. New York: Basic Books.

Gilbert, M. J. (1993). Anthropology in a multidisciplinary field, *Social Science and Medicine, 37*, 1–3.

Glaser, B. (1978). *Theoretical sensitivity*. Mill Valley, CA: Sociology Press.

Glaser, B. G., & Strauss, A. L. (1967). *The discovery of grounded theory*. New York: Aldine de Gruyter.

Griffin, L. J., & Isaac, L. W. (1992). Recursive regression and the historical use of "time" in time-series analysis of historical process. *Historical Methods, 25*, 166–179.

Griffin, L., & Ragin, C. (Eds.) (1994a). Formal methods of qualitative comparative analysis, *Sociological Methods and Social Research, 23*(1), pp.XX .

Griffin, L. J., & Ragin, C. (1994b). Some observations on formal methods of comparative analysis. *Sociological Methods and Research, 23*, 4–21.

Groves, W. B., & Lynch, M. J. (1990). Reconciling structural and subjective approaches to the study of crime. *Journal of Research in Crime and Delinquency, 27*, 348–375.

Guagliumi, A. (1994). Making small collages. *Connecticut Review, 16*, 47–52.

Guba, E. G., & Lincoln, Y. S. (1989). *Fourth generation evaluation*. Newbury Park, CA: Sage.

Hage, J., & Meeker, B. F. (1988). *Social causality*. Boston: Unwin Hyman.

Hammersley, M. (1991). *Reading ethnographic research: A critical guide.* New York: Longman.

Hammersley, M. (1992). *What's wrong with ethnography? Methodological explorations.* London: Routledge.

Hedburg, B. L. T., Nystrom, P., & Starbuck, W. (1976). Camping on seesaws: Prescriptions for a self-defining organization. *Administration Science Quarterly, 21,* 41–65.

Henry, D., Chertock, F., Keys, C., & Jegerski, J. (1991). Organizational and family systems factors in stress among ministers. *American Journal of Community Psychology, 19,* 931–952.

Hicks, A. (1994). Qualitative comparative analysis and analytic induction: The case of the emergence of the social security state. *Sociological Methods and Research, 23,* 86–113.

Hirsch, P., Michaels, S., & Friedman, R. (1987). "Dirty hands" versus "clean models." *Theory and Society, 16,* 317–336.

Holland, P. W. (1986). Statistics and causal inference. *Journal of the American Statistical Association, 81,* 945–960.

Homans, G. C. (1950). *The human group.* New York: Harcourt, Brace, & World.

House, E. R. (1994). Integrating the quantitative and qualitative. *New Directions in Program Evaluation, 61,* 13–22.

Howe, K. R. (1985). Two dogmas of educational research. *Educational Researcher, 14,* 10–18.

Howe, K. R. (1988). Against the quantitative-qualitative incompatibility thesis, or dogmas die hard. *Educational Researcher, 17,* 10–16.

Hoyle, R. H. (Ed.) (1995a). *Structural equation modeling: Concepts, issues and applications.* Thousand Oaks, CA: Sage.

Hoyle, R. H. (1995b). The structural equation modeling approach: Basic concepts and fundamental issues. In R. H. Hoyle (Ed.), *Structural equation modeling: Concepts, issues, and applications* (pp. 1–15). Thousand Oaks, CA: Sage.

Hoyle, R. H., & Smith, G. T. (1994). Formulating clinical research hypotheses as structural equation models: A conceptual overview. *Journal of Consulting and Clinical Psychology, 62,* 429–440.

Hu, L., & Bentler, P. M. (1995). Evaluating model fit. In R. H. Hoyle (Ed.), *Structural equation modeling: Concepts, issues, and applications* (pp. 1–15). Thousand Oaks, CA: Sage.

Huberman, A. M., & Crandall, D. P. (1982). Fitting words to numbers: Multi-site/multimethod research in educational dissemination. *American Behavioral Scientist, 26,* 62–83.

Huberman, A. M., & Miles, M. B. (1994). Data management and analysis methods. In N. K. Denzin & Y. S. Lincoln (Eds.), *Handbook of qualitative research* (pp. 428–444). Thousand Oaks, CA: Sage.

Isaac, L. W., Carlson, S. M., & Mathis, M. P. (1994). Quality of quantity in comparative-historical analysis: Temporally-changing wage labor regimes in the United States and Sweden. In T. Janowski & A. Hicks (Eds.), *The comparative political economy of the welfare state: New methodologies and approaches.* Cambridge: Cambridge University Press.

Isaac, L. W., & Griffin, L. I. (1989). Ahistoricism in time series analyses of historical process: Critique, redirection and illustrations from U. S. labor history. *American Sociological Review, 54,* 873–890.

Iverson, G. R. (1991). *Contextual analysis.* Newbury Park, CA: Sage.

Jaccard, J., Turrisi, R., & Wan, C. K. (1990). *Interaction effects in multiple regression.* Newbury Park, CA: Sage.

Jenkins, C., & Kposowa, A. (1990). Explaining military coups in Africa. *American Sociological Review, 55,* 861–875

Kaniasty, K., & Norris, F. H. (1993). A test of the social support deterioration model in the context of natural disaster. *Journal of Personality and Social Psychology, 64,* 395–408.

Kauffman, D. L., Jr. (1980). *Systems 1: An introduction to systems thinking.* Cambridge, MA: Pegasus Communications.

Kerlinger, F. N. (1986). *Foundations of behavioral research* (3rd. Ed.). New York: Holt, Rinehart & Winston.

Kim, J., & Mueller, C. W. (1978). *Introduction to factor analysis: What it is and how to do it.* Beverly Hills, CA: Sage.

Kincheloe, J. L., & McLaren, P. L. (1994). Rethinking critical theory and qualitative research. In N. K. Denzin & Y. S. Lincoln (Eds.), *Handbook of Qualitative Research* (pp. 138–157). Thousand Oaks, CA: Sage.

King, G. (1986). How not to lie with statistics: Avoiding common mistakes in quantiative political science. *American Journal of Political Science, 30,* 666–687.

Kirk, J., & Miller, M. L. (1986). *Reliability in qualitative research.* Newbury Park, CA: Sage.

Kornhauser, R. R. (1978). *Social sources of delinquency.* Chicago: University of Chicago Press.

Land, K. C. (1969). Principles of path analysis. In E. F. Borgotta (Ed.), *Sociological methodology* (pp. 3–37). San Francisco: Jossey-Bass.

Langbein, L. (1980). *Discovering whether programs work.* Santa Monica, CA: Goodyear.

Lieberson, S. (1985). *Making it count: The improvement of social research and theory.* Berkeley: University of California Press.

Lieberson, S. (1992). Einstein, Renoir and Greeley: Some thoughts about evidence in sociology. *American Sociological Review, 57,* 1–15.

Liem, J. H., & Liem, G. R. (1990). Understanding the individual and family effects of unemployment. In J. Eckenrode & S. Gore (Eds.), *Stress between work and family* (pp. 175–204). New York: Plenum.

Light, D. B., & Pillemer, R. J. (1982). Numbers and narrative: Combining their strengths in research reviews. *Harvard Educational Review, 52,* 1–26.

Little, D. (1991). *Varieties of social explanation: An introduction to the philosophy of social science.* Boulder, CO: Westview Press.

Little, D. (1995). *On the reliability of economic models.* Boston: Kluwer.

Lofland, J. (1995). Analytic ethnography: Features, failures and futures. *Journal of Contemporary Ethnography, 24,* 30–67.

Luskin, R. C. (1991). Abusus non tollit usum: Standardized coefficients, correlations and R^2s[*]. *American Journal of Political Science, 35,* 1032–1046.

Luster, T., & Okagaki, L. (1993). Multiple influences on parenting: Ecological and life-course perspectives. In T. Luster & L. Okagaki (Eds.), *Parenting: An ecological perspective* (pp. 227–250). Hillsdale, NJ: Lawrence Erlbaum Associates.

MacCallum, R. C. (1995). Model specification: Procedures, strategies and related issues. In R. H. Hoyle (Ed.), *Structural equation modeling* (pp. 16–36). Thousand Oaks, CA: Sage.

Mackie, J. L. (1965). Causes and conditions. *American Philosophical Quarterly, 2,* 254–264.

Maines, D. R. (1992). Theorizing movement in an urban transportation system by use of the constant comparative method in field research. *The Social Science Journal, 29,* 283–292.

Maines, D. R. (1993). Narrative's moment and sociology's phenomena: Toward a narrative sociology. *Sociological Quarterly, 34,* 17–38.

Marini, M. M., & Singer, B. (1988). Causality in the social sciences. In C. Clogg (Ed.), *Sociological methodology* (pp. 347–409). Washington, DC: American Sociological Association.

Mark, M. M., & Shotland, R. L. (Eds.). (1987). *Multiple methods in program evaluation* (new directions in program evaluation, No. 35). San Francisco, CA: Jossey-Bass.

Marsh, H. W., & Grayson, D. (1995). Latent variable models of multitrait-multimethod data. In R. H. Hoyle (Ed.), *Structural equation modeling* (pp. 177–198). Thousand Oaks, CA: Sage.

Marshall, C., & Rossman, G. B. (1989). *Designing qualitative research*. Newbury Park, CA: Sage.

Mathison, S. (1988). Why triangulate? *Educational Researcher, 17*, 13–17.

Maxwell, J. A. (1992). Understanding and validity in qualitative research. *Harvard Educational Review, 62*, 279–300.

McMillan, J. H., & Schumaker, S. (1993). *Research in education: A conceptual introduction* (3rd ed.). New York: Harper Collins.

McPhail, C., & Wohlstein, R. T. (1983). Individual and collective behavior within gatherings, demonstrations, and riots. *Annual Review of Sociology, 9*, 579–600.

Meehan, A. J. (1986). Record-keeping practices in the policing of juveniles. *Urban Life, 15*, 70–102.

Meeker, B. F., & Hage, J. (April, 1991). *Causality and theory construction in sociology.* Paper presented at the North Central Sociological Association, Dearborn, MI.

Merton, R. K. (1967). *On theoretical sociology*. New York: The Free Press.

Miles, M. B., & Huberman, A. M. (1984). *Qualitative data analysis: A sourcebook of new methods*. Beverly Hills, CA: Sage.

Miles, M. B., & Huberman, A. M. (1994). *Qualitative data analysis: An expanded sourcebook*. Thousand Oaks, CA: Sage.

Miller, W. L., & Crabtree, B. F. (1994). Clinical research. In N. K. Denzin & Y. S. Lincoln (Eds.), *Handbook of qualitative research* (pp. 340–352). Thousand Oaks, CA: Sage.

Mishler, E. G. (1979). Meaning in context: Is there any other kind? *Harvard Educational Review, 49*, 1–19.

Moore, B. (1958). *Political power and social theory*. Cambridge, MA: Harvard University Press.

Morse, J. M. (1991a). Approaches to qualitative–quantitative methodological triangulation. *Nursing Research, 40*, 120–123.

Morse, J. M. (1991b). *Qualitative nursing research: A contemporary dialog*. Newbury Park, CA: Sage.

Mulaik, S. A., & James, L. R. (1995). Objectivity and reasoning in science and structural equation modeling. In R. H. Hoyle (Ed.), *Structural equation modeling* (pp. 118–137). Thousand Oaks, CA: Sage.

Muller, E. N., & Seligson, M. A. (1994). Civic culture and democracy: The question of causal relationships. *American Political Science Review, 88*, 635–652.

Murphy, J. (1974). Teacher expectations and working class underachievement. *British Journal of Sociology, 25*, 326–344.

Musheno, M. C., Gregware, P. R., & Drass, K. A. (1991). Court management of AIDS disputes: A sociological analysis. *Law and Social Inquiry, 16*, 737–776.

Neuman, W. L. (1994). *Social research methods: Qualitative and quantitative approaches*. Boston: Allyn & Bacon.

Nevitte, N., & Kanji, M. (1995). Explaining environmental concern and action in Canada. *Applied Behavioral Science Review, 3*, 85–102.

Orum, A. M., Feagin, J. R., & Sjoberg, G. (1991). The nature of the case study. In J. R. Feagin, A. M. Orum, & G. Sjoberg, (Eds.), *A case for the case study* (pp. 1–26). Chapel Hill: University of North Carolina Press.

Parker, H., Casburn, M., & Turnbull, D. (1981). *Receiving juvenile justice*. Oxford, England: Blackwell.

Pearlin, L. I. (1983). Role strains and personal stress. In H. B. Kaplan (Ed.), *Psychosocial stress: Trends in theory and research* (pp. 3–32). New York: Academic Press.

Pelto, P. J., & Pelto, G. H. (1978). *Anthropological research: The structure of inquiry* (2nd ed.). Cambridge, MA: Cambridge University Press.

Phillips, D. C. (1990). Post-positivistic science: Myths and realities. In E. G. Guba (Ed.), *The paradigm dialog* (pp. 31–45). Newbury Park, CA: Sage.

Pietrkowski, C., & Baker, A. (1993). The effects of participation in HIPPY on children's classroom adaptation: Teacher ratings. *Report of the NCJW Center for the Child*. New York: National Council of Jewish Women Center for the Child.

Popper, K. (1959). *The logic of scientific discovery*. New York: Harper & Row.

Ragin, C. (1987). *The Comparative method: Moving beyond qualitative and quantitative strategies*. Berkeley: University of California Press.

Ragin, C. (1989). The logic of the comparative method and the algebra of logic. *Journal of Quantitative Anthropology, 1*, 373–398.

Ragin, C. (1993). Introduction to qualitative comparative analysis. In T. Janoski & A. Hicks (Eds.), *Comparative political economy of the welfare state* (pp. 299–319). New York: Cambridge University Press.

Ragin, C., (1994). *Constructing social research*. Thousand Oaks, CA: Pine Forge Press.

Ragin, C., & Bradshaw, Y. W. (1991). Statistical analysis of employment discrimination: A review and critique. *Research in Social Stratification and Mobility, 10*, 199–228.

Randers, J. (1980). *Elements of the system dynamics method*. Cambridge, MA: Productivity Press.

Reichardt, C. S., & Cook, T. D. (1979). Beyond qualitative versus quantitative methods. In T. D. Cook & C. S. Reichardt (Eds.) *Quantitative methods in evaluation research* (pp. 7–32). Beverly Hills, CA: Sage.

Reichardt, C. S., & Gollub, H. F. (1987). Taking uncertainty into account when estimating effects. In M. M. Mark & R. L. Shotland (Eds.), *Multiple methods in program evaluation* (pp. 7–22). San Francisco: Jossey-Bass.

Reichardt, C. S., & Rallis, S. F. (1994a). The qualitative–quantitative debate: New perspectives. *New Directions in Program Evaluation, 61*.

Reichardt, C. S., & Rallis, S. F. (1994c). The relationship between qualitative and quantitative research traditions. *New Directions in Program Evaluation, 61*, 5–12.

Reichardt, C. S., & Rallis, S. F. (1994b). Qualitative and quantitative inquiries are not incompatible: A call for a new partnership. *New Directions in Program Evaluation, 61*, 85–91.

Richardson, G. P. (1986). Problems with causal-loop diagrams. *System Dynamics Review, 2*, 158–170.

Richardson, G. P., & Pugh, A. L., III (1981). *Introduction to systems dynamics modeling with DYNAMO*. Cambridge: MIT Press.

Rosenthal, R., & Jacobson, L. (1968). *Pygmalion in the classroom*. New York: Holt, Reinhart & Winston.

Rossman, G. B., & Wilson, B. L. (1985). Numbers and words: Combining quantitative and qualitative methods in a single, large-scale evaluation study. *Evaluation Review, 9*, 627–643.

Rossman, G. B., & Wilson, B. L. (1991). Numbers and words revisited: Being "shamelessly eclectic." *Quality and Quantity, 28*, 315–327.

Salomon, G. (1991). Transcending the qualitative–quantitative debate: The analytic and systemic approaches to educational research. *Educational Researcher, 20(6)*, 10–18.

Sameroff, A. J. (1975). Transactional models in early social relations. *Human Development, 18*, 65–79.

Sameroff, A. J., Seifer, R., & Zax, M. (1982). Early development of children at risk for emotional disorder. *Monographs of the Society for Research in Child Development, 47*, 1–82.

Sampson, R. J. (1992). Family management and child development: Insights from social disorganization theory. *Advances in Criminological Theory, 3*, 63–93.

Sampson, R. J., & Laub, J. H. (1994). Urban poverty and the family context of delinquency: A new look at structure and process in a classic study. *Child Development, 65*, 523–540.

Schreckengost, R. (1980). *An introduction to modeling with DYNAMO*. Videotaped lecture given in Fort Lauderdale, FL.

Schwandt, T. A. (1994). Constructivist, interpretivist approaches to human inqury. In N. K. Denzin & Y. S. Lincoln (Eds.), *Handbook of qualitative research* (pp. 118–137). Thousand Oaks, CA: Sage.

Senge, P. M. (1990). *The fifth discipline*. New York: Doubleday.

Sieber, S. D. (1973). The integration of fieldwork and survey methods. *American Journal of Sociology, 78*, 1335–1359.

Silverman, M., Ricci, E. M., & Gunter, M. J. (1990). Strategies for increasing the rigor of qualitative methods in evaluation of health care programs. *Evaluation Review, 14*, 57–74.

Simons, R. L., & Whitbeck, L. B. (1991). Running away during adolescence as a precursor to adult homelessness. *Social Service Review, 65*, 224–247.

Singer, M. (1993). Knowledge for use: Anthropology and community-centered substance abuse research. *Social Science and Medicine, 37*, 15–25.

Sjoberg, G., Williams, N., Vaughn, T. H., & Sjoberg, A. F. (1991). The case study approach in social research: Basic methodological issues. In J. R. Feagin, A. M. Orum, & G. Sjoberg (Eds.), *A case for the case study* (pp. 27–79). Chapel Hill: The University of North Carolina Press.

Skocpol, T. (1979). *States and social revolutions: A comparative analysis of France, Russia, and China*. Cambridge: Cambridge University Press.

Smith, A. G., & Louis, K. S. (Eds.) (1982). Multimethod policy research: Issues and applications. Special issue of *American Behavioral Scientist, 26*, entire issue 1.

Smith, M. L. (1994). Qualitative plus/versus quantitative: The last word. *New Directions in Program Evaluation, 61*, 37–44.

Smith, R. B. (1982). Introduction: Linking quality and quantity. In R. B. Smith (Ed.), *A handbook of social science method,* Vol. 3 (pp. 1–52). New York: Praeger.

Strauss, A. L. (1987). *Qualitative analysis for social scientists*. Oxford, England: Cambridge University Press.

Strauss, A. L., & Corbin, J. (1990). *Basics of qualitative research: Grounded theory procedures and techniques*. Newbury Park, CA: Sage.

Straus, M., & Wauchope, B. (1992). Measurement. In E. F. Borgotta & M. L. Borgotta (Eds.), *Encyclopedia of sociology* (pp. 1226–1240). New York: Macmillan.

Telles, E. I. (1995). Structural sources of socioeconomic segregation in Brazilian metropolitan areas. *American Journal of Sociology, 100*, 1199–1223.

Tesch, R. (1990). *Qualitative research: Analysis types and software tools*. New York: The Falmer Press.

Trow, M. (1957). Comment on "Participant observation and interviewing: A comparison." *Human Organization, 16*, 33–35.

Tufte, E. R. (1983). *The visual display of quantitative information*. Cheshire, CT: Graphics Press.

Tufte, E. R. (1990). *Envisioning information*. Cheshire, CT: Graphics Press.

Tukey, J. W. (1962). The future of data analysis. *Annals of Applied Statistics, 33*, 1–67.

Uslaner, E. M. (1976). Introduction. In H. B. Asher (Ed.), *Causal Modeling* (pp. 5–6). Beverly Hills, CA: Sage.

Van Maanen, J. (1983a). The moral fix: On the ethics of fieldwork. In R. W. Emerson (Ed.), *Contemporary field research* (pp. 269–279). Prospect Heights, IL: Waveland.

Van Maanen, J. (1983b). *Qualitative methodology*. Beverly Hills, CA: Sage.

Van Maanen, J. (1988). *Tales from the field: On writing ethnography*. Chicago: University of Chicago Press.

Wainer, H. (1986). *Drawing inferences from self-selected samples*. New York: Springer-Verlag.

Wainer, H. (1992). Understanding graphs and tables. *Educational Researcher, 21*, 14–23.

Wheaton, B. (1990). Where work and family meet: Stress across the social roles. In J. Eckenrode & S. Gore (Eds.), *Stress between work and family* (pp. 153–173). New York: Plenum.

Wilson, L., & Allen, W. (1995). Urban education: Critical issues. A special issue of *Applied Behavioral Science Review, 3*.

Wolcott, H. F. (1994). *Transforming qualitative data: Description, analysis, interpretation*. Thousand Oaks, CA: Sage.

Woolfolk, E. (1995). *Comparative analysis*. Unpublished poem. Detroit, MI: Wayne State University.

Yancey, W. L., & Saporito, S. J. (1995). Racial and economic segregation and educational outcomes: One tale—two cities. *Applied Behavioral Science Review, 3*, 105–126.

Yin, R. K. (1984). *Case study research: Design and methods*. Beverly Hills, CA: Sage.

Yin, R. K. (1994). Evaluation: A singular craft. *New directions in program evaluation, 61*, 71–84.

Zigler, E., & Trickett, P. K. (1979). IQ, social competence, and evaluation of early childhood programs. *American Psychologist, 33*, 789–798.

Author Index

Subject Index